People for the People

. . . I pondered all these things, and how men fight and lose
the battle, and the thing that they fought for comes about in
spite of their defeat, and when it comes turns out not to be
what they meant, and other men have to fight for what they
meant under another name. . . .

WILLIAM MORRIS

A Dream of John Ball, 1888, Ch. IV

People
for
the People

radical ideas & personalities
in British history
edited by David Rubinstein

introduction by Michael Foot

London: Ithaca Press
New York: Humanities Press
1973

Published by Ithaca Press
15 Southwark Street
London SE1, England
&
Humanities Press
450 Park Avenue South
New York, NY 10016
USA

Acknowledgements and thanks are due to the
following for permission to reproduce pictures
in their possession: the Trustees of the British
Museum, The Mansell Collection, Victor Neuberg Esq.,
the Radio Times Hulton Picture Library, John Frost Esq.

Library of Congress Cataloging in Publication Data
Rubinstein, David, comp.
   People for the people.
   Include bibliographies.
   1. Radicalism—Great Britain—Addresses, Essays
      lectures.
   2. —Great Britain—Social conditions—Addresses,
      essays, lectures. I. Title
HN400.R3R8 1974   309.1'42   73—15894
ISBN 0-391-00331-3

Clothbound ISBN 903729 02 4
Paperback   ISBN 903729 03 2

Printed in Great Britain by The Anchor Press Ltd,
and bound by Wm Brendon & Son Ltd,
both of Tiptree, Essex

Contents

8 CONTENTS

Preface

Most of these articles first appeared in *Tribune*, in a series entitled *The People's Past* which was printed at intervals between 1969 and 1972. It is fitting that *Tribune*, founded in 1937 in the middle of a crowded period of socialist history, should play a role in illuminating the history of the British working class and its institutions. The book's first debt is to Elizabeth Thomas, the paper's former literary editor, and Richard Clements, its editor, for having conceived and carried out the project. My article on the 1886 West End riot also appeared in *Tribune*, in 1968, and Asa Briggs' article on H M Hyndman appeared in the same paper in 1965. Most of the articles have been revised, in some cases radically, since their original publication.

Edward Thompson's article on Peterloo is a shortened and edited version of one which first appeared in the *Times Literary Supplement* on 11 December 1969. It is here reprinted by kind permission of the editor of that journal. The articles by Anthony Arblaster on William Morris, John Lovell on the dock strike of 1889 and Philip Bagwell on the Left in the 1930's have been specially written for this volume. So too has Michael Foot's introduction.

My debts in the compiling of this book are few but heavy. I am grateful to the contributors and to Michael Foot for enthusiastic co-operation. John Saville has been a tower of strength, making many helpful suggestions throughout the preparatory period. Irene Baldwin did the necessary typing and managed to translate some hardly legible manuscripts into flawless English. David Lawton did much useful work in checking bibliographies. Finally, David Wolton, the publisher of this book, has been helpfulness personified, acting not only as publisher, but as editorial assistant in countless ways.

Any book by a variety of hands will fail to satisfy in some respects. That is bound to be true of this volume. But if it introduces to the history of the British people not only school, college and university students, but those within the ranks of the labour movement, if it acts as inspiration to any of these people, our purpose will be achieved.

DAVID RUBINSTEIN

Hull
May 1973

Introduction by Michael Foot

MICHAEL FOOT *has been an influential force in the Labour Party and in radical journalism since before World War II. He was an MP from 1945 until 1955 and succeeded Aneurin Bevan as MP for Ebbw Vale in 1960, a seat he still holds. He was editor of* TRIBUNE *from 1948 to 1952 and 1955 to 1960. He was for a number of years one of the principal leaders of the Campaign for Nuclear Disarmament. Besides a number of shorter works on current political topics, he is the author of a study of Jonathan Swift and his era,* THE PEN AND THE SWORD *(1957), and a two-volumed life of* ANEURIN BEVAN *(1962, 1973).*

How can Socialists achieve their aims in societies radically organised to bar the achievement of anything distantly worthy of the name of Socialism? The argument about strategy and tactics continues perpetually and becomes part of our conception of the aims themselves. Those laws, wrote John Warr, one of the lesser-known seventeenth-century pamphleteers, which "do carry anything of Freedom in their Bowels have been wrested from the Rulers and Princes of the World by Importunity of Entreaty or by Force of Arms". Unconsciously John Warr had turned to history for instruction, despite the difficulties he and his fellow-Leveller historians must have encountered in uncovering sources. Inevitably, if unconsciously, we do the same. In a sense, history is our only guide. Yet, for the most part, the record has been kept by our enemies, and although the charge of deliberate suppression or distortion may not be constantly proved, no doubt is possible about the manner in which all the arts of selection and emphasis have been used to bestow on biased judgements the stamp of un-challengeable authority. If Tories may complain about the Whig interpretation of history, how much grander is the working-class indictment.

Since Sedgemoor, in the year 1685, no great battle has been fought on English soil. Since the days of the first Queen Elizabeth Englishmen have settled by the arts of negotiation many issues which in other lands were only decided by the sword. The English tradition of parliamentary institutions is longer and stronger than that of any other country. Hence most of the heroes lauded by the official English historians of varying political affiliations have been the men who seemed to know how far they could go and how much they must concede if convulsion was to be avoided. We never cease to be congratulated on the English genius for compromise, and one result of this theme has been the denial of proper credit to the others who have supplied so much of the real engine power in our history—the rebels, the revolutionaries, the heretics who risked their necks, the prophets who understood more than the statesmen, the far-seeing, the eccentrics and the men of no-compromise. Because they were not blessed with suc-cess in their own generations, their historical stature has been shamefully diminished.

Yet the whole story can be written so differently. The boldest revolutionaries in Cromwell's armies had the whole wonderful logic of the democratic argument on their side, and the famous demand of Colonel Thomas Rainborough that "the poorest he that is in England has a life to live as the greatest he", resounds across the intervening centuries. A good case can be made for the view that Thomas Paine was the greatest Englishman of the eighteenth century; certainly he had a better understanding of his age than the rulers who hunted him for treason and burnt his books. He was proclaiming the age of democracy in better prose than Dr Johnson's and building a new nation across the seas while his triumphant enemies spent their best exertions to restore the Bourbons.

In the years that followed, the intrepid radicalism of the early nineteenth century—of William Cobbett and William Hazlitt, of Shelley and Godwin, of Thomas Spence and Orator Hunt—was swallowed up by the industrial revolution. The smug victors in that conquest have received their full meed of fame. "What has never been adequately written", wrote Professor Tawney, "is the history of the political philosophy which failed. For the victory of the panegyrists of the new industrial order was so complete as to obliterate the very remembrance of its critics, and to create the impression that Utilitarianism spoke with the voice of reason itself." The reputations of writers like Gray, Thompson, Hodgkin and Bray seemed sunk without trace. Even Sidney Webb, writing what he called "the historical view of Socialism" in the first *Fabian Essays*, published in 1889, managed to achieve the feat with only a footnote reference to the Chartists.

However, deliberate attempts to belittle some of the greatest figures in our history, even Fabian oversights or insults, may be repaired. Where the names are known and their writings are available and reinterpretations are possible much may be disinterred from beneath the weighty edifices of orthodox scholarship. The complacent worlds of the historians who worship the *fait accompli* may eventually be overturned. But the more this work is accomplished by the Socialist historians, by, say, E P Thompson and Christopher Hill, the more they give us glimpses of great companies of men and women who struggled and fought and were beaten, but whose names have been obliterated altogether : men whose aims, like those of the Luddites, have been bowdlerised and defamed, or whose revolutionary strength, like those charged with high treason in the 1790's, has been interestedly underrated.

Yet the news was handed down by word of mouth where it was not possible or safe to keep a written record or in what another historian has called "the underworld of largely-unrecorded thinking" or in the collective memory of the working class. Socialism began in Kent, said H G Wells, legitimately proud of his fellow-Kentishman, John Ball, but others peered further back still. The revolutionaries of the Commonwealth looked, without the assistance of historical archives, across six centuries to the way William the Conqueror, the landlord's God, had "made Dukes, Earls, Barrons, and Lords of their fellow Robbers, Rogues and Thieves", to Saxon times when, according to Thomas Scot, one of the Commonwealth regicides, "there was nothing but a House of Commons".

And when Thomas Paine wished to renew the battle in language which Englishmen—and Americans—could understand he knew which chords to touch: "A French bastard landing with an armed banditti and establishing himself King of England, against the consent of the natives, is, in plain terms, a very paltry, rascally original. It certainly has no divinity in it. The plain truth is that the antiquity of English monarchy will not bear looking into." The very words Paine invoked were minted for him by the Levellers—that word *consent*, for example, so debased in modern times, was a favourite of Thomas Rainborough's, and to-day Paine's *Rights of Man* still has a steady sale because it can restore to the jaded idea of democracy its vibrancy and freshness and power. But again, with Paine, we are back with those whose greatness can be recorded. Clearly he was so greatly feared because he spoke for millions in his own age and seemed to summon to his aid more millions of the forgotten, suppressed voices of the past. "In 1792", wrote Hazlitt, "Paine was so great, or so popular an author, and so much read and admired, that the Government was obliged to suspend the Constitution, and to go to war to counteract the effects of his popularity."

Historians invent theories of history to justify their craft, but the Labour movement—English, Welsh, Scots and, let us not to our shame forget, the Irish, since their contribution has been so disproportionately conspicuous—had hit upon this excellent and necessary device even in pre-Marxist times. For working-class movements, history has always been a weapon, the best at their disposal to sustain their pride, their refusal to be broken by exploitation, their fighting solidarity, their shared aspirations.

It is, of course, for this reason that every Socialist newspaper, *Tribune*, like its forbears, the *Clarion* in the age of Robert Blatchford or the *New Leader* in the age of H N Brailsford, has sought to recite in the differing idiom of each new age the great working-class tradition. Such an indulgence may run the risk of being nostalgic or escapist, but not for long, surely. Turn where one will, the drum-beat of militancy re-emerges more strongly than ever. "I knew", wrote William Cobbett, "that all the palaver in the world, all the wheedling, waxing, praying: I knew that all the blustering and threatening; I knew that all the teachings of the Tract Societies; that all the imprisoning, whipping, and harnessing to carts and wagons; I knew that all these would fail to persuade the honest, sensible industrious English labourer, that he had not *an indefensible right to live.*" "Till *man*", wrote Thomas Hodgkin, "shall be held more in honour than the clod he treads on, or the machine he guides—there cannot, and there ought not to be either peace on earth or goodwill among men."

At which point let me add hastily that I am not wishing to pre-judge nor accept uncritically the conclusion of the reflections on violence by David Rubinstein in the essay which concludes this book. The theme of *consent* weaves throughout our history, from Saxon times if our Leveller ancestors are to believed, partly at least because those Alfredian revolutionaries were convinced that matters could be better settled that way than by clash of arms. Dilemmas not so different provoked the great debates among the Chartists, and anyone foolish enough to dismiss too whole-heartedly the "moral force" claims of William Lovett should not forget that "physical force" Julian Harney himself came to acknowledge William Lovett as "first in honour" in that famous company. The same essential controversy acquires a fresh shape at every period. The victories of the 1920's and 1930's—and there were some to set alongside the defeats—were achieved only when agitation outside the House of Commons was combined with intelligent action within it, and yet the lesson, at any rate one lesson, of the defeats was that industrial leadership must be com-bined with political leadership, that the syndicalist revulsion against all forms of parliamentary activity could be a sectarian snare. The ambitions of the Chartists themselves were certainly not limited by the political letter of their Charter, but they would have been both scornful and incredulous if anyone had fatuously argued that the case for representative institutions should be sur-rendered to the reactionaries who had striven so strenuously to prevent them ever being established. The ideas of Socialism and democracy, like liberty, equality and fraternity, came into the world joined together, and woe to those who would put them asunder.

Rodney Hilton
The Rebellion of 1381

RODNEY HILTON *comes from a family active in the labour movement in Lancashire since before the foundation of the Labour Party. He was a member of the Communist Party from his student days just before the Second World War until 1956. He is professor of medieval social history at the University of Birmingham. His main public activity at the present time is with the Council for Academic Freedom and Democracy. He has written a number of books and articles on the history of the medieval peasant, among them* A MEDIEVAL SOCIETY *(1966),* THE DECLINE OF SERFDOM IN MEDIEVAL ENGLAND *(1969) and* BOND MEN MADE FREE *(1973).*

The English rising in 1381 was the first major social upheaval in English history. In that year, the lowest classes of English society took political action of the most extreme kind, that is, the occupation of the capital, the execution of leading members of the Government, and the formulation of plans for the subversion of existing institutions and relationships.

England was then a predominantly peasant society, that is, 80 per cent of the population were peasants, living in villages and hamlets and, for the most part, engaged in a primitive form of mixed husbandry. Most rural households depended for their subsistence on the produce of a holding, which would seldom exceed 20 acres of arable, with appurtenant common pasture rights.

There were, of course, a few richer peasants with perhaps as many as 100 acres; and there was an important population of cottagers and wage labourers. These last, however, were fewer in number than the land-holding peasants. Most peasant farms were worked without wage labour.

In East Anglia, the home counties and Kent, but to a lesser
extent in the midlands, the south west and the West Riding of
Yorkshire, artisan industry, mainly in the production of woollen
cloth, had spread from the towns to the countryside. This production was partly for the home market, but perhaps four-fifths
of it was exported. The European market for English cloth was
very disturbed by war and political uncertainties; export figures
fluctuated violently from year to year, so that there must have
been much temporary unemployment in the cloth manufacturing
towns and villages.

Medieval peasants were not faced simply with problems of production for subsistence or for the market. The peasants also had
to bear the burden of other social classes. The majority of the
peasants were the servile tenants of land-owners, and had to pay a
considerable proportion of the income from the peasant holding
in the form of rents, tithes, fines imposed in manorial courts and
taxes to the King's Government.

The landowners varied in character. Some were enormously
wealthy dukes, earls, barons, bishops and abbots, others were
local gentry and lesser religious houses. The most influential sat as
Lords of Parliament or as members of the House of Commons,
and some of them were the close advisers and officials of the
Crown.

After the Black Deaths (bubonic plagues) of 1349, 1361-2,
1369 and 1375, as a result of the shortage of labour and of tenants, wages naturally tended to go up and rents and services owed
by tenants to go down. Parliament enacted a Statute of Labourers
which attempted to freeze wages, and which was strongly enforced by restricting the movement of labour and imposing fines
on workers and employers who ignored it. The gentry, in their
role as Justices of Labourers and Justices of the Peace, were effectively in charge of the enforcement.

At a local level, landowners everywhere tried to step up rents
and servile obligations in order to compensate for the loss of tenants through death and migration from village to village. These
two policies were not completely successful : wages did go up and
rents did go down, but the coercion exercised by the JPs in the
Quarter Sessions and by the lords' stewards in the manor courts
exacerbated existing social tensions. Added to this were the

Government's financial difficulties, largely due to the increasing unsuccessful war with France.

The successive Poll Taxes of 1377, 1379 and 1380 precipitated the rising, especially that of 1380. This was levied at one shilling a head, three times that of 1377. It was equivalent to three days' wages, and naturally there was much evasion. The Government was aware of the evasion and in the first few months of 1381 sent a series of collectors, assessors and enforcers into the towns and villages, to the increasing rage of the peasants and artisans who bore the heaviest burden of this regressive tax.

The revolt began at the end of May in a number of Essex fishing villages, soon followed by risings in Kent on the other side of the river. It spread quickly throughout these two counties, to Suffolk, Norfolk, Cambridgeshire and Hertfordshire. Smaller towns, especially those dominated or even owned by unpopular church landowners, such as Canterbury, Bury St Edmunds and St Albans, also joined the rebels. Peasants as far away as Worcestershire began to refuse to pay rents and dues. Eventually the county armies joined together and entered London with the support of the city's lower classes (June 13).

The chief government officials, the Chancellor and the Treasurer (both churchmen) were executed, and two programmes of demands were put to the King and his councillors. The demands were presented on the rebels' behalf by Wat Tyler of Maidstone, Kent, who was murdered during the course of negotiations at Smithfield on June 15.

Many of the rebels, especially those from Essex, had gone home the previous day, deceived by charters of freedom from serfdom which the King had granted with the intention of later revocation. After Tyler's death, the peasants in London dispersed, though the rebellion continued in East Anglia and elsewhere for another week, until crushed by the Bishop of Norwich and other aristocrats.

The social composition of the many rebel bands, some of which joined together to take London, others of which operated regionally in the Eastern counties, was mixed. Many village and urban artisans were involved, as one would expect given the industrialised character of the main areas of the revolt.

Leadership at all levels was provided by (among others) members of the lower clergy, ranging from John Ball, one of the principal organisers with Tyler, through John Wrawe, the Suffolk leader, to local clerics such as those who served the Church of St John, Thanet, and were active in mobilising the Isle's population for the rebellion. Some well-to-do yeomen joined in. The main body of rebels, however, must have been peasants, as their demands indicate.

If we leave aside demands for the execution of corrupt Ministers of the Crown, which would be supported by many who were not rebels, the demands which were presented at Mile End (June 14) and Smithfield (June 15) were primarily aimed at the reconstitution of rural society. Most prominent was the demand for the end of serfdom, the culmination of a century and a half of sporadic local actions, some through the law courts, some by individual village rebellion. Next was the demand for the end of all obligations, whether monetary or personal, to landowners.

At Mile End, the rebels offered to pay a rent of fourpence an acre, but the implication of the Smithfield demands was the abolition of all landlords' power, and other evidence also indicates that the rebels envisaged the end of the class of landowners.

Other demands reflect the interests of wage earners, both agricultural and industrial. The abolition of forced service was aimed at the Statute of Labourers, as may have been the demand for the abolition of outlawry as a process of law. The rebels also recognised the importance of the part played by the wealthy hierarchy of the church in the existing social order.

In the more far-reaching Smithfield programme, they demanded the dispossession of church landowners, the division of their lands among the common people, and the elimination of the hierarchy. Monks and priests were to have no more than reasonable sustenance. There should be only one head of the church, that is one bishop over all the clergy, just as there should be only one head of state with greater power than other men, that is the King.

All our evidence about the aims of the peasants comes from hostile sources, that is chronicles written by monks and other clerics and indictments in the law courts after the revolt was suppressed. The sources are therefore biased; most of what was written about the rebels must have been hearsay and some of it must have been sheer invention. The way in which we have to judge their aims is by putting them in the context of what we know in general about peasant society at this period and by checking independent sources of information against each other.

The items reported as demands at Smithfield and Mile End are taken from the soberest of the Chronicles (the so-called *Anonimalle*) and are reinforced by reports by other chroniclers, such as the very prejudiced monk of St Albans, Thomas Walsingham. From these, it seems that, insofar as the rebels had a general idea of the society they would wish to live in, it would be a popular monarchy in which there would be no social class in between the King and the peasant masses.

Freedom is the keynote of this society, and although equality is not formulated in social and economic terms, it is clearly stated as far as political rights were concerned. Their popular monarchy is obviously quite different from the feudal monarchy as they had experienced it, and there are indications that some of them may have wanted to set up regional or county monarchies, the local kings being those popuar leaders who had emerged in the course of the rising.

What were the ideological influences on the peasant and artisan rebels in 1381? There seem to have been two distinguishable strands of thought which affected them, though these two strands often seem to be intertwined. The first, which is best known, is the radical Christian tradition which is expressed in the sermon which the priest John Ball is said by the chronicler Froissart to have been in the habit of preaching. Ball simply asked why there should be serfs and gentry, rich and poor, when all were descended from Adam and Eve. He also suggested that things would not go right for England until all things were held in common.

His rhyming letters which were preserved in some chronicle accounts of the rising are more cryptic, but suggest an acquaintance with William Langland's religious poem *The Vision of Piers Plowman*, which exalts the peasant as a social type. It is possible that Ball, whom we know to have been preaching since the 1360's, may have echoed many of the social and religious views of continental heretics such as the Waldensians, and there may have been many like him.

The other strand of thought is legal, rather than specifically religious. It emerged in the course of litigation between landlords and peasants in which the point at issue was whether the peasant was free or serf. Peasants hired lawyers, who (whatever their personal opinions) formulated arguments in court to the effect that freedom was man's natural condition.

Peasants understood well enough what free status meant in practice. and must also have been reinforced in their desire for freedom by listening to their lawyers' arguments. The combination of legal and religious justifications for freedom in the conditions of England in 1381 evidently produced an explosive mixture.

Some historians say that the revolt achieved nothing, either because it was completely suppressed and all concessions revoked, or because economic trends were going to bring about what the peasants wanted anyway. The indications are, however, that it was the revolt which *ended* the post-Black Death feudal reaction, and that the defeat of the rebels did not start another one.

The Government and the lords were too frightened to begin a reign of terror. The rise in wages and the fall in rents is most noticeable *after* 1381, and some have thought that the century following the revolt was the golden age of the peasantry. There is something in this—though it soon came to an end and, from the sixteenth century, an era of repression of peasants set in which did not even end with their disappearance as a class in the eighteenth century.

It is, however, worth remembering that the late medieval peasant had a much better position in society than the downtrodden agricultural labourer of modern times, and that this was largely due to his capacity for organised resistance to the state, the church and the landowning class.

E POWELL   *The Rising in East Anglia in 1381* (Cambridge, 1896)
C OMAN   *The Great Revolt of 1381* (1906, reprinted 1969)
R H HILTON   *The Decline of Serfdom in Medieval England* (1969)
R D DOBSON   *The Peasants Revolt of 1381* (a collection of documents) (1970)
R H HILTON   *Bond Men Made Free* (1973)

Andrew Boyd
Sir Thomas More's Utopia

ANDREW BOYD, *a graduate of Queen's University, Belfast, is a lecturer, author and journalist. He was Irish organiser for the National Council of Labour Colleges, 1954–64. He has contributed to* TRIBUNE *since 1955, and is a frequent contributor to the* NATION *of New York. He contributes to leading newspapers and journals in Ireland and also appears on radio and television. Among his publications are* HOLY WAR IN BELFAST *(1969),* THE RISE OF THE IRISH TRADE UNIONS *(1970) and* BRIAN FAULKNER AND THE CRISIS OF ULSTER UNIONISM *(1972).*

Sir Thomas More has been described—perhaps misleadingly—as a socialist born out of his time, and for that reason a tragic figure. But Thomas More was not a man of the common people; he was Lord High Chancellor of England in the reign of Henry VIII and Speaker of a House of Commons whose membership was restricted to a few very wealthy men. Moreover, he was a devout Catholic, was executed for his devotion to the Pope and now abides in glory among the saints and martyrs of the Church.

Yet for all his piety Sir Thomas More was anything but a narrow-minded bigot. It is true that in conscience he could not support King Henry in his quarrel with Rome nor could he condone the divorce of Queen Catherine, yet he believed that in a truly just society all religions would be treated with equal respect.

In his *Utopia* all religions are allowed. Sectarian agitators of the kind that have recently been given so much publicity in Ulster were banished from Utopia as seditious persons who raised up dissensions among the people. And it is noteworthy that the one instance of such a banishment mentioned by More concerns a fanatical convert to Christianity who preached all other religions were wicked and devilish and that their adherents were condemned to everlasting damnation.

If the religious bigots find themselves portrayed in the pages of *Utopia*, so too might those racialist bigots who wish to banish immigrants and to keep "England for the English". In More's Utopia there are two kinds of bondsmen, criminals sentenced to periods of servile work as a punishment, and poor strangers from other countries who work for wages. The criminal bondsmen are dealt with harshly as they deserve, but the immigrants are treated honestly and given the same status as free citizens. If they want to return to their own homes, which More states is seldom, they are not restrained, nor are they "sent away with empty hands".

Thomas More had much experience of intolerance; he saw riots when he was Under-Sheriff of London on May 1, 1517, a day that was long to be remembered as the Evil May Day, he was called out to quell an angry demonstration directed against the continental aliens then in the city. The demonstrators complained that these aliens were devouring the good food of Englishmen and introducing their own inferior continental diets into the country. His eloquence and courage, it is said, brought the mobs under control.

An Elizabethan play, *Sir Thomas More*, part of which was written by Shakespeare, puts this eloquence into moving poetry:

"Grant them removed, and grant that this your noise
Hath chid down the majesty of England.
Imagine that you see the wretched strangers
Their babies at their backs, and their poor luggage,
Plodding to the ports and coasts for transportation,
And that you sit as kings in your desires
Authority quite silenced by your brawl
And you in ruff of your opinions clothed,
What had you got? I'll tell you. You had taught
How insolence and strong hand should prevail,
How order should be quelled; and by this pattern
Not one of you should live an aged man;
For other ruffians, as their fancy wrought

With self same hand, self reasons and self right
Would shark on you; and men like ravenous fishes
Would feed on one another."

For 20 years before his execution in 1535 More's reputation as
the author of *Utopia* had spread throughout Europe. *Utopia*
from its first edition in 1516 was what would nowadays be called
"a best-seller". "The million sales of a modern novel", wrote Goi-
tein in an introduction to the Broadway edition of *Utopia*, "pale
into significance beside the reception it met with."

As Marx in the nineteenth century synthesised the immature
socialist philosophies of the Industrial Revolution to formulate his
theory of scientific socialism, so More in his day synthesised the
communist theories of the Middle Ages and the humanism of the
Renaissance in pursuit of the ideal society, Utopia, where all property is common property and everybody is, therefore, wealthy
and secure.

But *Utopia* cannot be dismissed as an idle philosophical dream.
It is full of practical proposals, many of which, the abolition of
chattel slavery, for example, were eventually accepted by the civilised world. For three and a half centuries before the publication
of the *Communist Manifesto*, it was read and studied by the most
learned men in Europe.

Utopia consists of two parts, the first of which deals with the
economics, criminal laws, and politics of Tudor England, while
the second describes the economy, the government, and the cus-
toms of the people who live on the Island of Utopia, an imagin-
ary place which is presumed to be located somewhere in the
Americas.

The Utopians live in a society of the kind that socialists everywhere have argued for. Utopian society is Clause Four of the
British Labour Party's constitution, i.e. "the common ownership
of the means of production, distribution and exchange". It is the
society of the communist formula, "from each according to his
ability; to each according to his needs".

Labour in Utopia is obligatory on all healthy, able-bodied citizens. However, people are free to change from one occupation to
another though every citizen is obliged to be proficient in agri-
culture and to spend some time, as on national service, working
on the land. Those citizens who have a natural aptitude for

learning and study are freed from manual work and employed in scholarship.

The working day is six hours and so Utopians have ample leisure time in which to further their education and cultural interests. Adult education is widespread. There are no brothels, gaming houses or other debased attractions.

The constitution of Utopia, though based primarily on the Platonic theory of the properly ordered society, is democratic and republican. The national parliament is so organised that it is impossible for it to become the breeding ground for factions and rival political parties.

"And it is provided that nothing touching the common wealth shall be confirmed and ratified, unless it have been reasoned of and debated three days in the council before it be decreed. It is death to have any consultation for the commonwealth out of the council or the place of the common election."

This statute, More explains, was to prevent the more powerful politicians conspiring "to oppress the people by tyranny" or to change the constitution of the country.

Other aspects of Utopian society were population control, euthanasia, and the marriage of priests—all of which are matters being fiercely debated by Christians in the modern world. Utopian law laid down a standard population for each city or community. If the population of any place rose above this legal level the extra people were moved to new communities or sent to cities where the population had fallen below the standard figure. Euthanasia applied only to old people, suffering from diseases that were painful as well as incurable; it was entirely voluntary.

The first book of Utopia is not however about the ideal socialist society; it is concerned mainly with the effects of the Tudor agrarian revolution on the common people of England. Wool had become a profitable commodity; at that time the export of cloth was the most important item in England's foreign trade. And so, to provide the wool in the increasing quantities that were demanded, men were evicted from their farms and the land stocked with great flocks of sheep.

"Your sheep that were wont to be so meek and tame, and so small eaters, now, as I hear say, become so great devourers and so wild that they eat up and swallow down the very men themselves. They consume, destroy and devour whole fields, houses and cities."

So Thomas More denounces the Tudor enclosures. In the next paragraph he condemns the idle rich and their retainers and attacks the clerical landowners—"those good holy men who turn all dwelling places and all glebe land into desolation and wilderness".

More was distressed at the sight of his fellow-countrymen and their families being forced to wander through the land as beggars and perhaps to be hanged when they stole to keep themselves alive. He considered hanging a barbarous custom; its abolition was one of the reforms he advocated in the Utopian penal code.

Open prisons and the remission of sentences for good conduct are familiar aspects of the penal code in modern societies; they were advocated by Thomas More four and a half centuries ago, along with old-age pensions and sickness benefits "for those people who were not able to work for their living".

Fr Bernard Basset in his book, *Born for Friendship; The Spirit of Sir Thomas More*, sees More's philosophy as relevant in the present-day world. "The present search for peace, the groping towards world government and peaceful co-existence must make us regard Utopia with far greater honour and respect. This little book, so long regarded as a delightful extravaganza, now appears as one of the wisest contributions to sane living devised by man ...

"With the increase of leisure thanks to automation, the need for true education must become increasingly felt. Life will prove unbearable for those who have been educated for one purpose only, to get and to hold a job. The right use of leisure, the value of crafts, the danger of idleness, in a word, the full implications of education were elaborated in theory and in practice at Chelsea four hundred years ago.

"Sir Thomas More has increased in stature now that so many men have lived under dictatorships and tyranny and know better the importance of human liberty. It has taken 400 years for us to grasp the wisdom and courage of his attitude to kings."

THOMAS MORE   *Utopia* (first published in Latin in Louvain, 1516; first English translation, 1551. There have been very many subsequent English editions)

THOMAS MORE   *Dialogue of Comfort Against Tribulation* (written 1534, published 1553, new edition 1937. Published in Everyman edition with *Utopia* in 1910, last reprinted 1970)

The English Works of Sir Thomas More (first published 1557, reprinted 1931)

WILLIAM ROPER   *The Life of Sir Thomas More* (written by More's son-in-law in the mid-sixteenth century, published Paris 1626, many later editions)

NICHOLAS HARPSFIELD   *The Life and Death of Sir Thomas More* (written in the mid-sixteenth century, published 1932)

CRESACRE MORE   *The Life and Death of Sir T More* (n.d., 1626)

R W CHAMBERS   *Thomas More* (1935)

STANLEY MORISON   *The Likeness of Thomas More* (n.d., 1963)

E E REYNOLDS   *The Trial of St Thomas More* (n.d., 1964)

BERNARD BASSET   *Born for Friendship: The Spirit of Sir Thomas More* (n.d., 1965)

Christopher Hill
The Levellers

CHRISTOPHER HILL *obtained a first in modern history at Balliol College, Oxford, in 1934, and has taught modern history at Oxford since 1938, apart from military service during the Second World War. Since 1965 he has been Master of Balliol. His many books include* THE ENGLISH REVOLUTION *(1940)*, ECONOMIC PROBLEMS OF THE CHURCH *(1956)*, PURITANISM AND REVOLUTION *(1958)*, THE CENTURY OF REVOLUTION *(1961)*, SOCIETY AND PURITANISM IN PRE-REVOLUTIONARY ENGLAND *(1964)*, INTELLECTUAL ORIGINS OF THE ENGLISH REVOLUTION *(1965)*, REFORMATION TO INDUSTRIAL REVOLUTION *(1967)*, GOD'S ENGLISHMAN: OLIVER CROMWELL AND THE ENGLISH REVOLUTION *(1970)*, ANTICHRIST IN SEVENTEENTH-CENTURY ENGLAND *(1971) and* THE WORLD TURNED UPSIDE DOWN *(1972)*.

The Levellers were a party of democrats who emerged at the conclusion of the civil war of 1642–5. This war had been waged against King Charles I in the name of the Parliament and people of England. In London in 1645–6, among the supporters of Parliament, men began to appear who suggested that now the King had been defeated, Parliament should be made truly representative of the people, by a wide extension of suffrage, a redistribution of seats, and that sovereignty should be transferred to the House of Commons, to the exclusion of King and House of Lords. (In seventeenth-century England the franchise was about as restricted as it is in Rhodesia today.)

"The poorest that lives", wrote John Lilburne, the Leveller leader, "hath as true a right to give a vote as well as the richest and greatest." But the Parliament of gentry proved singularly unresponsive to such arguments. The Levellers came to believe that the rank-and-file fighters for Parliament in the civil war had been had for suckers. "All you intended when you set us a-fighting", Lilburne told the Lords, "was merely to unhorse and dismount our old riders and tyrants, that you might get up and ride in their stead."

Side by side with their political programme the Levellers were working out a series of economic and social demands expressing the needs of the small men in town and country—complete equality before the law and drastic law reform, the decentralisation of justice to local communities, election of sheriffs and Justices of the Peace, abolition of the trading monopolies of the rich City companies and protection of the interests of small masters and journeymen, the laying open of enclosures, security of tenure for small proprietors, no conscription, billeting or excise, abolition of tithes (and so of the state church which they financed), complete toleration and freedom of religious worship and organisation. Their design, said a hostile pamphleteer, was "to raise the servant against the master, the tenant against the landlord, the buyer against the seller, the borrower against the lender, the poor against the rich".

Lilburne boasted that his support came from "the hobnails, clouted shoes, the private soldier, the leather and woollen aprons, the laborious and industrious people in England". Rebuffed by the Parliament of gentry, the Levellers turned directly to the people of London and to the New Model Army. This remarkable force, which had won the war for Parliament, was unlike any army which had previously existed. Partly composed of, and mainly officered by, picked volunteers, who, in Oliver Cromwell's phrase, "knew what they fought for and loved what they knew", all ranks had enjoyed an unprecedented amount of freedom of organisation and discussion. Promotion went by merit, not birth, and Cromwell defended "russet-coated captains" who were no gentlemen, and officers who were "Anabaptists"—the seventeenth-century equivalent of "Reds".

In 1647, the war over, Parliament foolishly attempted to disband this army without even providing for arrears of pay. The army revolted, "hooted divers officers out of the field, unhorsed some and rent their clothes and beat them". Delegates ("Agitators") were elected by the regiments. "Every foot soldier gave 4d. apiece towards defraying the charges", which argues a considerable degree of organisation : 4d. was half a day's pay. The soldiers attended meetings with red ribbons tied on their left arms, to show "that we will defend the equity of our petition with our blood". The Agitators included many who had been influenced by Leveller ideas. In June they sent Cornet Joyce to seize the King as a hostage, and told their Commander-in-Chief to order a general rendezvous of the army : otherwise "we shall be necessitated to do such things ourselves".

At this rendezvous an Army Council or Soviet was set up, in which Agitators sat side by side with officers. ("The officers at that time", said Lilburne later, "could have no power but what was entrusted to them by the soldiers.") The Army Council proclaimed that "we were not a mere mercenary army, hired to serve any arbitrary power of a state", but civilians in uniform, retaining the rights of citizens. At Parliament's invitation they had taken up arms "in judgment and conscience to preserve the nation from tyranny and oppression, and therefore were pledged to insist upon our rights and freedoms as commoners". The united army marched on London.

The fate of England now depended on a struggle for power within the army. In the Putney Debates of October 1647 the future constitution was discussed. A Leveller draft, the Agreement of the People, was put before the Army Council by spokesmen of the rank and file and some officers. It was opposed by a preponderantly conservative group of higher officers, whose spokesman was Commissary-General Ireton, soon to marry Cromwell's daughter. Ireton defended the existing narrow Parliamentary franchise by saying that only men of property had a right to rule : political democracy would inevitably lead to economic democracy, to communism.

Colonel Rainborough replied in the famous words, "the poorest he that is in England has a life to live as the greatest he; and therefore truly, sir, I think it's clear that every man that is to live under a government ought first by his own consent to put himself under that government, and I do think that the poorest man in England is not at all bound in a strict sense to that government that he hath

not had a voice to put himself under". "I should doubt whether
he was an Englishman or no that should doubt of these things."
"If the people find that [the laws] are not suitable to freemen
as they are, I know no reason that should deter me . . . from endeavouring by all means to gain anything that might be of more
advantage to them than the government under which they live."
Otherwise "I would fain know what the soldier has fought for
all this while? He has fought to enslave himself, to give power
to men of riches, to men of estates, to make him a perpetual
slave."

"Our very laws were made by our conquerors", said the Leveller John Wildman when Ireton appealed to established law.
"Whatever our forefathers were," a Leveller *Remonstrance* of
July 1646 had proclaimed, "or whatever they did or suffered or
were enforced to yield unto, we are the men of the present age,
and ought to be absolutely free from all kinds of exorbitancies,
molestations or arbitary power."

Historians disagree on whether the Levellers really wanted to
establish manhood suffrage, and later receded from this ideal only
for tactical reasons; or whether they always thought that servants and paupers should be excluded from the franchise. Given
an illiterate population and no secret ballot, it was not unreasonable to suppose that the very poor would vote as their landlords
and employers told them. Some Levellers indeed argued that
servants and paupers had lost their birthright, their property in
their own persons and labour. But probably the Levellers were
divided on this issue. None of them, I am sorry to say, ever suggested votes for women, though Mrs Lilburne and other women
were very active petitioners.

The Putney Debates ended in deadlock. Charles I escaped from
captivity just in time to suit the generals, who restored "discipline" by force. The outbreak of the Second Civil War reunited
the army against the royalists. Feeling ran high against Charles
among the rank and file as they tramped over England pursuing
the enemy through a wet summer. Leveller influence began to
grow again. But in a swift *coup* the generals brought the King
to trial and execution. Stealing some of the Levellers' ideas they
abolished the House of Lords and proclaimed a republic. Then
they turned on the Levellers on their left flank in an equally swift

series of repressive blows. A last revolt of Leveller regiments was put down at Burford and Banbury in May 1649.

The Levellers existed for barely three years as an organised political force; and they started absolutely from scratch, with no predecessors as a democratic political party. But in that period they left their mark on history. They evolved many of the techniques which modern democracy still uses—the mass petition, the demonstration, lobbying Parliament. They had their own newspaper, *The Moderate*, with correspondents in many parts of the country. Their leaders included the irrepressible John Lilburne, who, when he was flogged through the streets of London and pilloried by command of Charles I's Star Chamber, used the occasion to distribute seditious literature and to address an admiring crowd; when he was gagged he stamped with his feet.

John remained the darling of the people of London. The Long Parliament in 1652 exiled him under pain of death. He returned next year, and all that should have been necessary was to prove that he was the John Lilburne named in the act. But the jury found him "not guilty of any crime worthy of death". Lilburne had a splendid knack of making his clumsily powerful enemies look ridiculous. Playing for time during his trial he asked for a respite, if only to relieve himself. When this was refused, he called for a chamber-pot to be brought into court—and used it.

There was the gentle William Walwyn, who was accused of communist leanings. "It would never be well until all things were common", he was alleged to have said. "Then there would be no thieves, no covetous persons, no deceiving and abusing of one another, and so no need of government . . . no need of judges etc., but if any difference fall out, . . . take a cobbler from his seat, or a butcher from his shop, or any other tradesman that is an honest and just man, and let him hear the case and determine the same, and then betake himself to his work again." When Cromwell's army was conquering Ireland, Walwyn's voice was one of the few raised in England against it, in words which are still relevant. "The cause of the Irish natives in seeking their just freedoms . . . was the very same with our cause here in endeavouring our own rescue and freedom from the power of oppressors."

There was the acute and witty Richard Overton, who argued that the soul died with the body, and proclaimed that "by natural birth all men are equally and alike born to like property, liberty and freedom; and as we are delivered of God by the hand of nature into this world, every one with a natural, innate freedom and property (as it were writ in the table of every man's heart, never to be obliterated) even so are we to live, every one equally and alike to enjoy his birthright and privilege; even all whereof God by nature hath made him free".

There was the Agitator Sexby, who bearded Cromwell at Putney in 1647, and 10 years later, when Oliver was Lord Protector, impudently dedicated to him a pamphlet advocating his assassination, declaring that Oliver was "the true father of your country; for while you live we can call nothing ours, and it is from your death that we hope for our inheritances".

The Levellers never won support on a national scale. Their seagreen colours held the London streets, but it was difficult to get their message across to the masses of the population, largely illiterate, used to taking ideas from parson and squire. Their failure to capture the Army was decisive. But had they been given more than three years in which to educate a democratic electorate, their programme was well calculated to appeal to farmers, small tradesmen and artisans—the overwhelming majority of the people. "They cannot expect [success] in a few years", said *The Moderate* in August 1649, "by reason of the multiplicity of the gentry in authority, command etc., who drive on all designs for support of the old government, and consequently their own interest and the people's slavery; yet they doubt not but in time the people will herein discern their own blindness and folly."

In 1649 the Levellers were turning to propaganda activities outside London, as well as suggesting that the Irish and English peoples had common enemies. Cromwell may have been right when he shouted to the Council of State, not knowing that Lilburne's ear was at the keyhole, "You have no other way to deal with these men but to break them in pieces. . . . If you do not break them they will break you." The Levellers' was "a pleasing voice to all poor men", he said a few years later, "and truly not unwelcome to all bad men". "It is some consolation, if a commonwealth must needs suffer, it should rather suffer from rich men than from poor men." It has so suffered ever since.

Although the Levellers were defeated. many of their ideas lived on among the Quakers, whose use of the word "thou" to all and their refusal to take off their hats to their betters were acts of social defiance. The Levellers were rediscovered in the eighteenth century by the republican historian Catherine Macaulay, Wilkes's friend. They were quoted in the American, French and Russian Revolutions, by the Chartists, and by Marx and Engels as "the first who proclaimed the social question". In our own time H N Brailsford wrote a magnificent book on them. Lilburne had reason to be confident that "posterity . . . shall reap the benefit of our endeavours, whatever shall become of us".

A S P WOODHOUSE (ed.) *Puritanism and Liberty* (1938)

D W PETEGORSKY *Left-wing Democracy in the English Civil War* (1940)

W HALLER & G DAVIES (eds) *The Leveller Tracts (1647–53)* (New York, 1944)

D M WOLFE (ed.) *Leveller Manifestoes of the Puritan Revolution* (1944)

MONTAGUE SLATER *Englishmen with Swords* (1949) (a novel)

JOSEPH FRANK *The Levellers* (Cambridge, Mass., 1955)

C HILL *Puritanism and Revolution* (1958)

H N BRAILSFORD *The Levellers in the English Revolution* (1961)

P GREGG *Free-born John: A Biography of John Lilburne* (1961)

C HILL *The World Turned Upside Down* (1972)

Henry Collins

Thomas Paine and the Beginnings of Modern Radicalism

HENRY COLLINS *was a distinguished member of that generation of socialist historians who, during the past twenty years, have finally established the history of Socialism and labour movements as a "respectable" field of study. He was secretary of the Society for the Study of Labour History between 1961 and 1964. He was a Labour candidate in the 1964 General Election, acted as economic adviser to the Malta Labour Party and was economic correspondent of* TRIBUNE. *He was the author (with H. J. Fyrth) of* THE FOUNDRY WORKERS: A TRADE UNION HISTORY *(1959) and (with Chimen Abramsky) of* KARL MARX AND THE BRITISH LABOUR MOVEMENT *(1965). Among his many shorter works was an article on "The English Branches of the First International" in* ESSAYS IN LABOUR HISTORY *(eds. Briggs and Saville, 1960). He was senior tutor in social studies for the Oxford University Delegacy for Extra-Mural Studies. He died aged 52 in 1969, soon after the publication of his edition of Thomas Paine's* RIGHTS OF MAN. *Anthony Arblaster has supplemented the original version of this article, mostly with material from Dr Collins' introduction to that book.*

In 1776 a war of national liberation broke out in America to be followed, 13 years later, by a social revolution in France. Both events had repercussions in England. The success of America's revolutionary war discredited George III and forced his Ministers to go through the motions of reforming the administration. In Ireland there was even a pretence of granting home rule but in the kingdom as a whole there was little change because the class struggle was at a low ebb.

The American revolution jolted men's minds and the decade

immediately following saw the first stirrings of a reform movement though it was mainly confined to the aristocracy and the
middle class. The French Revolution had a much deeper impact.

Almost at once the European monarchies rallied to support the
French crown. In 1791 the Emperor of Austria and the King of
Prussia actually called for a crusade of sovereigns to restore the
authority of the King of France, thus inadvertently making sure
of his execution. It occurred to the democrats in England that if
their rulers could make common cause with crown and nobility
in France, the English people had a stake in the success of the
French Revolution. The idea of an international solidarity of peoples appeared, probably for the first time in history.

Reform societies sprang up in Britain and began to exchange
friendly messages with the Jacobin Clubs in France. By coinci-
dence a number of societies had been formed in 1788 to com-
memorate the centenary of the "Glorious Revolution" which had
chased James II from the throne and established the supremacy
of Parliament in England. In 1789 they had another revolution
to celebrate and the London Society heard an address from the
Unitarian Dr Richard Price, one of the leading statisticians of his
day, "On the Love of Our Country". Dr Price argued that the
French Revolution was an assertion of basic human rights, in
particular "the right to liberty of conscience in religious matters
. . . the right to resist power when abused and . . . the right to
choose our own governors, to cashier them for misconduct and
to frame a government for ourselves".

This nearly drove Edmund Burke to distraction and was directly responsible for his *Reflections on the Revolution in France*
which has served as a handbook for conservatives down to the
present day. What particularly upset Burke was the assertion
that the people had a right to rise against their sovereign. This
seemed strange because Burke had justified the English Revolution of 1688 and sympathised with the American revolution of
1776. But, as he explained, it was in order for the right sort of
people to rebel against a very bad monarch as a matter of last
resort. It was quite different, in fact completely intolerable, if
every Tom, Dick and Harry was to start claiming his alleged
"rights" and begin issuing instruction to his sovereign.

A number of replies to Burke appeared but the most effective and the most lasting was written by Thomas Paine, whose *Rights of Man* appeared in two parts in 1791 and 1792. Paine was one of the most original thinkers who have ever lived and his writings, though they have remained in print and been widely read, have been pretty consistently under-rated. One reason was that his style, though plain and powerful, was out of key with the florid and rhetorical writings in vogue at the time. "I scarcely ever quote", he wrote at the time of the American revolution; "the reason is I always think."

After scratching a living as a corset-maker and exciseman, Paine had left England for America in 1774. At the age of 37 he had shown talent but no sign of anything more and Benjamin Franklin wrote him a reference saying he would give satisfaction as a clerk or tutor in a private home. On arriving in Philadelphia he found a revolution in the making and plunged straight in. Six months before the Declaration of Independence, which contained many of his ideas, Paine published a pamphlet, *Common Sense*, which rallied opinion behind the still unfamiliar and terrifying idea of national liberation. The *Crisis* papers, published intermittently throughout the war, saved American morale more than once when it was close to breaking point.

When General Howe's advance forced Congress to abandon Philadelphia for Baltimore, Paine announced that a nation in arms could defeat superior professional forces if it learned the lessons of revolutionary warfare. At the beginning of 1777 he told the English commander that he would be beaten by mobile warfare—"By the time you extended from New York to Virginia, you would be reduced to a string of drops not capable of hanging together"—and some months later he explained that America, with "but few towns" was better placed than England to sustain a war economy. At the same time he prophesied that "The 'UNITED STATES OF AMERICA' will sound as pompously in the world or in history, as 'the kingdom of Great Britain'." Paine was in fact the first to use the term "United States of America".

He also predicted, and helped to secure an alliance between revolutionary America and monarchical France, pointing out that national interests were more powerful than ideological differences.

After the end of the Anglo-American war, in 1783, Paine

turned from politics to take up his scientific and technological projects. He designed an iron bridge and tried to invent a smoke-less candle. The candle was a failure, but his bridge design formed the basis of the famous bridge over the Wear at Sunderland, which became one of the wonders of the new industrial age, and was pictured on many popular commemorative jugs and mugs.

Returning to Europe in 1787, Paine foresaw the danger of war between England and France and wrote *Prospects on the Rubicon* in an effort to avert it. He divided his time between France and Britain. He was in England when the French Revolu-tion began in July 1789, but by September he was in Paris again, from where he wrote exuberantly to George Washington that "a share in two revolutions is living to some purpose".

Paine, an Englishman who was involved in revolutions in America and France, could well be called the first international revolutionary, and in 1791, at a dinner held by the radicals to celebrate the anniversary of the so-called "Glorious Revolution" of 1688 in England, he proposed a toast to "The Revolution of the World". His *Rights of Man*, in reply to Burke, not only de-fended the French Revolution but argued the case for democracy in England. Part Two went further and explained that demo-cracy would be incomplete unless it provided for economic wel-fare and social security. Expounding this theme Paine worked out the details of a system of welfare services, including retirement pensions and child allowances, to be financed by progressive taxa-tion.

Rights of Man and other democratic writings were circulated by the hundred thousand and a number of organisations appeared concerned to disseminate radical ideas. The most important of these was the London Corresponding Society founded by the Scot-tish shoemaker, Thomas Hardy, at the beginning of 1792. In con-trast to the other reforming bodies, which were confined to the aristocracy and middle classes, the LCS recruited working men and small shopkeepers, deliberately keeping its subscription rate down to a penny a week.

Hardy was one of the first to see the link between democracy and economic reform. He argued that poverty could no longer be excused by backward technology. He knew that the country was productive and that its citizens were hard-working and inventive, so that the distress which he saw on all sides was due neither to the soil nor to those who worked it, but to a faulty economic and social system.

The LCS fought for peace and democracy against poverty and exploitation. One of its best known publications, *An Address to The Nation from the London Corresponding Society on the Subject of a Thorough Parliamentary Reform*, which appeared in 1793, is worth quoting at some length because its remarks on counter-revolutionary war have not, unfortunately, lost their relevance. "British gold now subsidises armies of continental slaves and the blood of half Europe is pledged for the destruction of France! Supplies of every kind are sent from hence! . . . Provisions rise in price! The Revenue decreases and fresh Taxes are wanting! For fresh supplies of blood the liberties of our country are invaded . . . If such, O much oppressed Britons, are the effects of a four months' war, what are you to expect when it shall have lasted as many years?"

Inevitably, this radical agitation was met by government repression. And, as *Rights of Man* was the major written source of this agitation, it was equally inevitable that the government should try to put Paine in prison. They planned to put him on trial in 1792, but Paine was in Paris, having been chosen as a member of the French National Assembly. So he was declared an outlaw by the British government at the end of 1792, and never again returned to the country of his birth.

One of the weaknesses of the reform movement was that, while the industrial towns which had begun to appear in the north and midlands were centres of poverty, they were not yet centres of a working-class movement. The London Corresponding Society corresponded with like-minded clubs in the provinces (national political organisation was illegal), public meetings were held and literature circulated, often on a considerable scale.

But with the peasantry largely destroyed by the Enclosures—a situation peculiar to England—the working class small, scattered and raw and the middle class frightened out of its wits, there was no possibility of forming alliances with other classes. The radicals of the LCS and one or two of the provincial societies like Sheffield were largely lower middle class, thoughtful rather than revolutionary and the sort of men who, especially in London, made up the "moral force" wing of Chartism half a century later.

By October 1795, the war with France had been fought for nearly four years and hunger had become a major force in politics. The LCS called a big meeting at Copenhagen Fields and three days later the King's coach was attacked as he was on his way to open the new session of Parliament. The Government, already alarmed by the state of feeling, was only too happy to find a pretext for strengthening its already considerable powers of repression. Two Acts were passed increasing the power of magistrates and banning all unlicensed meetings of more than 50 people. The radicals showed enormous courage in continuing their agitation but the tide was now moving powerfully against them and some responded to repression by going underground and preparing for insurrection.

In 1799 the London Corresponding Society was suppressed by name, along with a number of other organisations, while the Combination Acts simultaneously suppressed trade unions. These were still few and scattered and there is no evidence that they were touched by the radical political movement, but there had been a few strikes in the skilled trades and the Government decided on a clean sweep. For the moment, the working-class movement was crushed, politically and industrially. After the rising of the United Irishmen had been suppressed in 1798 there was no base from which opposition could be organised.

Paine, meanwhile, had continued to live dangerously. Represented by Pitt's government as a bloodthirsty Jacobin, Paine was in fact a Girondin moderate in the context of the French Revolution, who, because of his opposition to the execution of Louis XVI, came under suspicion in France as a royalist! He was imprisoned for a year, being released in November 1794.

It was at this time that he wrote what was to become his second most influential work next to *Rights of Man, The Age of Reason*. This was an attack on Christianity and established religion, which gave Paine the reputation, again mistaken, of being an atheist. Paine was in fact a deist, in the traditional eighteenth-century style. But the effect of the book in England was undoubtedly to strengthen the popular secularist movement against religion and the churches.

In 1802, Paine, disenchanted with Napoleon, returned once

more to America, where he was welcomed by the President, Thomas Jefferson, but by few others. He continued to write and engage in political controversy, but the country which he most admired and for which he had done so much rewarded him with hostility and neglect. His last years were a sad epilogue to an astonishing life. He died in New York in 1809. Ten years later William Cobbett, like Paine a victim of British governmental repression, dug up Paine's bones and took them back to England.

It was a political gesture which had less effect than Cobbett had hoped. But it was symbolically important, for Paine's crucial role in the development of English popular radicalism was already clear. *Rights of Man* was, as Edward Thompson has said, "one of the two foundation texts of the English working-class movement" (the other being *Pilgrim's Progress*). It continued to be read, and Paine's name was not forgotten. Indeed, it is hardly an exaggeration to say that Paine has remained a controversial figure to this day. For when it was proposed to erect a statue to him in his birthplace, Thetford in Norfolk, the plan met with fierce opposition. The statue was finally set up in 1964, but Paine would undoubtedly be better pleased by the fact that his books, especially *Rights of Man*, continue to be widely read. "Mankind", he wrote there, "are not now to be told they shall not think, or they shall not read." Words such as those have hardly lost their relevance.

THOMAS PAINE   *Rights of Man* (1791). The Penguin edition (1969) has a valuable introduction by Henry Collins.

THOMAS PAINE   *The Complete Writings* in two volumes edited by Philip S Foner (New York, 1945).

H N BRAILSFORD   *Shelley, Godwin and their Circle* (1927). Has a good chapter on Paine.

ALFRED O ALDRIDGE   *Man of Reason* (Philadelphia, 1959).

E P THOMPSON   *The Making of the English Working Class* (1963, revised ed. 1968). Chapter Four includes a fine critique of Paine, and Chapter Five says much about his influence in the 1790's and thereafter.

E J HOBSBAWM *Labouring Men* (1964). Contains a short but stimulating essay on Paine.

DAVID THOMPSON (ed.) *Political Ideas* (1966). Useful short essay on Paine by J Hampden Jackson.

AUDREY WILLIAMSON *Thomas Paine: His Life, Work and Times* (1973). Published as this book went to press.

A J Peacock
Luddism and the Early Trade Unions

A J PEACOCK *was born in Cambridge in 1929, on the day that the Labour Government of that year was elected. He became an electrician and in 1952 went to Ruskin College, Oxford, where he studied Politics and Economics. He then read history at Southampton University and is now completing a PhD at York University. He is a magistrate for the City of York. He has been warden of the York Educational Settlement since 1960. Among his publications are* BREAD OR BLOOD *(1965),* GEORGE HUDSON OF YORK *(with David Joy, 1971), and "Revolt of the Fields in East Anglia" in Lionel Munby (ed),* THE LUDDITES AND OTHER ESSAYS *(1971).*

When the nineteenth century began, trade unions were illegal. The Tory Government of the late eighteenth century had passed the Combination Acts which rendered union activity almost impossible. Under these circumstances, working-class movements of protest were of a violent nature, secretive and, of necessity, backward looking. They were movements to stop innovation, movements of people afraid of the future, looking back sadly to a pre-industrial past; they usually took the form of violent attacks on machinery.

In 1811, during a year of industrial depression and following a succession of dreadful harvests, the first outbreaks of "Luddism" occurred (The name is said to derive from a Leicester stockinger's apprentice, who in a fit of temper smashed his employer's frames with a hammer.) These took place among the workers in the lace and hosiery trades of the midlands. Machine breaking had been a fairly commonplace occurrence amongst the framework knitters, but never on the scale of the last years of the war with France. Hundreds of frames, whereon cheap and shoddy goods were made, were smashed by armed bands of men who assembled at night, allegedly under their mythical general, Ned Ludd. In 1812 frame-breaking was made a capital offence.

The Act of 1812 had little deterrent effect, and Luddism spread to the croppers and weavers of Lancashire and Yorkshire. The stockingers had been protesting against sharp practices; these people were protesting against the introduction of weaving and cropping machinery. Attacks on the "obnoxious" looms took place in Stockport, Manchester, Bolton and many other places, and eight people were sentenced to death at Lancaster Assizes, another 15 at Chester.

In Yorkshire Luddism in 1812 was centred in the Spen Valley, between Huddersfield and Leeds, the heart of the cropping branch of the woollen industry. Suffering from the effects of bad trade, the croppers saw the new machines as a threat to their very existence. Men with blackened faces went round the villages at night breaking the "detestable shearing frames". A particular object of hatred was William Cartwright of Rawfolds, and in an armed attack on his mill, two persons were killed.

An attempt to assassinate Cartwright was made a week later, and William Horsfall, another employee, *was* killed, for which crime three people were eventually hanged, after a trial at York Assizes in January, 1813. The Horsfall murder lost the Luddites a great deal of sympathy, and the gangs were broken up. There were a few more isolated incidents in Yorkshire, but the area was pacified. Over 1,000 troops were moved into Huddersfield alone.

In the agricultural villages at this time rural Luddism was by no means absent. Rick burning, and the smashing of threshing mills and mole ploughs were common occurrences. In East Anglia there were serious riots among the fenland labourers and a number were executed at Ely.

No one had been killed by the rioters during the troubles of 1816, but 24 were sentenced to death. Eventually 19 were reprieved, many of them receiving long sentences of transportation. The five left to die were executed on a specially constructed drop which, it was said, would launch "the unhappy men . . . into eternity without that horrible pause attending the usual mode of execution . . . from a cart". From the scaffold John Dennis made a speech to the crowd which was reported at great length in the newspapers—as an awful warning to other would be protesters. "I exhort you in the name of God", Dennis said, "that God before whom I shall shortly appear, to avoid drunkenness, Sabbath-breaking, whoremongery, bad company : oh! beware of these sins, I pray you also to avoid rioting!—and in every respect refrain from breaking the laws of your country!—Remember the words of the Judge, that tried us for the crimes for which we are now going to suffer, who said, 'The law of the land will always be too strong for its assailants, and those who defy the law will, in the end. be subdued by the law, and be *compelled* to submit to its justice or its mercy!' We stand here a melancholy example of the power and justice of the law. I freely forgive those who gave evidence against me : and may the God of mercy forgive me and have mercy upon my soul!"

The next wave of Luddism took place in the mid 1820's. This time the handloom weavers, whose numbers had greatly swollen during the previous decades because of the increased supply of yarn made possible by the mechanisation of spinning, were the people most affected. In 1822 a Bradford manufacturer "constructed a power-loom as secretly as possible to evade any attack which might be made to destroy it, and sent it to be worked at Shipley". To no avail. Weavers from the surrounding villages caused it first to be dismantled, then destroyed it. In other parts of the country also machines were smashed. The weavers, however, were unable to stop their introduction, and their craft entered its death throes. They were finally squeezed out of existence during the years of Chartism.

The handworkers, in fact, formed the depressed masses who were among the most enthusiastic Chartists. Some hung on a miserable pittance; some went into the factories; many, in Yorkshire, became woolcombers.

The woolcombers in the early 'twenties were the élite of the working class engaged in the worsted trade, able to earn as much as 23 shillings a week. Unlike the weavers who worked alone, they worked in batches and were extremely radical, "the combing shops rang with wild denunciations of wrongdoers, and . . . fervid

admiration of the champion[s] of democracy," a historian of
Bradford recalled.

Their trade was easily learned, however, and easily equipped.
The influx of weavers and others brought wages down, and made
work hard to get. They did not finally disappear until the early
'fifties, but for almost 30 years before that suffered appallingly. In
November, 1839, the month of the Newport rising, it was reported
that they could earn no more than eight shillings a week in Bradford, and many could not get employment even at that rate. Trade
in Bradford was getting worse, the *Northern Star* reported on
23rd November: "Thousands upon thousands of human beings,
in this large and populous district, know not when they go to bed
where the morning's breakfast is to come from. . . . The general-
ity of woolcombers are stinted to earn not more than from six
shillings to eight shillings per week, and in a great many cases the
employers either cannot or will not find work for their men to
earn the sum stated". A month later the same newspaper reported that "Woolcombers, weavers, &c, are in a great state of
actual 'Privation'," and just before Christmas prominent Chartists presided at a meeting of the unemployed. Henry Hodgson
proposed a resolution saying "that the distresses of the labouring
classes call for the interference of the authorities to provide them
with food or employment". A petition was taken to the magistrates, who refused to help, and the deputation went to the Vicar
—who "promised to preach a sermon for the good of their souls".
Fifteen years later still, in 1854, the *Bradford Examiner* carried
a heartrending account of the conditions of the combers then.
There were 942 heads of families and single men in the Bradford
district, it reported, all getting under two shillings a week from
all sources.

Until 1824 these people, fighting a painful, losing battle with
machinery, were forbidden to unite in unions, and their protests,
perforce, were unorganised and violent. The Combination Acts,
however, had not been entirely successful, and there is evidence
of the existence of unions in many towns while the Acts were in
existence. In York, for example, an unindustrialised city, the
building workers almost certainly had a union, and in July
1810, Thomas Townend was given two months' hard labour for
"having on the 18th of June last, prevailed on the workmen em-

ployed on the Minster, to leave their work for an advance of wages". In Bradford, too, there must have been an organisation in existence during these years which was able to come out into the open after repeal.

In August 1824 what was to become the Union Association of Woolcombers and Stuff Weavers came into existence, and in the following June there commenced "the bitterest strike of Bradford's history". Starting with wage demands the strike developed into one for union recognition, and as many as 20,000 weavers and combers were involved in it. Contributions poured into Bradford, and John Tester, the leader of the union, said that expenditure on people "out of employ" was over £14,000. All to no effect. The employers used "the document," and the men (and women and children) were utterly defeated, and forced back to work.

The "document" was a regular feature of labour disputes— "a pledge which all employees were required to sign . . . [which] bound them to renounce the Union and to refrain from supporting other members of the Union". It was used everywhere as an instrument of oppression; and not only by employers. The *Yorkshireman* of 10th May 1834 said that "even in York" feelings were running high, and that it had "been requested to state that the overseers of one parish . . . [had] come to the determination of refusing relief to any person who belongs to the Unions. No doubt the same principles will be acted upon", the paper concluded, "in all other parishes". On 28th September 1839 the *Northern Star* reported that, in response to a strike by the carpet weavers of Heckmondwike, the employers there had "formed a most *disgraceful and diabolical* combination for the purpose of *reducing* their workmen's wages, and to compel them to sign their names against all Trade Unions &c."

The year after the defeat of Tester's union another attempt was made by the firm of J G Horsfall to introduce machinery in the Bradford district. This led to a celebrated incident. Unionism had failed, and the methods of pre-union days were tried once more. On May Day a crowd of 240 smashed the mill windows. Two days later it was attacked again. On this occasion the mill was defended and two of the crowd were killed. Eventually John Holdsworth and five others were tried at York Assizes. Holdsworth, a woolcomber, said that he told Colonel Pumbe Tempest: "It was hard to wind, weave, dress and carry home 30 yards for 6d." According to other reports he adopted a far more high-handed tone. "Silence, sir, until I have done," he is alleged to have said, "meat is high, wages are low, and it is time something should be done—are we to starve?"

Nothing was done, of course, but the events of 1824–6 had a profound effect. Luddism—which was to be very prevalent in the agrarian districts for at least another 20 years—decreased, and unionism amongst the woollen and worsted workers went underground. Nevertheless it remained, and in 1832 there was in existence a Bradford branch of the famous Leeds Clothier's Union, which sent no less than £1,822 to workers on strike at Dolphinholme, near Lancaster.

Political activity absorbed the energy of the working classes in the industrial districts during the early 'thirties, but in the aftermath of the "great betrayal" of 1832 there was an upsurge of unionism again. In late 1833 the enormous Grand National Consolidated Trades Union came into being, into which unions of every sort of trade were swept. Into it went the woolcombers and weavers of Bradford, at a time when they were again being threatened with wage reductions. Their leader in Bradford, and eventual secretary of the local organisation of the GNCTU, was Peter Bussey. Bussey was to become one of the best known of the "physical force" section of the Chartist movement.

Several other groups joined the Grand National in Bradford. Among them the tailors, who very quickly engaged in a strike for "equalisation of wages", and lost. In York, too, a city tremendously different from Bradford, the tailors joined "the unjustifiable combination", were sacked, and successfully resisted attempts to bring in blacklegs from Leeds.

The building workers were also prominent in the Grand National. They had had a national organisation which attracted Robert Owen's attention very early on in the history of the GNCTU, and building workers were in a very strong position in the fast-growing towns of the West Riding. Bradford's population increased by over 250 per cent between 1801 and 1841, and the need for buildings put the bricklayers, carpenters, and masons in a very strong position. While the *Bradford Observer* and the

Northern Star reported wage cuts for weavers and combers in
the 'thirties and 'forties, it reported successful strikes by builders
for wages of as much as 24 shillings. The position was the same
in York. In some places, skilled building trade workers became
prominent (usually moral force) Chartists a little later on.
William Lovett had been a cabinet maker, William Cordukes of
York was a joiner.

The GNCTU was a nine-days' wonder and disappeared rapidly
after the Government attacked it by prosecuting the six agricultural labourers of Dorset. The "Tolpuddle Martyrs" were arrested for swearing men into a lodge which was intending to join
the Nation. They had not started or even threatened a strike, but
in March 1834 they were sentenced to seven years' transportation, a sentence which finally alienated the working class from
the Whig Government which they had done so much to bring to
power, a sentence which is important in the story of subsequent
independent working-class activity. Chartism, the great attempt
at comprehensive political reform, was only a few years away.
The sentence on the Dorchester labourers had a great effect upon
people like Bussey (and apparently Feargus O'Connor), impress-
ing upon them the need to create movements of their own, and
to desert the Whigs. On Monday 28th April 1834 a crowd esti-
mated at between 15,000 and 20,000 met on Wibsey Low Moor
to protest at the treatment of the Tolpuddle labourers. Captain
Wood of Sandal presided and Bussey and Joshua Jobson, editor
of *The Voice of the West Riding*, were appointed to present a
petition to the King. The notice calling the meeting shows the
disillusionment the working class felt with its allies of a few short
years ago.

"Freedom or Slavery.—West Riding Meeting.—In compliance
with the unanimous Requisition of the Meetings held in the
several towns comprising the West-Riding of this county, a
public meeting will be held on Wibsey Low Moor, near
Bradford, on Monday, the 28th day of April, 1834, (the
Chair to be taken at twelve o'clock,) to take into further
consideration the most adviseable means of restoring to their
homes the six unfortunate and unjustly banished Dorchester
labourers. The time has at length arrived, when it behoves
every man who values the last remaining vestige of British

liberty, to come forward, and openly and fearlessly declare his sentiments. Now, then, speak out! Say yea or nay. Say you will be slaves, or act as freemen! If you will do your duty, come to the meeting. Men and women, Unionists and Non-Unionists,—Operatives come, one and all; leave your looms, your mills, your lapstones, and needles; and show that you feel for your fellows, and that you are determined to present a bold front to tyranny."

Working-class activity in the early years of the nineteenth century shows a steady progression from machine smashing to experiments in political organisation and unionism. As soon as the new methods failed, however, there was a reversion to the methods of the Luddites. Tester's union was followed by Luddism, and the same pattern can be seen in the Chartist movement later on. When peaceful agitation failed, there was a move towards "direct action" : when the great National Petition was rejected, the physical force men took over.

THOMAS BAINES   *Yorkshire Past and Present* (2 vols., 1871, 1877)

RAYMOND POSTGATE   *The Builders' History* (nd, 1923)

G D H COLE & RAYMOND POSTGATE   *The Common People* (1938)

C H DRIVER   *Tory Radical, The Life of Richard Oastler* (1940)

G D H COLE   *Attempts at General Union 1818–1834* (1953)

J C GILL   *Parson Bull of Byerley* (1963)

E P THOMPSON   *The Making of the English Working Class* (1963)

A J PEACOCK   *Bread or Blood, A Study of the Agrarian Riots in East Anglia in 1816* (1965)

A J PEACOCK   *Bradford Chartism 1838–1840* (York, 1969)

M I THOMIS   *The Luddites, Machine-Breaking in Regency England* (1970)

LIONEL M MUNBY (ed.)   *The Luddites and Other Essays* (1971)

Margaret Cole
Robert Owen

MARGARET COLE, *eldest child of Professor J P Postgate, took First-Class Honours in Classics at Cambridge. As the wife of G D H Cole she collaborated with him in books on Socialism and labour history, and detective novels. She is the historian of the Fabian Society and its President. She served on the Education Committee of the London County Council, 1943–64 and was chairman of its Further Education Committee. She was an Alderman of the LCC, 1950–64. She is a journalist and has lectured in university tutorial classes in Cambridge and London. Her books include* BEATRICE WEBB *(1945),* MAKERS OF THE LABOUR MOVEMENT *(1948),* GROWING UP INTO REVOLUTION *(1949),* ROBERT OWEN OF NEW LANARK *(1953),* THE STORY OF FABIAN SOCIALISM *(1961),* THE LIFE OF G D H COLE *(1971) and many others.*

Robert Owen was born over 200 years ago in Newtown in mid-Wales, He went to the village school, where he was so bright a little boy that when he was only seven, Mr Thickness, the principal, made him a pupil-teacher. He was a popular child, good at dancing and athletics; but—and this is important—he hated all competitive effort because it made the losers so unhappy. When he was just 10 years old he persuaded his parents to let him go away to earn his living, and with £2 in his pocket and his coach fare to London paid, he went to stay with an elder brother while he looked for a job. Within six weeks he found one with a Stamford linen-draper named McGuffog. So he started life as a shopboy; but unlike Britain's other famous shopboy, H G Wells, he was extremely efficient—so good, in fact, that his first employer considered offering him a partnership and the hand of his niece.

His third shop job was in Manchester, in the midst of the already booming cotton trade. Exports of cotton goods rose about
five-fold in the ten years between 1780 and 1790; and Owen
observed this. In his first venture into business—with the help of
£100 borrowed from his elder brother—he was let down by his
partner; but, recovering, he struck out on his own, and though
in a small way he did well enough to secure, at twenty years old
and when he had been five years in Manchester, the post of
manager of one of the most up-to-date cotton-spinning mills in
the country, owned by the well-known Peter Drinkwater. He still
knew very little about the industry as a whole—his own little venture had been confined to the making of "rovings"; but by continuous application, by arriving early and staying late, by study-
ing closely the machinery and the workers, and by confining his
own function for the first weeks to the making of only such decisions as were absolutely essential, he had effectively mastered
the whole business of the factory, including the purchase of machinery and raw materials and the day-to-day finance. He further
added, as his own contribution, a knowledge of fine materials
which he had learned while in the service of Mr McGuffog:
this enabled him to see at a glance the possibilities of the famous
Sea Island cotton which, uninviting as it appeared at first sight,
produced finer and stronger thread than any other. After only
six months with Drinkwater, he was offered a permanent post
with the promise of a partnership. Drinkwater, however, for financial reasons of his own, reneged on this offer, and though he
tried to retain Owen's services as manager for any salary he
cared to name, Owen refused, "because I will never connect myself with any partners who are not desirous to be united with me".

This display of independence did Owen no harm and he found
other partners immediately, and during the ensuing years built
himself up a reputation as an industrial and business expert which
got him elected in 1793 to the Manchester Lit. & Phil. (see below) and three years later to the newly-formed Manchester
Board of Health : he also became personally prosperous enough
to buy a largish house—Greenheys, which had been built by the
father of Thomas De Quincey the essayist. The next important
date in his history is, however, 1798.

In that year, while visiting Glasgow as the representative of the

Chorlton Twist Company, he met a girl called Caroline Dale, who decided she would like to marry him, and asked him if he would like to see her father's mills at New Lanark by the Falls of Clyde. Indeed he would : all that he had heard of the philanthropic cotton-master David Dale (who had no son of his own) made the young man of twenty-seven feel that New Lanark was just the right place for him to put into practice ideas of organisation which he had been working out in his own mind during the years in Manchester, and had already tried out to some extent in Drinkwater's factory.

Unfortunately, we do not know exactly what those ideas were at that time or who influenced them; for Owen did not write them down until a dozen years later, by which time he had convinced himself—as he remained convinced until the end of his life—that he had thought out his New View of Society, as he called it, all by himself, and owed nothing to anyone else. Of course this was not true : as a bachelor in Manchester, he had early been elected to the famous Literary and Philosophical Society where so many of the most informed minds of the age met for weekly discussions—Lavoisier, Dalton, Erasmus, Darwin, Benjamin Franklin, Joseph Priestley, Josiah Wedgwood, Count Volta, Gilbert Wakefield, to take only a few names at random, were among those who addressed it—and though young Owen was welcomed as a successful businessman, his colleagues presumably talked to him; it is probable also that he read Godwin's *Political Justice* and some of the works of the Scottish radical humanists. At any rate, he had enough confidence in his ideas, and his ability to call upon David Dale and ask to buy his mills. After some brief discussion, he and his partners secured the mills and shortly afterwards he married Caroline. It was not a close union, for Caroline was no intellectual; and though she loved him dearly and was a good mother and housekeeper, and carried out his precepts with regard to the villagers and children of New Lanark insofar as she understood them, she did not share his opinions. But his seven children (the first-born died in infancy) did; they were devoted to him, and several of them when they grew up took part in his major work.

He started immediately to reform what he afterwards described as "a very wretched community". This was not quite fair to his father-in-law, who had been rightly known as an enlightened and philanthropic employer. But David Dale was getting old; and though his workers liked him, they were not a very enlightened lot, drawn as they were from all over the place, sometimes by "press-gang" methods, and including in their numbers the unfortunate "pauper apprentice" children sent out by the administrators of the Poor Law; and they had many of the anti-social habits of the Scottish working class at that date. Owen was determined to reclaim them; but he was not in too great a hurry. He had of course to make the mills—which were very large for the time—earn enough money to keep his partners happy. This was at first the least of his troubles; but he had also to persuade the workers to accept him—a foreigner from the south—and to collaborate in his many experiments for improving methods and standards of work, and reorganising living conditions in the village without ever using big stick methods. Much of this he did himself, by altering lay-out and check-points for materials and products, and by paving the roads, building better houses, and buying in bulk coal, pure food (and pure whisky!); some, such as the internal cleansing of the houses, he persuaded the workers themselves to take on—though what some of them rudely called *The Committee of Bughunters.* But he did not really gain their confidence until 1806, when the American embargo on the export of raw cotton forced the mills to close, and Owen persuaded his partners to pay full wages to all thrown out of work—for over four months, during which time they had a good chance to watch what Owen was doing with his most memorable experiment— the schools.

Immediately, he had ended the system of taking in apprentices from the workhouses, and he refused to have in the factory any child under ten years old—he would have preferred twelve, but in the days when children normally went to work at six or younger he could not manage this—and gradually he developed for the young creatures a school regime astonishingly modern. To mention only the principal points: Owen absolutely forbade punishment of any kind, or even "scolding"; he insisted on complete truthfulness in answering—or saying that one could not answer —the children's questions. He did away with set lessons and periods (though he allowed lectures from time to time) holding that children wanted to learn and would learn if you provided them with plenty of material to learn with and from, excited their interest and left off teaching when it flagged; he also believed that instruction should be related to reality, to things which they knew or could find by exploring the neighbourhood, and that music, dancing, and play should be a regular part of their education; and above all that they should be helped throughout "to think and act rationally". By 1815 or 1816 the New Lanark schools, and the happy children in them, had become an admired port of call for visitors from all walks of life, and for persons from all over the civilised world—and only less so the community of New Lanark itself.

This, as I have said, was not achieved all at once. Owen had to grapple with a succession of partners who thought he was trying to spend too much on what they considered frills and fads. At one time they nearly ruined him, and it was not until 1814, after he had published his essays on *A New View of Society*, in which he expressed his conviction that men were naturally good, but distorted by bad education and bad institutions, which ought to be and could be completely changed, that he acquired a new set, including rich Quakers, who were prepared to put up plenty of money and to give him, for some years at least, a completely free hand. At once he began to complete the building of the schools and of the new community centre, called the Institution for the Formation of Character, at the opening of which, in January 1816, he gave the first public signs that he hoped to apply the principles of New Lanark to the country at large—and showed, also, the beginnings of a dangerous self-confident optimism.

But it did seem time for new principles.

The horrors of the early factories, combined with the cost to the Poor Law of relieving unemployment caused by enclosures and the disbandment of the armies after Waterloo, were shocking "enlightened" persons; and many were willing to believe that Owen, the highly successful manufacturer, had a recipe for the troubles which the government's repressive legislation had failed to find. He was invited to draw up a Factory Bill which Sir Robert Peel, himself a manufacturer, would steer through Parliament, and to prepare a comprehensive plan for dealing with the Poor Law and the unemployed. Eagerly he undertook both, and came slap against the hard cruel world outside New Lanark. The factory-owners ganged up against his Bill, gathering evidence to show that a twelve-hour day of breathing cotton fluff was very good for small children (who otherwise would be learning to be criminals!) and succeeded in taking the guts out of the Bill. The House of Commons Committee which was considering the Poor Law left him in an anteroom for two days before refusing even to see him. Thus checked, he turned himself into a one-man band, published his Plan for Villages of Co-operation to organise production throughout the kingdom, with a full complement of schools and communal institutions based on what he was doing so successfully at New Lanark. He had it printed at length in *The Times* and other leading London papers, and bought, out of the money made in his own New Lanark works, thirty or forty thousand copies of each of the journals for mass circulation. In the summer of 1817, he called huge meetings at the City of London Tavern to discuss the plan.

These meetings ended in confusion, partly through his own fault. For he had called them, not for discussion, but to expound what he felt certain must be instantly accepted by everyone of sense and goodwill; and he chose to expound it in highly Messianic language, incidentally remarking that all revealed religions had been proved to be untrue and must be abandoned in favour of a rational humanist system of education. Worse still, he infuriated political Radicals like "Orator" Hunt (who had already called his Villages "parallelograms of paupers") by declaring that political democracy and Parliamentary voting were of no importance. The result was to lose him some middle and upper-class support, though not as much as might have been expected, for three years later it was the Scottish farmers and landowners who asked him to prepare the best and clearest exposition of his by now socialist ideas of reform, which is called the *Report to the County of Lanark*. More important, the publicity then secured for his vision of a good and just society found a strong welcome in the hearts of a great many of the thinking working-class, where it continued to grow, almost unperceived, for the next dozen years.

Unperceived, certainly, by Owen himself, who was busy in the years immediately following the war first, in touring Europe, being lionised and trying to convert European VIPs like Louis Philippe and Metternich(!) to his proposals, and secondly, in Britain, lecturing and expounding to groups large and small. This meant that he was less on the spot in New Lanark, and his backers, particularly the Quaker William Allen (founder of Allen & Hanbury) were getting alarmed at his large ideas, his attacks on religion and the unconventionality of some of the school practices, and were starting to push him out into the unfortunate adventure of New Harmony.

Harmony was a village in Indiana, owned by a community of God-fearing German peasants who wanted to move to another site. There were many "communities" in the New World at that date, and if Europe appeared not to be ready for Villages of Co-operation, America was the obvious country to receive them. So Owen, who felt that he had got as far in New Lanark as he could, bought the Harmony estate pretty well on the nod, and instantly started to set up an Owenite community there. Within three years he had written it off as a failure, and this disappointment was due almost entirely to his own indecent hurry.

After he had completed the *Report to the County of Lanark*, Owen seems to have lost almost all sense of the practical—in financial affairs, but also, and more important, in his power to judge men, to discriminate, and so to manage them or help them to manage themselves. In filling up the community, for example, he accepted all who volunteered without any selection, with the result that along with many individuals of talent and value there were some who had neither, and worse still there was a fearful shortage of those with the practical skills, such as cooks, masons, bricklayers, &c., which were needed if the community was to be a going concern. Also, as founder and in effect director of the community, he felt certain that it should adopt, and adopt *quickly,* all the principles and practice of living which he had thought out for himself—he kept devising new constitutions for it. Everyone can now see the many mistakes which were made —nevertheless, Robert Dale Owen, who wrote of the first months there, testified to the enormous and enthusiastic excitement of the pioneers. It must have been something like a cross between an early kibbutz and a socialist summer-school.

When it came to pieces, Owen was not deterred; he went

around speaking to crowds, and we next meet him in conversation with the government of Mexico, offering to run the whole territory of Texas for them on Owenite lines. When that offer was declined he went back to England where he found a whole host of small co-operative societies, all impressed by Mr Owen's Plan, and anxious to play a part in turning Britain into a co-operative socialist society.

Owen himself was not at first impressed by them; as Lovett the Chartist tells us, he found them pretty small beer after Texas. But suddenly, as it seems, he saw in the co-operative movement a possible means of spreading socialism; he went to a co-operative movement conference at Bristol, was received with huge enthusiasm and acclaimed as their new leader; shortly afterwards he became leader, in like fashion, of the Building Trade Workers, whom he persuaded to set up a National Guild of Builders, and only a few months later, gathered most of the Trade Unions set free by the repeal of the Combination Acts into the Grand National Consolidated Trades Union, which claimed a million or so members and was slain, when it had barely come into existence, by the combined onslaught of the employers and the Whig Government which had just passed the Reform Act.

The fate of the Grand National, its constituents and its branches at Tolpuddle and elsewhere, is part of Trade Union history, and nobody doubts that Owen was a very bad leader for a revolutionary movement of the downtrodden; he did not understand the tactics of strikes or negotiations; his methods exasperated those who most passionately admired him; and he never listened (except politely) to what anyone else had to say. Because he *knew*; and if people—workers, employers, ministers with a large M or a small one—would only listen to him they could establish the New Moral World "like a thief in the night". What must be understood however, is that neither co-operative societies nor Trade Unions meant anything to him *as themselves*, only as possible agents for the establishment of socialism. He did not ask to be their leader; they carried him on their shoulders to that position—and this for three main reasons. First, because they believed that what he said about society was *right* and *ought* to come about, secondly, because they knew something of what he had done at New Lanark and thought that he could show them how to do it in their own spheres; and thirdly, because they could see for themselves that, whatever he might have thought about formal democracy, he was in practice the most courteously egalitarian of men, whose "fine manners" were an example to anyone and whose plain honesty and kindness could put others to shame and fill them with a desire to be as good, and as selfless and as unpretentious as he was.

Aside from his major Plan, one has to record that he threw out, by the way as it were, dozens of suggestions for the improvement of life. He was the first, in this country, to advocate town-planning and a Green Belt : in addition to his own educational innovations he called for teacher-training, for a census of production, for economic planning, for public works and bulk purchase of supplies, and for prison reform. Some, but not all, of his suggestions have been put into effect—often after so long an interval that everyone had forgotten who first made them; others have yet to be tried. His bicentenary celebrations hardly began to cover what we owe to Robert Owen.

ROBERT OWEN   *A New View of Society* (1813; Everyman edition, edited by G D H Cole, 1927; latest edition, 1970)

ROBERT OWEN   *Report to the County of Lanark* (Glasgow, 1821 reprinted with *A New View of Society*, 1970

ROBERT OWEN   *The Life of Robert Owen written by himself* (first published 1857, reprinted 1971)

ROBERT DALE OWEN   *Threading My Way* (1874, reprinted New York, 1967)

FRANK PODMORE   *Robert Owen, A Biography* (1906, reprinted New York, 1969)

G D H COLE   *Life of Robert Owen* (1925, reprinted 1965)

G D H COLE & RAYMOND POSTGATE   *The Common People* (1938, many times reprinted)

G D H COLE   *A Century of Co-operation* (n.d., 1945)

MARGARET COLE   *Robert Owen of New Lanark* (1953)

JOHN BUTT (ed)   *Robert Owen, Prince of Cotton-Spinners* (Newton Abbot, 1971). Essays dealing mainly with the period before Owen left New Lanark.

S POLLARD & J SALT (eds)   *Robert Owen, Prophet of the Poor* (1971)

Edward Thompson
Peterloo

EDWARD THOMPSON *was born in 1924 and read history at Cambridge. Between 1948 and 1965 he was extra-mural lecturer for Leeds University in the West Riding. Subsequently he became Reader in the Centre for the Study of Social History at Warwick University. He now writes full-time from his home near Worcester. He is the author of* WILLIAM MORRIS, ROMANTIC TO REVOLUTIONARY *(1955) and of* THE MAKING OF THE ENGLISH WORKING CLASS *(1963), the editor of* OUT OF APATHY *(1960), joint editor of* THE NEW REASONER *(1957–60), contributor to the* MAY DAY MANIFESTO *(1968) and editor of* WARWICK UNIVERSITY LTD *(1970). He has also published many articles dealing with English social history.*

The 150th anniversary of the massacre at St Peter's Fields, in Manchester, on August 16, 1819, saw the appearance of three new publications, two of which may be described as occasional. The first is a well-presented folder of plans, prints, and broadsides, prepared by the Manchester Public Libraries. The second is a popular account ("the first book for the general reader", as the blurb has it) by Miss Joyce Marlow. The bias of her book appears to be, like her maternal descent, of "Radical, Unitarian, small mill-owning stock"; and the general reader may sometimes find that her folksy narrative—"Bamford's wife, Mima, a sterling character, made determined efforts to ascertain what had happened to 'our Sam' . . ."—tends to cloy. Miss Marlow offers some general background to explain what led up to Peterloo; this is second-hand and generally over-simplified; but her narrative of the events of the day itself is closely-observed, well-written, and deftly employs a little original material. On this account her book deserves to find some readers; although the *first* book for the general reader must remain, as it has always been, Samuel Bamford's *Passages in the Life of a Radical*.

Bamford's evidence is not, of course, privileged and beyond reach of examination. He was one of the crowd ridden down by Yeomanry and Hussars—a thing likely to induce bias in the victims. And he was later found guilty before a special jury at York Assizes for "assembling with unlawful banners, at an unlawful meeting, for the purpose of inciting the subjects of our lord the king, to contempt and hatred of the government", and sentenced to one year's imprisonment. This clear decision in an impartial court of justice suggests him not only as a biased but also as a compromised witness. No matter such as this escapes the watchful eyes of Mr Robert Walmsley.

Mr Walmsley's *Peterloo: The Case Reopened* is not so much occasioned by the anniversary; it is, in itself, an occasion, and is —the blurb tells us—"the fruit of half a lifetime's research". The 585 pages of this fruit swing from the impeccable bough of the Manchester University Press. Mr Walmsley, a Manchester antiquarian bookseller, first had his interest in Peterloo aroused some thirty years ago during the course of research into the family history of the Hultons of Hulton. William Hulton (1787–1864) was chairman of the magistrates who overlooked the field of Peterloo and gave to the Yeomanry the fatal order to advance. In the course of his researches Mr Walmsley became convinced, not only that William Hulton had been unfairly treated by historians, but that he and his fellow magistrates were the victims of nothing less than a Radical conspiracy to falsify the events of that day—a conspiracy fostered by Hunt, Bamford, and Richard Carlile, furthered by Archibald Prentice (author of *Historical Sketches of Manchester*) and John Edward Taylor (before he sobered down and founded the *Manchester Guardian*), and in which John Tyas (the correspondent of *The Times* who witnessed events from the hustings), the Rev. Edward Stanley, and dozens of others were witting or unwitting accessories—a conspiracy so compelling that even Donald Read, in his sober and by no means radical study of *Peterloo* (1958), failed to detect it.

It is necessary to make clear what Mr Walmsley's book is not, as well as what it is. It is not a general interpretative account of Peterloo within its political or local background. Nothing is said of radicalism or reaction before January, 1819; very little is said about the government of Manchester in 1819, or to explain the character, role, or reputation of such important actors as Joseph Nadin or Henry Hunt before they emerge on the 1819 stage. This is not a book for the general reader, unless he has taken the precaution of reading (at least) Bamford—or Prentice—and Dr Read beforehand. Nor is it, altogether, a book for the scholar, although it has competent scholarly apparatus, adequate foot-notes and bibliography, and a very good index. It is not based on extensive newly discovered evidence, although Mr Walmsley introduces interesting new material from the Rev. W R Hay (the prominent clerical magistrate) and from William Hulton himself. In particular there has been no new search of Home Office, legal, or military papers in the Public Record Office.

Mr Walmsley is interested, chiefly, in the events of the day of Peterloo, and even more closely in the events of one half-hour of that day—between 1.14 and 1.45 pm—from the time when Henry Hunt arrived on the hustings to the time when the field was empty of all but shawls, bonnets, sticks, and cavalry adjusting their saddle-girths. Obsessively he rides up and down that field and its environs, obsessively he rides up and down the five or ten minutes between the arrival of the Yeomanry at the edge of the field and the dispersal of the crowd, summoning witnesses in the newspaper press of the weeks following, dragging them back by their collars, making them pace over the yards before and behind the hustings, cross-examining reminiscences and confronting them with conflicting depositions, galloping off into the suburbs of the twentieth century to interrogate suspicious stragglers, like F A Bruton, the author of the careful *The Story of Peterloo* (1919).

At the centre of his obsession is this: what happened on that day was unintentional, and the crowd (or part of it) was the first aggressor. The magistrates in their house overlooking the hustings were justly alarmed by the proceedings, both by tumults which had preceded August 16 and by the radical rhetoric and military array of the crowd on the day. With a nice sense of legalistic propriety they waited until Hunt and his fellow speakers were on the hustings and then ordered the constables to arrest them; this Joseph Nadin, the deputy-constable, refused to do without military aid; the magistrates sent for Yeomanry and Hussars, and the Yeomanry arrived first, fortuitously; the Yeomanry were ordered to support the constables in the execution of the warrant, and they advanced in reasonable order and without aggressive intention or action into the crowd; but the crowd then closed in upon them in a menacing manner and the Yeomanry were assailed, at some point close to the hustings, by brickbats and sticks hurled by a portion of the crowd; most of the Yeomanry kept their heads until Hunt and his fellows had been arrested, and then, increasingly assailed by brickbats and hemmed in on all sides by a threatening crowd, were forced to beat off their attackers (with the *flats* of their sabres) in self-defence. The magistrates, observing their predicament in the midst of a threatening multitude, were forced to order the Hussars to come to their rescue and to clear the field. All followed on. And the radicals have made party-political propaganda out of their own aggression ever since.

Did the Yeomanry ride quietly up to the hustings to effect the arrests, or did they (as "radicals" mythologise) begin to strike out with their sabres from their first entry into the crowd? Were they attacked, before they reached the hustings, by sticks and brickbats? The overwhelming majority of witnesses to these events may be suspected of "prejudice", as parties to the event, since the greater part belonged to the crowd who were ridden into, and the remainder belonged to the magistracy, special constables, and the Yeomanry who did the riding. Their evidence is not therefore worthless, since they were subject to cross-examination in the courts, and betrayed the customary signs of veracity or inconsistency. However, historians, from 1819 until 1969, have attempted to simplify the extreme difficulties of sifting this evidence (and the reports of partisan newspapers, on either side) by looking for witnesses who cannot be accused of belonging, in any obvious sense, to either contesting party. There *are* a few such observers : uncommitted and merely curious spectators on the fringes of the crowd : householders whose windows overlooked the field : and (notably) several press reporters who were afforded places on the hustings—John Tyas of *The Times*, John Smith of the *Liverpool Mercury*, Edward Baines of the *Leeds Mercury*—and the

Rev. Edward Stanley, a clergyman who had private business on that day with Mr Buxton, who owned the house which the magistrates chose as their headquarters, and who stayed on to observe the whole affair from a window directly above the magistrates.

Mr Walmsley's infinitely nice legalisms and remorseless battering away at the evidence accusatory of the Yeomanry almost impels us to fall into the trap which he has spent half a lifetime in baiting. He almost succeeds in distracting our attention from the actual attack on the crowd, and the nature of that attack. Give or take some emphasis this way or that, the events that preceded this attack are as follows.

A peaceable and fairly good humoured crowd was assembled, and Hunt began to address it. Immediately the magistrates sent for the Yeomanry to assist the civil power to arrest the speakers in the midst of the assembly. The Yeomanry—local shopkeepers, dealers, dancing-masters and the rest (several of whom were probably drunk)—rode fast towards the hustings, fanning out in disorder among the crowd as they came into it. As they reached the thickest part of the crowd the more disciplined or more humane probably only brandished their swords to make the crowd give way, but others struck out, and not only with the flats. The evidence of any brickbats, &c., being thrown at them until at least several minutes after they had reached and surrounded the hustings is excessively thin. Hunt—who until that moment had exerted himself for order and to prevent panic—was then arrested. Up to that moment the situation had still not passed beyond control, but simultaneously with that moment (Hunt disappeared as if he had been shot, said one witness) the cry went up from the Yeomanry—"Have at their flags!"—and the Peterloo Massacre really began. Some feeble attempts were made by the crowd to defend the costly embroidered banners and Caps of Liberty which the female reformers had worked over so carefully, and which the reformers had carried so many miles to the meeting. The Yeomanry struck out right and left and the special constables, not to be deprived of their share of the trophies of the field, joined in. The magistrates, seeing the Yeomanry in "difficulties", ordered the Hussars to clear the field. On the edge of the field, some of the people, finding themselves still pursued, made a brief stand.

Mr Walmsley, who has so much to say about unidentified Stockport militants, has almost no comment to offer on this—a moment of unrestrained aggression which cannot by any special pleading be offered as self-defence. Nor is there much conflict of evidence about this, the real "flashpoint". Scarlett, who led the prosecution against Hunt, remained unconvinced about any attack upon the Yeomanry until this moment, and declared in a subsequent parliamentary debate: "Had they [the Yeomanry] stopped then no real damage would have been done, but they then began to attack." Tyas reported:

"As soon as Hunt and Johnson had jumped from the waggon a cry was made by the cavalry, 'Have at their flags'. In consequence, they immediately dashed not only at the flags which were in the waggon, but those which were posted among the crowd, cutting most indiscriminately to the right and to the left in order to get at them. This set the people running in all directions, and it was not until this act had been committed that any brickbats were hurled at the military. From that moment the Manchester Yeomanry Cavalry lost all command of temper."

Not even Captain Birley, the scarcely impartial witness who commanded the Yeomanry on the field, disputed the fact of this attack on the flags. His account (through the medium of Lord Stanley) declared that, when the magistrates' warrant had been executed,

"considerable tumult prevailed, and a struggle ensued between the constables and those persons in the cart, who wished to save the caps of liberty, banners, &c. Some of those who resisted were taken into custody, and the soldiers cut with their sabres. In doing this, it was possible that some persons had been hurt, but not intentionally."

It would perhaps be legalistic to point out that the magistrates' warrant was for the arrest of Hunt and not of a Cap of Liberty. We are bereft of independent witnesses to describe the sensation of being "hurt, but not intentionally", since neither Tyas (who himself had been arrested, in error) nor the Rev. Edward Stanley was fleeing on the field. We must, perforce, supply the hiatus in Mr Walmsley's account, by drawing upon the evidence of some of these biased victims to describe the temper of these moments:

"William Harrison (cotton spinner) : . . . We were all merry in hopes of better times.

Coroner : Were you not desired to disperse?

Harrison : Only with the swords—nobody asked us to disperse—only trying to cut our heads off with their swords."

"The soldiers began cutting and slaying", went on Harrison, "and the constables began to seize the colours, and the tune was struck up; they all knew of the combination." Amidst such music, few paused to distinguish between flats and sharps :

"Coroner : Did they cut at you near the hustings?

Harrison : No; as I was running away three soldiers came down upon me one after another; there was whiz this way and whiz that way, backwards and forwards . . . and I, as they were going to strike, threw myself on my face, so that, if they cut, it should be on my bottom.

The Coroner : You act as well as speak?

Harrison : Yes; I'm real Lancashire blunt, Sir; I speak the truth; whenever any cried out 'mercy', they said 'Damn you, what brought you here'."

Another witness related how a special constable jumped on the hustings, "took up the President's chair, and beat it about those who remained". Some of the crowd, hemmed in on all sides by Yeomanry, crawled under the carts which formed the platform for the hustings. According to one witness, John Lees (who later died) was one of these :

"Jonah Andrew (cotton spinner) : I saw several constables round him, and beating him with truncheons severely. One of them picked up a staff of a banner that had been cut with a sword, and said, 'Damn your bloody eyes, I'll break your back'."

This "self-defence" was pursued by Yeomanry and specials to the edges, and beyond the edges, of the field. Hunt, as he was taken to the magistrates' house, ran the gauntlet of special constables' batons, and (according to an independent witness, J B Smith) "General Clay with a large stick struck him over the head with both hands . . . The blow knocked in his hat and packed it over his face." Even in the side-streets around the field the cavalry pursued the people, cutting at them and saying, "Damn you, I'll reform you;—You'll come again, will you?" Outside one house in Windmill Street, "special constables came up in great triumph, before my door, calling out 'This is Waterloo for you! This is Waterloo'."

Mr Walmsley is of course wrong to suppose that the sober accounts of Peterloo by Bruton and Read represent, even if unwittingly, a perpetuation of the "radical" myth. A radical interpretation of the day, derived in part from witnesses such as those just quoted, would be far more savage than anything published since Bamford or Prentice. It would see it as a clear moment of class war. Nor were the warriors only on the side of the magistracy. If Mr Walmsley had examined the Home Office papers he would have found evidence that both before the day (among those drilling on the moors) and afterwards (among those threatening vengeance) there were indeed most unpacific "militants" among the reformers. Bamford was—at least after Peterloo—very probably among them, although he gives himself a more sober character in his reminiscences. If the report of a spy is to be credited, he was still, three months later, venting his feeling in revolutionary rodomontade, and giving in a tavern the toast: "May the Tree of Liberty be planted in Hell, and may the bloody Butchers of Manchester be the Fruit of it!" As late as April, 1820, there was a fierce tavern brawl in Oldham between soldiers and townsmen, when one of the latter proposed the toast: "May the skin of every loyal man be taken off his back and made into parchment to beat the Reformers to arms!"

Undoubtedly among the huge crowd which assembled on that day there were some who felt obscurely that something large might come of it, and come suddenly to the raising of the poor and the throwing down of the rich. As one of the contingents marched in that morning they passed Roger Entwisle, an attorney and clerk to the race-course, and later a witness against Hunt: "Thou hast got a good coat to thy back", one of the marchers shouted, "but I shall have as good a one as thee before tonight is over."

All this was around, before and after Peterloo. But on the day itself the vast crowd was, definitively, under Hunt's control and subjected to his egotistical but emphatically constitutionalist strategy. He had spent the previous week in Manchester, seeing some of the leaders of contingents, and ensuring that his orders for peace and discipline were understood and would be obeyed. They were obeyed, and women and children came with the men upon the field. Hence Peterloo was not only a massacre, but a peculiarly cowardly one. Miss Marlow has discovered letters of Major Dyneley, who commanded the two field-pieces which were held in readiness in the wings on the day: "The first action of the Battle of Manchester is over", he wrote, "and I am happy to say has ended in the complete discomfiture of the Enemy." He had been "very much assured to see the way in which the Volunteer Cavalry knocked the people about during the whole time we remained on the ground: the instant they saw ten or a dozen Mobbites together, they rode at them and *leathered* them properly".

A radical interpretation, however, would re-examine with the greatest scrupulousness those parts of the received account which exonerate from blame in these events, not only the government but also the magistracy; or which assume that the magistracy were guilty only of panic or ill-judgment, and that once they had sent the Yeomanry upon the field, all happened fortuitously. Both Prentice and J E Taylor offered arguments against this at the time. The official *Papers Relative to the State of the Country*, published by government in November, 1819, and offering a selection of the letters of magistrates to the Home Office, depositions, &c., should be regarded as being just as much a party statement—and should be examined as scrupulously—as any radical account. Historians have not, generally, done this; although the *Papers* were selected and published in order to prevent any parliamentary enquiry; the information (Lord Liverpool admitted privately) "may be laid safely, and much more advantageously, by Government directly rather than through the medium of any committee". Many of the questions asked by John Edward Taylor in his brilliant and scathing *Notes and Observations, Critical and Explanatory on the Papers Relative to the Internal State of the Country* (1820) have never found a satisfactory answer.

These questions are of the order most difficult to resolve; questions of intention—did the magistrates intend beforehand that an armed dispersal should take place?—and of complicity—did Sidmouth (the Home Secretary) assent to, or know of, any such intention? Mr Walmsley himself quotes important passages from a private, justificatory account which the Rev. W R Hay drew up

for Sidmouth on October 7, 1819, and which was hitherto un-
published. In this he described the actions of the select committee
of magistrates which was in almost continuous session in the days
leading up to August 16 :

"The Committee continued to meet, and did so on Saturday,
[August] the 14th, Sunday, and Monday. Prior to the
Saturday, different points had been discussed as to the
propriety of stopping the Meeting and the manner of doing
so. They were of opinion that Multitudes coming in columns
with Flags and Marching in military array were even in the
approach to the Meeting a tumultuous assembly; and it was
for a little time under consideration whether each Column
should not be stopped at their respective entrances into the
Town, but this was given up—it was considered that the
Military might then be distracted and it was wished that
the Town should see what the Meeting was, when assembled,
and also that those who came should be satisfied they were
assembled in an unlawful manner."

"Being satisfied", the account continues, "that in point of Law
[the Meeting] if assembled as it was expected, would be an illegal
Meeting, we gave notice to Lieut.-Col. L'Estrange . . . of our wish
to have the assistance of the Military on the 16th."

This is a clear enough statement of the magistrates' intention,
although it does not amount to proof. It is abundantly evident
that magistrates and military had a contingency plan for dispersing the meeting; and, at the very least, it would appear that Sidmouth was informed of this plan, from a letter in the Home Office
papers dated August 18, in which Sidmouth conveyed to General
Sir John Byng his satisfaction in the judgment of Colonel
L'Estrange, the military commander on that day : "His Judgment has in Lord S.'s mind been evinced by his employing the
Yeomanry in the Van agreeably to the Plan on which I know you
intended to act." A contingency plan, it is true, does not amount
to a fully-proven intention, even when the first part of it—the
assembling of the military forces—is put into effect. But there is
altogether too much circumstantial evidence, as well as rumour,
circulating on the Sunday and the Monday morning, to allow one
to discount the possibility of such a fully-formed intention : the
clearing of the field by the authorities, early on Monday morning,

of all stones: the industrious preparation by the magistrates of depositions from prominent citizens that they were alarmed by the banners and military array of the crowd: the rumours such as those which reached the ears of J E Taylor:

> "... early in the forenoon on August 16th persons supposed to be acquainted with the intentions of the magistrates distinctly asserted that Mr Hunt would be arrested on the hustings, and the meeting dispersed. I myself was more than once told so, but could not conceive it possible ..."

The fact that such rumours (and, perhaps, specific instructions) were well-known to the friends of authority can be detected in the evidence of an "official" witness, Roger Entwisle, the attorney, in the unschooled days of the Oldham inquest, held soon after Peterloo, when under cross-examination by Mr Harmer (on behalf of the family of John Lees):

> "Q. Now, how is it, Sir, that after all your dreadful apprehensions of danger you go immediately into the midst of it [the meeting]?
>
> A. I was close to the special constables all the time. I was well aware that there was an understanding between the military and civil power, and that they would not act against the civil power—(*hesitatingly*)—I mean, that they would not act unless there was occasion.
>
> Q. Oh! then, you knew there was an understanding between the military and civil power, did you?
>
> A. I knew that the special constables were to be upon the ground, and I knew that as long as I was with them I should not suffer. I knew they were to be there, and I saw them come close in.
>
> Q. Who told you of the arrangement, upon your oath?
>
> A. I saw the arrangement. I knew they were summoned to meet in the morning.
>
> Q. Where did you say the arrangement was made between the military and special constables?
>
> A. Why I knew the military would be—No, I did not say an arrangement between the military and the civil power."

The counsel acting for the authorities extricated, for a time, the twisting and turning Entwisle. But Mr Harmer, many pages afterwards, switched back to the point:

"Q. Well then I will ask you no more.—Stop, I will just ask you now, whether the *understanding* that you have talked of, was not that the people were to be dispersed?

A. No. I heard of no understanding of that. It was merely from common report, that I heard the understanding was, the civil power was to be there; and if they could not disperse them, the military were to do it.

Mr Harmer (to the Witness)—Well, I shall ask you no more questions, Sir."

The intention was expressed, the contingency plan was prepared, the military forces were assembled, the rumours and more-than-rumours were circulating : and yet we are *still* invited to believe that the dispersal of the crowd was fortuitous, and that the magistrates determined to send cavalry into the midst of it to arrest the speakers because one Richard Owen, a pawnbroker, swore an affidavit that Hunt had arrived and that "an immense job is collected and he considers the town in danger". (The affrighted Richard Owen, in his alternating role as a special constable, is supposed to have signally distinguished himself on the field by capturing the black flag of the Saddleworth contingent— "Equal Representation or Death"—the mere sight of which so many official witnesses at subsequent proceedings testified as having thrown them into consternation and alarm.)

There is a simpler explanation than Mr Walmsley's for Peterloo. There was a plan. It was put into operation. The magistrates knew, for some hours, and perhaps days, before Hunt arrived on the hustings, what they intended to do; the special constables were expecting the arrival of the Yeomanry; the Yeomanry did, on the field, very much what was expected of them, although neither as efficiently nor as decorously as the authorities might have wished; and the regulars performed a part in which their officers (like Major Dyneley) were well versed.

This case has not been established, but it seems, at the least, open to enquiry. If established, it would not necessarily exclude the authorities from any larger historical defence. The magistrates were faced with a new phenomenon of which they had no understanding. The crowd was not attending a Whitsun walk nor even a miners' gala. Its size, its discipline, its high morale, were ominous to the old order. Neither in the magistrates' room nor in the crowd did men look forward complacently to 1832 and all that; it was more natural, in 1819, when two incompatible social forces confronted each other, to remember 1789.

Some such historical defence might be offered. Mr Walmsley, however, would not wish to offer it. His zealous partisanship is, in a serious sense, worthy of the Peterloo tradition; and his book, which has turned over the ground freshly, will certainly join the enduring literature of the event. But he cannot allow a line of investigation, nor even of defence, which must also show that Hulton of Hulton (who denied that the magistrates had any prior intention of dispersing the crowd) was a liar. But Mr Walmsley, in his zeal, has provided evidence for this as well. William Hulton had some sort of stiffening about him which some of his fellow-magistrates lacked—an absence of humanitarian cant and a contempt for general opinion. He offered no maudlin apologies for Peterloo; indeed, he later recalled it as the "proudest day" of his life, and many years afterwards he kept a Cap of Liberty, captured upon the field, in his study. A gentleman of Hulton's breed and station does not lie; he merely has so great a hauteur, so great a distance between himself and the seditious plebs, that it is a matter of utter indifference to him whether this or that is true of them or not.

Twelve years after Peterloo, and after fact upon fact had been disputed for as long, Hulton could throw off a public letter containing a manifest farrago of mis-statements about the day—"two people were killed in St Peter's Field—one, a woman, who having personated the Goddess of Reason, was trampled to death in the crowd. . . . On the succeeding day, an old pensioner was beaten to death with portions of his own loom, because he had expressed a loyal attachment to the King". He was as inflexibly convinced, in 1831 as he had been in 1817, that the defence of "this vast aegis" of our liberties required the hunting of Jacobins and the sharpening of swords. The defeat of the Tories in South Lancashire in the Reform election of 1832 led only to an adjustment of tactics. "A few despondent individuals", Hulton of Hulton later recalled, then met in a common pot-house in Newton-le-Willows: "It occurred to them that it was their duty to call up every friend to the monarchy and the Church to counteract the machinations of the enemies to both." As a result of that meeting

"the foundations of the South Lancashire Conservative Association were laid . . . and from that stem at Newton, Conservative
associations had branched out all over Her Majesty's dominions."
It is well to remember that British Conservatism has not only
been made by the great, the well-endowed, the fluent. It has also
had its stubborn provincial grass-roots.

JOHN EDWARD TAYLOR   *Notes and Observations Critical and
          Explanatory on the Papers Relative to the Internal State
          of the Country . . .* (published anonymously, 1820)
SAMUEL BAMFORD   *Passages in the Life of a Radical* (published
          Heywood, Lancs, 1841; published with *Early Days* in two
          volume edition in 1893; reprinted in abridged edition in
          1967)
ARCHIBALD PRENTICE   *Historical Sketches and Personal Recol-
          lections of Manchester* (Manchester, 1851, reprinted
          1970)
F A BRUTON   *The Story of Peterloo* (Manchester, 1919)
DONALD READ   *Peterloo* (Manchester, n.d., 1958)
E P THOMPSON   *The Making of the English Working Class*
          (1963)
JOYCE MARLOW   *The Peterloo Massacre* (1969)
ROBERT WALMSLEY   *Peterloo: The Case Reopened* (Manches-
          ter, 1969)

Anthony Arblaster

William Cobbett and the Struggle for Parliamentary Reform

ANTHONY ARBLASTER *is a lecturer in Politics at Sheffield University. He was a journalist on the staff of* TRIBUNE *from 1965 until 1968, after which he was for two years a lecturer in Philosophy at Manchester University before moving to Sheffield. He has contributed many books reviews to* TRIBUNE *and more recently to the* NEW STATESMAN, *and has written a number of articles for the* SOCIALIST REGISTER. *Together with Steven Lukes he edited* THE GOOD SOCIETY *(1971), an anthology of political and social thought since Rousseau.*

William Cobbett was one of the greatest, if not *the* greatest, journalist England has ever seen; and far and away the most influential. This influence was exercised chiefly through his famous weekly paper, the *Political Register*, which first appeared in 1802, and which he continued to produce and largely write, with very few gaps, until his death in 1835. The *Register* was essentially a one-man band, and that was the secret of its enormous success. As G D H Cole wrote in his life of Cobbett :

"... from the first number the *Register* possessed, what so many papers lack and what is the surest key to journalistic success, the clear impression of a personality. Cobbett talked rather than wrote to his readers : his articles always had the vividness of a personal conversation."

He was able to preserve this extraordinary individual vividness, which is the most obvious and enjoyable feature in all his writing, because he took great care to preserve his independence as a journalist. "From my very first outset in politics, I formed the resolution of keeping myself perfectly independent." At great personal and financial cost to himself, he held fast to that resolution :

"I set out as a sort of self-dependent politician. My opinions were my own . . . I scorned to follow anybody in matter of opinion. Before my time, every writer of talent enlisted himself under the banners of one party, or one minister, or other. I stood free from all such connections; and, therefore, though admired by many, I was looked upon with an evil eye by all."

He is famous, above all, in fact as a great radical journalist. But he began his pamphleteering career as an aggressive anti-radical, and both when he was in America in the 1790's, and when he returned to England in 1800, Pitt's anti-French, anti-radical Government offered him financial support as a journalist. He refused these offers, for, as he said, "the pen of a slave seldom produces effect".

Later on, when he had moved over to a radical position, he became the target of continuous harassment and persecution by successive governments, as were all radical writers in those years. For Cobbett lived through a period of some of the most vicious repression of popular political activities and opinions in English history. It was a period when a hard fight had to be put up to win even the most elementary political rights, both for the press and the people as a whole. Cobbett himself went to prison for two years in 1810, convicted of "sedition" for having protested against the flogging of soldiers who had mutinied for lack of food. A second attempt to send him to prison was made by the Whigs in 1831 (Cobbett was then 67) when he was accused of inciting farm labourers to riot and violence. The attempt failed, although another radical journalist, Richard Carlile, was imprisoned for two years for the same offence. On another occasion, in 1817, Cobbett fled to America for two years, suspecting with a good deal of justice, that the suspension of *habeas corpus* in that year was principally directed against him.

In addition to all this, the Government continually used taxes on newspapers in an effort to put Cobbett and other radicals out of business, while "often Cobbett's parcels of *Registers* to country subscribers simply failed to arrive—they were 'lost' in the mail" (E P Thompson). In 1817 a Shropshire magistrate had two men "well flogged" for distributing Cobbett's pamphlets, and that was by no means an isolated incident. In 1819 a man went to prison for 10 weeks for spreading the news of Cobbett's return from America. Thus is was dangerous to write, or even to read, the *Political Register*. Yet despite this, despite general political repression, despite widespread illiteracy, this radical weekly, in the cheap form in which it appeared from 1816 onwards (*Twopenny Trash*, it was contemptuously labelled, but Cobbett adopted it as a badge of honour) sold at its peak between 40,000 and 60,000 copies each week. Particular issues, such as the first twopenny one, the *Address to the Journeymen and Labourers of England*, were even more successful. This sold more than 200,000 copies in two months.

Some of his books, such as his *Grammar of the English Language*, which was a political as well as a linguistic work, and his *Cottage Economy* sold in comparable quantities in the 1820's. These figures alone bear witness to the degree of popular political involvement at that time. But we should remember, too, that the *Register* was, in many cases, taken by an individual subscriber, and then read aloud to a group of sympathisers. So its circulation figures do not represent its readership or its impact. It formed a focus for groups of radical working people all over the country.

Cobbett's enormous influence was recognised by his contemporaries. His great radical contemporary, William Hazlitt, said of him :

"he is too much for any single newspaper antagonist, 'lays
waste' a city orator or Member of Parliament, and bears hard
upon the Government itself. He is a kind of fourth estate in
the politics of the country."

It was precisely because of this wide influence, because of what Cobbett represented, that the Government was forever trying to silence, terrify or suppress him.

What *did* he represent? At first sight his importance appears paradoxical. He has been called "the first great tribune of the industrial proletariat," yet he was born a farmer's son, at Farnham in Surrey in 1763, and remained all his life a countryman by nature and inclination.

Sitting at the window of a Wiltshire downland inn, on one of his famous *Rural Rides* in the summer of 1826, he found himself filled "with wonder, that a heart and mind so wrapped up in every thing belonging to the gardens, the fields and the woods, should have been condemned to waste themselves away amidst the stench, the noise and the strife of cities . . ." For, he wrote on another occasion, "I hated the life of the great cities; I hated their everlasting noise and bustle : my taste, all my own personal enjoyments would have led me far away from them for ever."

It was characteristic, too, that he should admit to being more concerned with the plight of agricultural than industrial workers :

"the deplorable descriptions of the distresses in the manufacturing districts, though very afflicting, are not, however,
those which produce the most serious impression upon my
mind. I am much more deeply affected by the general, though
silent distresses of those whom we call the country people."

And it can fairly be said that normally and instinctively he looked backwards, to the stable and relatively contented essentially *rural* social order which he believed to have existed when he was born :

". . . you may cry Jacobin and Leveller as long as you please. I
wish to see the poor men of England what the poor men of
England were when I was born; and, from endeavouring
to accomplish this wish, nothing but the want of means should
make me desist."

Such quotations, which can easily be multiplied, lend plausibility to Cole's claim that "he was really an agrarian tribune."

This apparent paradox of a backward-looking countryman, who even, as Hazlitt tells us, dressed like a "gentleman-farmer in the last century," becoming the spokesman of radical industrial workers is deepened when we recall that Cobbett began his political life as a fervent monarchist, patriot and anti-Jacobin. He loudly proclaimed his hatred of "the anarchical and blasphemous principles of the French Revolution," and even in 1804, when he was over 40 years old, still wanted "to check the spirit and progress of levelling innovation". Only gradually did he move away from this position, first into opposition to Pitt's Government and the war against France, later developing his attack on the entire unreformed political system, and the economic policies which produced such appalling misery for millions of working, or workless, men and women in Britain.

But the paradox is, I think, only an apparent one. For, however unprogressive Cobbett may have seemed to those like the Utilitarians who saw the whole process of industrialisation as essentially one of general improvement and progress, the fact is that even in his prejudices and old-fashionedness Cobbett reflected the common experience of industrialisation in a way that the preachers of the gospel of "progress" never did.

For what reason did working people then have to believe that all was for the best in the best of all possible worlds? What grounds had they for anticipating a brighter, more prosperous future? What many of them knew was their own bitter experiences of industrialisation, the experiences, which Cobbett understood so well, of being forced off the land and into the factories, or of being put out of work by the development of new machinery. However deplorable it might appear to the "enlightened", many ordinary people looked back, as Cobbett did, because the future was dark with oppression and the past was at least familiar. They shared his impatience with those who tried to mitigate the miseries of the factory system by suggesting that the past had been so much worse :

> "Talk of *vassals*! Talk of *villains*! Talk of *serfs*! Are there any
> of these, or did feudal times ever see any of them so debased,
> so absolutely slaves, as the poor creatures who, in the
> '*enlightened*' North, are *compelled* to work fourteen hours
> in a day, in a heat of *eighty-four degrees*; and who are liable
> to punishment *for looking out at a window of the factory!*"

Cobbett was not exaggerating. He obtained his facts and figures about factory conditions from published sources, and he never allowed his readers to forget them. The same point can be made about Cobbett's move to radicalism. Probably no other single person did more than Cobbett to convince people, in the 20 years before Parliamentary reform eventually arrived in 1831–2, that such a reform was both necessary and inevitable. Yet Cobbett's own conversion to the cause was a sign of the times.

He did not simply adopt the principles of Thomas Paine, or attempt to import Jacobin recipes into England. It was his *experience* of the failure of the unreformed political system which pushed him into radicalism, and he was able to carry so many others with him to the point where they accepted his conclusions, because they knew, or could understand, that experience. So that

Cobbett, in his complexity, his prejudices, and his very practical, empirical approach, is *more* representative than he would have been had he been more consistent.

Cobbett was not a revolutionary. On the contrary, he usually argued that "We . . . wish for a Reform that shall *prevent* Revolution." And, like many reformers before and since, he was apt to argue that "nothing new" was being asked for, but simply the restoration of ancient constitutional rights that had been lost. On the other hand, as a radical he had no doubt that the French Revolution had been, on balance, a "good thing"; ". . . the state of France is a state of *blessedness*, compared to what it was before the Revolution". It can also be suggested that if Cobbett had been able to foresee how little would be done for working people either by the Reform Bill itself or by the legislation which followed it, he might have taken a different attitude at the moments in this period, such as the months after the Peterloo massacre in August 1819, or the crisis over reform in 1831–2, when, in the words of the Benthamite, Francis Place, "we were within a moment of general rebellion".

Cobbett was one of those who really did believe that the key to relief of the terrible sufferings and hardships of the time lay in parliamentary reform, in purging the system of corruption and sinecures that weighed so heavily on the country in the form of taxation :

"Why did we cry for *Reform*? Because the people were
suffering and because no hope was entertained that the
Parliament, as now constituted, would afford us relief."

Some radicals realised even before the Whigs put through their Bill that it would enfranchise the middle class, but not working people; but Cobbett gave his full support to the Bill, believing it to be the most that could then be obtained. It was only afterwards, when he sat in the "reformed" House of Commons as one of the Members for Oldham, that he realised how little, how very little, had changed. He spent much of his energy in the last years of his life in a rather lonely, losing battle in Parliament against the horrors proposed under the New Poor Law, one of which the reformed Commons produced.

So William Cobbett went down to his death, still fighting for the working people of England. It was a sad, but characteristically brave end to an astonishing life. He wrote on one occasion in his Register :

"I say WE, because I never do and I never can separate myself
. . . from the labouring classes. I never can think myself *well
off* while they are oppressed. I never can be contented,
never can be easy, must be '*disaffected*' and '*designing;*'
always '*rebelling*', as my good Lord Castlereagh calls it, as
long as millions of Englishmen are degraded and in misery.
And what man *can* think that he *ought* to be *contented*,
while nineteen out of twenty of his countrymen have just
cause for *discontent*? Of what value is abundance in the midst
of famishing millions?"

He spoke only what was true about himself, and his readers knew that it was true and trusted him accordingly. To my mind, it is the kind of epitaph which any Socialist would be proud to earn.

WILLIAM COBBETT *Rural Rides* (first published 1830). The Penguin edition (1967) has excellent notes and an introduction by George Woodcock. The two-volume Everyman edition is more complete.

WILLIAM HAZLITT *The Spirit of the Age* (first published 1825, Reprinted Menston, Yorkshire, 1971). This contains a characteristically sharp, acute, if sometimes unfair, short study of Cobbett.

G D H COLE *The Life of William Cobbett* (1924). This standard biography, which is out of print, can be found in some libraries.

WILLIAM COBBETT *The Progress of a Plough-Biy to a Seat in Parliament* (1933); reprinted 1947 as *The Autobiography of William Cobbett*. This is a compilation of passages from various works put together by William Reitzel.

RAYMOND WILLIAMS *Culture and Society, 1780–1950* (1958). This book contrasts Cobbett's response to the development of industrial capitalism with that of some of his contemporaries.

E P THOMPSON *The Making of the English Working Class* (1963). This outstanding work is indispensable for an understanding of Cobbett's historical role, and he is assessed very acutely in Chapter 16, section 2.

George Rudé
Captain Swing & the Uprising of 1830

GEORGE RUDÉ *taught history and modern languages in London schools. Subsequently he was professor of history at Adelaide and Flinders Universities, Australia, and a visting professor in Britain, Japan and the United States. At present he is professor at Sir George Williams University in Canada. Among his books are* THE CROWD IN THE FRENCH REVOLUTION *(1959),* WILKES AND LIBERTY *(1962),* THE CROWD IN HISTORY *(1964),* REVOLUTIONARY EUROPE *(1964),* CAPTAIN SWING *(with Eric Hobsbawm 1969),* PARIS AND LONDON IN THE EIGHTEENTH CENTURY *(1970),* HANOVERIAN LONDON *(1971) and* EUROPE IN THE EIGHTEENTH CENTURY *(1972).*

The years 1830 and 1831 were among the most convulsive in British history. G D H Cole and Raymond Postgate wrote in *The Common People* that "never since 1688 had Great Britain been so near actual revolution as in 1831"; and the country has probably never been so near to it since. It was the time of the agitation for the great Reform Bill; of the Bristol and Nottingham riots; and the first great strikes and industrial movements in the coal fields and factory towns of the Midlands, the north and the west. But none of these movements were as widespread, none were as violent and sustained, and none aroused such panic and vindictive ardour in the Government, Parliament and the Bench as the great country labourers' rising of 1830, which was associated with the "mythical" Captain Swing.

The movement took its name from the swing of the flail of the threshing machine; and it spread, within a space of three months, over more than 20 counties in the Midlands, the south and east of England, stretching from Kent to Cornwall in the south, as far east as Norfolk and Suffolk, and as far north as Yorkshire and Cumberland.

It took various forms: marches on workhouses; wages meetings; assaults on overseers, parsons and landlords; arson; threatening letters; seditious and "inflammatory" handbills and riots over rent, tithe, taxes and enclosure. But most characteristic of all was the destruction of agricultural machinery; particularly of threshing machines, of which several hundred were destroyed between August and December of that year.

The riots grew out of the misery and degradation of the village labourers at the end of the Napoleonic Wars. Long before the wars, the old peasantry had already been disappearing from the Midlands and southern counties and was being rapidly transformed into hired men or rural proletarians, whom a social gulf divided from their employers, whether landlords, farmers or Church of England parsons.

Thus the labourers' new-found "liberty", for which he had traded his old security, left him exposed both to the whim or rapacity of an employer and the growing hazards of the rural economy. The wars, whatever hardships they inflicted, had given the old village a temporary reprieve: for the farmer it was a golden age and even the labourer's wages and employment were protected. But the end of the wars brought a sudden depression and widespread rural distress.

The landlords, after the initial shock, quickly recovered by means of the Corn Laws and by imposing high rents on the farmers. The farmer, squeezed by the landlord's rent on the one hand and the Church's tithe on the other, riposted by cutting his labourer's wages or, when work was scarce, putting him on the parish. This had become a regular practice, in many villages, in the winter months.

Moreover, the parish allowance, far from staying at its original "Speenhamland" level, had been progresively reduced to something below half the prevailing wage; and after the disastrous harvest of 1829, thousands of unemployed labourers were drawing an allowance of something like three or four shillings a week. So the fear of another such winter was already a potent stimulus to rebellion.

But further factors were needed to set the movement alight, to generalise it and to drive it across half the counties of England. In part, this stimulus was provided by the outbreak of revolution in Paris in 1830, which served to stoke up the Radical agitation that had already begun over Parliamentary reform, and was already, through pamphlets and press, involving many of the literate craftsmen who often acted as the labourers' spokesmen. More precisely, it was afforded by the introduction of threshing machines—already familiar in Lincoln and Norfolk—in East Kent and in the summer of 1830. On the night August 28, a machine was destroyed by labourers at Lower Hardres near Canterbury. It was followed by others; and by the third week in October almost a hundred machines had been destroyed, mainly in this corner of the county.

Meanwhile, there had been an outbreak of threatening letters (often signed "Swing") and fired hayricks and barns on the borders of Surrey and Kent. It was noted that the villagers frequently gave their moral support to the incendiaries, and from Orpington *The Times* reported that, after a barn had been set ablaze, the labourers stood calmly by, saying, "D——n it, let it burn, I wish it was the house."

By early October, arson had spread to East Kent, and a *Times* leader spoke of an "organised system of stack-burning and machine-breaking". Two weeks later the movement had swung to the Maidstone area, and here it took the form of great wages meetings, usually held in broad daylight, where the labourers demanded a minimum daily wage of 2s 3d in winter and 2s 6d in summer.

In early November, as the riots spread westwards into the Kentish and Sussex Weald, new issues were raised. Sometimes it was tithes, sometimes taxes or rents, and the labourers, often in collusion with the local small or "middling" farmers, demanded that the parson reduce his tithe and the landlord his rent so that the farmer could pay his labourer a higher wage. Round Battle and Rye, in East Sussex, the main demand was for better allowances to be paid by the overseers of the poor; and, in the village of Brede, an unpopular overseer was wheeled out of the parish in the parish cart and dumped unceremoniously across its border.

So the movement continued, with increasing momentum, into West Sussex, Hampshire and the counties of the west. In Horsham, then described as "a hotbed of sedition", the marching labourers joined with the farmers and townspeople in packing the vestry meeting and insisting on a reduction in rents and tithes and a rise in wages. The riots reached Hampshire on November 18 and Wiltshire a couple of days later. In both, they barely lasted a week but left a heavier toll of broken machines, forced levies of money and arrested labourers than in any other county. They reached east Dorset on November 23 and south Gloucestershire on November 26 and, after a pause in this area, Worcester, Devon and Cornwall in early December. The most westerly point touched by the movement was the village of Whitney in Hereford, where a "Swing" letter, addressed to a considerable farmer on November 17, urged him to "pull down your Threshing Machine or else Bread or Fire without delay".

Meanwhile, a new focus of rebellion had opened in Berkshire. It began as a wages demonstration by the labourers of Thatcham and developed quickly into a far wider movement, in which threshing machines were destroyed and farmers were held to ransom and compelled to contribute money for food and beer as a reward for "services rendered". One local leader, a bricklayer from Kintbury, near Hungerford, was, when arrested, found in possession of £100, including a couple of IOUs.

The Berkshire movement spread southwards back into Hampshire, westwards into Wiltshire, eastwards into Oxford and Buckinghamshire, and northwards into Bedfordshire and Northampton. Once more, the main targets were the hated threshing machines. But there was an important exception : between Loudwater and West Wycombe, along the Thames, the unemployed paper workers, in some cases with the village labourers' support, destroyed the machinery in half a dozen paper mills. Forty-five prisoners were taken after damage had been done to a value of over £3,000.

A third main centre of rioting was East Anglia, where there had been earlier attacks on machinery in the agrarian riots of 1816 and 1822. Here the movement started at North Walsham, a village in the north-eastern corner of Norfolk. It began with the destruction of threshing machines but developed, as it swept southwards towards the Suffolk border, into riots against tithes and assaults on Church of England parsons. In West Suffolk and Essex, the disturbances were generally over wages. In the woodlands of west Norfolk, northern Cambridgeshire, in Lincoln, the Isle of Ely and along the Huntingdonshire border, the emphasis was all on arson; in Lincoln alone, there were over twenty fires in a single month.

"Swing's" influence was felt as far north as Carlisle, where it played a part in local Radical agitation. In early December, after two ricks had been fired, a handbill was posted, offering "£1,000 reward, in the apprehension of Borough-mongers, Stock-jobbers, Tax-eaters, Monopolizers, Special Constables, and the Extinguishers of freedom by order of the SWING UNION." There was a brief revival of machine-breaking in Kent and Norfolk in the late summer of 1831; and a final threshing machine was broken at Tadlow, in Cambridgeshire, in September 1832.

But, long before this, the movement had run its course or been broken by the repressive intervention of the military and courts of justice. Wellington's Tory Ministry, with Peel at the Home Office, were at first more concerned about the strikes and discontents in the manufacturing districts, not to mention the events in France, and reacted without much energy; but they attempted to enrol special constables among the farmers (often with little success), appealed to local voluntary bodies to take action, and sent troops into Kent, Sussex and Hampshire. Wellington's Ministry fell and was succeeded by Grey's Whig Government as the riots swept into Wiltshire. On November 23, the day after taking office, Lord Melbourne, the new Home Secretary, issued a Proclamation, offering rewards of £500 for bringing rioters and incendiaries to justice, and urged justices to act with greater vigour. A fortnight later, seeing that some magistrates were half-hearted in their efforts to protect threshing machines, Melbourne sternly reminded them that it was "their Duty to maintain and uphold the Rights of Property, of every description, against Violence and Aggression".

Meanwhile, by one means or the other, the prisons had been filled and, in mid-December 1830, there were nearly 2,000 prisoners awaiting trial in more than a score of counties. To set a stern example and encourage the local magistrates to act with greater severity, the Government set up Special Commissions at Winchester, Salisbury, Reading, Dorchester and Aylesbury to judge those arrested in the major areas of disturbance. In three weeks, they tried 992 cases, at first sentencing 227 men to death (101 in Hampshire alone), though of these only 11 were "left for execution". The remaining thousand prisoners were tried in a further 85 courts sitting in 30 counties. When they completed their work, 644 were sentenced to jail and 19 were hanged, all but three of them for arson.

But the most vindictive act of all was the transportation of 479 men and two women to the Australian colonies for terms varying between seven years and "life", and with virtually no hope of returning to their homes. On no other protest movement of the times—on neither Luddites, nor Chartists, nor trade union pioneers—was such a bitter blow inflicted. It was a measure of the panic that the labourers' action had inspired among the land-owning classes of England, and it has done much to tarnish the reputation of Grey and Melbourne and the Whig "Reform" Go-vernment of the 1830's.

What had the labourers' movement achieved? In strictly poli-tical terms, they achieved nothing at all. This is hardly surprising as they had set themselves no political goals; least of all had they attempted to start a revolution. Besides, their movement was iso-lated, confined to the wheat-growing counties or regions of the Midlands, the south and the west and cut off from the manu-facturing districts and the Reform Bill agitation of the cities and large towns. They had carried no arms and had behaved with con-siderable restraint. Their language was violent enough, it is true : there was much talk of "bread or blood" and even of "blood for supper" or "blood for breakfast". But their violence was limited to machine-breaking, rick-burning and strong words : not a single farmer, overseer, landlord or parson was killed or even sustained serious injury at their hands.

Moreover, their organisation had been of the most casual and primitive form; they were not members of trade unions, like their Dorset successors of 1834 or of the far wider "Revolt of the Field" of the 1870's. Their object had been to win back some of the lost security of the past, to restore their wages and poor law allowances, and to destroy the machines which threatened to dis-place their labour and which to them appeared as obnoxious and unlawful as Ship Money had appeared to Sir John Hampden 200 years before; and, like him, they believed that right and jus-tice—and even the law—were on their side.

And, in this last respect at least, they achieved a remarkable success. In many districts, the threshing machine, destroyed or removed in the course of the riots, did not return at all; and, a dozen years later, an observer of the countryside wrote that "in a large part of the Agricultural Districts of the South, the Thresh-ing Machine cannot be used, owing to the destructive vengeance with which the labourers resisted its introduction". So "Swing", though his methods were the same, did considerably better than "Ludd". And this alone entitles him to be drawn from his present obscurity and raised to an honourable place in the annals of labour history

J L AND B HAMMOND *The Village Labourer* (1911, frequently reprinted)

LORD ERNLE (Rowland Edmund Prothero) *English Farming Past and Present* (1912, frequently reprinted)

M K ASHBY *Joseph Ashby of Tysoe, 1859–1919* (Cambridge, 1961)

J P D DUNBABIN "The 'Revolt of the Field': the Agricultural Labourers' Movement in the 1870's", *Past and Present*, (26 November, 1963)

E J HOBSBAWM & G RUDÉ *Captain Swing* (1969, revised ed. 1973)

Dorothy Thompson
Chartism, Success or Failure?

DOROTHY THOMPSON *is lecturer in modern history at the University of Birmingham. She has taught in adult education and has written, edited or collaborated in several books of history and sociology, among them* THE BRITISH PEOPLE, 1760–1902 *(1969) and* THE EARLY CHARTISTS *(1971). She is at present engaged on a full-length study of Chartism.*

The Reform Bill of 1832 was an event of supreme importance in the history of British government. The beacons and feasts with which its passing was celebrated in the provincial towns of England were no mere bread and circus-type rejoicing by an ignorant and deceived people. Many radicals took part in the rejoicing in all sincerity, celebrating, as they thought, the first example in Europe of an *ancien régime* giving in peacefully to the forces of constitutional democracy.

For the working-class reformers, the 1832 Bill was to be merely the beginning. They hoped, and many believed, that the middle classes who had asked for their help to achieve their own political emancipation would now go on to press, in and out of Parliament, for the extension of Reform to include at least all adult males in the franchise. Only a small number of men, Henry Hunt and the leaders of the National Union of the Working Classes in London being the best-known of them, maintained from the beginning that the middle-class reformers had no intention whatever of including working men in their new political fellowship. The years between 1832 and 1837 saw the gradual realisation by a substantial part of the working class of the deep conflicts which divided them from the middle class, and of the need to form their own organisation if they were to achieve political emancipation.

The men who led the early Chartist movement, in the years 1837–40, included many who were already well-known as radical leaders during the reform agitation of 1831–2. Men like Peter Bussey of Bradford, Matthew Fletcher of Bury, John Reginald Richardson of Salford, John Frost of Newport, and others in the main provincial centres up and down the country, had been agitating for manhood suffrage during the reform activity. They had organised petitions and meetings for the extension of the suffrage as soon as the Bill was passed, and they had argued, what others were to learn from experience, that the actions of a Parliament responsive to a middle-class electorate were unlikely to be of great benefit to the working classes.

The middle classes wanted cheap and efficient government. They also wanted a cheap and efficient labour force. Parliament, still made up largely of members of landowning and wealthy merchant families, but very much aware now of an electorate which included small and large manufacturers and shopkeepers, proceeded to enact a series of measures to support these demands. The Factory Act of 1833 represented the minimal concession to the factory reformers, defining the age for the end of childhood as 13 and restricting its provisions to the cotton, wool and worsted industries.

The Poor Law Amendment Act—the most contentious piece of social legislation passed by any nineteenth-century Parliament, seemed to be taking away from the people such provision as existed for assisting them in periods of sickness, unemployment and old age, and substituting a system of punishments intended to "deter" them from poverty, surely the ultimate insult to people whose whole lives were spent in its shadow. The 1835 Municipal Reform Act, while abolishing many of the abuses of the old corrupt corporations, put the middle classes more firmly in control of local government, whilst two notorious legal cases—that of the Tolpuddle labourers in 1834, and that of the Glasgow Cotton Spinners in 1837, showed that the authorities were determined to prevent the working men from building up their own protective organisations of trade unions.

None of these acts passed unnoticed. In 1834 30,000 Londoners marched in disciplined procession to protest against the sentences on the Dorchester labourers; the North of England sprang into angry life to oppose the New Poor Law—in parts of Lancashire and the West Riding attempts to implement it were held at bay for years. 1837 saw a nationwide campaign in support of the Glasgow cotton spinners, and of trade unionism in general.

The Chartist movement, united around the six points of constitutional reform—manhood suffrage, the ballot, payment of MPs, the abolition of property qualifications for MPs, equal electoral districts and annual parliaments—is usually considered to have been the first national working-class movement in the world. In recent years historians have, rightly, shown that Chartism in various parts of the country had different emphases. In London the anti-poor law element was far less strong than in the Northern manufacturing districts, for example. London was still largely a pre-industrial city, whose working people were organised in very small units, depending for their livelihood on the production of goods and services for the wealthy metropolis rather than on the basic industries of the country. Here Chartism tended to be led by the skilled artisans, who were concerned more with questions of political and religious liberty and the protection of trade and friendly societies than with the poor law or the protection of factory children.

But it was a difference of emphasis only. What is in fact really remarkable, at a time when regionalism was still very marked in Britain, is the extent to which Chartism *was* a national movement. Far more so than the political organisations of the middle and upper classes, which continued to be divided by basic regional differences until after the Chartist period.

This national quality can perhaps be attributed mainly to the fact that Chartism was an extremely literate and articulate movement. Anyone who thinks that the British working people only began to read after the Liberals educated them in 1870, should read some of the hundreds of thousands of journals, pamphlets, posters, handbills and broadsides which were produced up and down the country. Thus the Ashton-under-Lyme strikers, in 1842, end their case, for restoration of wage cuts, on a poster:

"Whether we succeed or not, we shall have the satisfaction of knowing that we have asked for nothing unreasonable or

unjust. We want a uniform price for the whole of the
manufacturing districts; and it is in the interests of the masters
to have it, in order that one man cannot undersell another
in the market. Much is said about over-production and about
the market being glutted. In order to obviate the past, let
us all work 10 hours per day, and we are sure it will lessen
the amount of goods in the market. The home consumption
will also be considerably increased by increasing the wages
of the labourer.

Chartist newspapers and journals carried on a continuous argument with their opponents, as well as stating the case for reform,
and reporting the news, including news of the activities of local
Chartist groups. The *Northern Star*, most important of the newspapers, and a unifying force in the movement, sold at its highest
more than 50,000 copies weekly. It was read in groups—aloud
or passed from hand to hand, and was to be seen in beer houses
and coffee shops, so that its actual readership was undoubtedly
many times that number.

The areas of the greatest Chartist activity were the industrial
townships and villages of the manufacturing areas. It was here
that the tone was set, rather than in the cities or villages, although
it is possible to find examples of Chartist activity in almost every
kind of community. These industrial areas were the growing
points of nineteenth-century urban development. Many of them
had traditions of social behaviour going back into pre-industrial
society, and they often had a large Irish population, many of
them first generation industrial workers.

At its strongest, in these industrial areas, Chartism was a movement involving whole communities. The weavers, combers, stockingers, cotton-spinners, artisans and other workers who led the
local organisations tended also to be the leaders in their trades
and in their communities. Evidence against arrested Chartists was
always difficult, sometimes impossible to obtain. A brewer who
gave evidence against John Frost in 1840 was driven out of business within a year, since no local people would drink his beer, and
many others—like the shopkeepers who gave evidence against
Joseph Rayner Stephens in 1838—had similar experiences. On
the other hand shopkeepers and publicans who supported Chartism did a roaring trade.

Chartism, then, had two main characteristics. It was a defensive movement, based on the belief that the reformed Parliament planned a determined attack on working-class standards and institutions. To re-read the documents of the early years—documents like the manifesto of the Chartist Convention, signed by William Lovett and Hugh Craig, two of the most "moderate" of the Chartist leaders—is to realise the extent to which the Chartists expected an all-out attack on free speech, the freedom of the press and the radical movement generally. The continual assertion of the right to´arm, the appeal to Chartists to acquire and understand arms, the expectation of provocation of a "Peterloo" kind at all the large meetings, and above all the intense distrust of all the authorities, including most of the so-called Radicals in Parliament, all indicate the defensive nature of the early years of Chartism.

In the end, however, the authorities did not provoke a conflict. The only major confrontation of the period took place at Newport, on November 4, 1839, the time and place chosen by the Chartists themselves. There is little doubt that this was intended to be part of a more widespread rising, but the decisive defeat inflicted by the small body of soldiers on the Welsh Chartists, and the excuse which the affair gave to the authorities to round up Chartist leaders in the main provincial centres on conspiracy and sedition charges, effectively prevented further risings.

Perhaps the most difficult thing to find out now, 130 years after the events, is the extent of the insurrectionary plans of the Chartists. Even Newport took most of the authorities by surprise, although there was a general anticipation of some kind of outbreak. But traces were destroyed in the aftermath, and although there was a great deal of talk of action to free the arrested Welsh leaders, John Frost, Zephaniah Williams and William Jones, the attempts at risings after their trial and sentence—notably in Sheffield and the textile districts of the West Riding—were on a small scale and totally without success. The most serious attempt to examine what evidence still remains about the insurrectionary attempts in the West Riding has been made in a recently-published pamphlet by Alf Peacock on Bradford Chartism—very much the best account yet written of a local Chartist centre.

Very significant for the subsequent development of radical and working-class movements in Britain was the fact the Welsh leaders, although sentenced to death, were finally reprieved and their sentence commuted to transportation. The possibility of obtaining a pardon and the return of the prisoners, and the apparent respect which the decision to commute the sentences showed for popular opinion, gave great strength to moderate and constitutional policies as against those of insurrection.

On the positive side, Chartism was the demand for recognition by articulate and self-conscious working people. It was not a demand for the replacement of existing institutions by new ones which would be totally controlled by the working class; it was not, in that sense a revolutionary movement. It was the demand for the inclusion in a political system, in whose efficacy they believed, of labourers who could see themselves as part of an expanding economy, but as the victims of the system they were helping to create. It was the fear of being used by the industrialists which above all led to the hostility between the Chartists and the anti-Corn-Law League.

Free Trade, in particular the abolition of taxes on food, had long been part of the radical programme. But the Chartists were not going to allow themselves to be drawn into the employers' campaign against the Corn Laws, as they had been drawn into the Reform agitation, without guarantees that their political rights would also form part of the programme. Perhaps nowhere is the essential class line-up of the period seen as clearly as in the hostility between the Chartists and the Leaguers, nor is the new political climate and the optimism and self-confidence of the Chartists anywhere more evident than in the picture of the Chartist working man publicly debating the corn-law question with his employer or his representative, and speaking against his employer's candidate at the hustings.

The Chartists presented their petition to Parliament three times. They held a series of Conventions, and thousands of meetings up and down the country. They even got their leader, Fergus O'Connor, elected to Parliament in 1847. In the localities they carried on education classes, promoted co-operative societies and trade unions, as well as the more militant activities of demonstrations, exclusive dealing and electioneering. As local government developed and the smaller towns got their charters, Chartists and former Chartists became members of local councils, where a radical voice could often do a great deal to question corruption. The Liberal Party watched the local radicals, and finally absorbed a number of them into the radicalised Liberal Party which appealed for the working-class vote after the 1867 Reform Bill—a measure which itself owed quite a lot to the activities of former Chartists.

Nevertheless, by the end of the 1850's, when the last Chartist journals ceased to exist, and the name dropped out of the political vocabulary, not one of the six points had been gained. If a movement is to be judged by the success of its programme, then Chartism had failed. But this is, of course, too crude a way to assess 20 years of experience, which marked an essential phase in the growth of working-class consciousness in Britain. Whether Chartism's contribution helped or hindered the final emancipation of the British workers will remain a subject of debate as long as alternative strategies are debated.

Local Studies
ASA BRIGGS (ed.)   *Chartist Studies* (1959). This should be supplemented by some of the excellent local studies published since, of which the two outstanding ones are
A J PEACOCK   *Bradford Chartism 1838–40* (York 1969)
I PROTHERO   "Chartism in London" in *Past and Present No. 44* (Aug 1969)

Biographical Studies
DAVID WILLIAMS   *John Frost* (Cardiff, 1939)
G D H COLE   *Chartist Portraits* (1941)
A R SCHOYEN   *The Chartist Challenge, A Portrait of George Julian Harney* (1958)

Documents
JOHN SAVILLE (ed.)   *Ernest Jones Chartist* (1952)
F G & R M BLACK (eds.)   *The Harney Papers* (Assen, Holland, 1969)
DOROTHY THOMPSON (ed.)   *The Early Chartists* (1971)

In addition there are a number of reprints of journals, and of R G Gammage's *History of the Chartist Movement* (first published 1854, reprinted 1969) which is of great interest and importance, but should not be regarded as an objective history.

Royden Harrison
The Hyde Park Rail-Way to Reform

ROYDEN HARRISON *was formerly Reader in Political Theory and Institutions at Sheffield University and is now professor of social history at the University of Warwick. In 1960 he was the co-founder and has remained the co-editor of the* BULLETIN *of the Society for the Study of Labour History. He is also a member of the editorial board of the* POLITICAL QUARTERLY *and of the advisory boards of* VICTORIAN STUDIES *and* TRIBUNE. *His principal published work is* BEFORE THE SOCIALISTS: STUDIES IN LABOUR AND POLITICS, 1861–1881 *(1965). He has been commissioned by the Passfield trustees to write the life of Sidney and Beatrice Webb. He was the first president of the Socialist Charter and has frequently addressed the Labour Party Conference as the delegate of the Sheffield (Hallam) Constituency Labour Party. In 1970 and 1971 he stood for the Labour Party's National Executive Committee, obtaining well over one hundred thousand votes on each occasion.*

The "Great" Reform Act of 1832 ended the rule of "Old Corruption" and conferred increased power upon the landed gentry and the urban middle class. Bertrand Russell's grandfather, Lord John Russell, declared that this must be regarded as a final measure of Reform. Alas for "Finality Jack"! Demands for a further extension of the franchise continued to agitate British politics for the next 30 years. Until 1848 the demand came mainly from "without": the Chartists held the field. After 1848 "Reform" was reintroduced into parliamentary politics and there was a succession of abortive Reform Bills: in 1852, 1854, 1859 and 1860.

Before 1848 Reform was not carried because it would have been too dangerous to concede it. After 1848 it was not conceded because the House of Commons was too comfortable to move. The House was ready to take up Reform as a subject for petty party manœuvres, but such manœuvres never caught the imagination of the people. It was not until 1866–7 that Reform became the decisive question both within Parliament and out of doors. The success of the post-Chartist agitation lay in the manner in which it exhibited a number of contradictory characteristics. It was these characteristics which made it dangerous for the ruling classes to resist Reform and safe for them to concede it.

Despite important continuities, the British Labour movement in the third quarter of the nineteenth century looked very different from what it had done in the second. Co-operation abandoned community building in favour of shop-keeping and exchanged the new moral world for "the divi". Trade unionism became less of a school of war and more of a workman's equivalent of the public school. From aspiring to the control of industry, it limited itself to attempting to control the supply of labour. Its new leaders taught it, not militancy, but how to be respectable and respected : to practise, not the class war, but industry, chastity and sobriety.

Labour leaders themselves ceased to be inspired "outsiders"; visionaries and demagogues : Robert Owen : Bronterre O'Brien : Fergus O'Connor. They were increasingly "insiders" : products of the new Labour bureaucracies : great men of business : Allan of the Engineers : Applegarth of the Carpenters and Joiners.

The very rhythm of the Labour movement changed. Whereas it had advanced most markedly during the troughs in the trade cycle, after 1850 new departures tended to be associated with the upswing in the cycle. Throughout the second quarter of the century organised Labour had generally been open to dreams of a total reconstruction of existing society. During the third quarter its concern became more with securing its own incorporation within that society.

These large changes in attitudes and institutions have to be understood in relation to the altered composition of the working classes. The fiercest and most turbulent element in Chartism had been supplied, not by the artisans nor by the factory operatives, but by the depressed domestic outworkers : handloom weavers and framework knitters who were being extinguished by the competition of machine industry.

After 1850 the skilled engineers and the relatively privileged aristocrats of Labour ceased to be despised as "pukes" or "exclusives" and took the place of the domestic outworkers as the stratum which set the tone and the pace for the Labour movement as a whole. The new institutions presupposed the presence of this relatively privileged stratum. The Co-operative store which refused credit and the trade union which was built on high contributions and high benefits effectively shut out the great mass of the labouring population.

This new Labour movement which attained maturity in the 1860's was both frightening and reassuring to the propertied classes. It was reassuring to have a working class whose leaders boasted that their people were themselves becoming capitalists. In a society which lacked a peasantry it was comforting to think that part of the working class was acquiring a stake in the country and learning the corporate management of vast sums of money through the unions and the Co-ops. It was agreeable to have workmen who wanted the vote, not as a hammer to knock property on the head, but as a means of rising in the social scale.

When Mr Gladstone was reproached by one of his aristocratic relatives with encouraging the demand for Reform he replied : "Please to recollect that we have got to govern millions of hard hands. That it must be done by force, fraud, or good will. That the latter has been tried and is answering, that none have profited more by this change of system since the Corn Law and the Six Acts than those who complain of it."

There were plenty of men who understood the conservative possibilities of democracy. Provided the mere labourers, the dangerous classes, the "residuum" could be excluded, there was not too much to fear. The power of property was recognised to depend less upon privileged access to political decision-taking than upon "those occult and unacknowledged forces that are not dependent upon any legislative machinery." In other words, upon the power of deference. Upon the readiness of a substantial number of working men to look upon the world of the gay and the splendid not with a jealous envy, but with admiration.

The trouble was that the skilled workmen did not claim to speak for themselves alone. They demanded manhood suffrage and vote by ballot. In practice, they showed a greater readiness to settle for the half loaf than the Chartists had done. But they were much more perfectly organised.

The Reform League which numbered its members in over 600 branches was the most complete political machine that had yet been created. If this League was ready to co-operate with middle-class radicals, as the Chartists had not been ready to, it nevertheless insisted upon own organisational and programatic independence. If it had given up the vision of working-class ascendancy it was determined upon securing political equality. If Parliament continued to trifle with the question of Reform then there was every reason to believe that the workers would display an increasing contempt for authority and would become more and more unmanageable. This is evident from the progress of the Reform agitation which may be seen to have passed through three major stages in terms of its relationship to established power.

In the spring of 1866 the Russell-Gladstone administration introduced a Reform Bill. It was such a limited measure that it failed to inspire any public enthusiasm. However, it went far enough to alarm the most reactionary Whigs. They succeeded in bringing the Government down. A minority Tory administration led by Derby and Disraeli took its place.

These developments aroused Reformers in the country. The Reform League announced its intention of holding a mass meeting in Hyde Park. When the police closed the gates against the crowd the pressure on the railings caused them to give way. For three days and nights rioting occurred. John Stuart Mill described how he had to use all his persuasive powers to induce the Labour leaders to avoid a revolutionary confrontation. In the end the Home Secretary, powerless to restore order without his help, had to enlist the assistance of Beales, the President of the League, so as to clear the park.

The next stage was reached in the winter of 1866–7. There was an outbreak of cholera in London and unemployment was rising at the same time as the price of bread was increasing. The legal status of trade unions was being called into question by decisions in the courts and by the establishment of a Royal Commission.

The metropolitan police advised the Government that it could no longer guarantee the maintenance of order if massive Reform demonstrations were permitted in London. The response of the League was to project the creation of its own Reform constabulary. The middle-class Radical leader, John Bright, was seriously alarmed and suggested that if this were done the country would find itself on a soil "hot with volcanic fire". Mill, finding himself unable to dissuade the League leaders from dangerous courses, ended his association with them.

In February 1867 Disraeli began to venture along the tortuous parliamentary path that eventually led to Reform. By April his Bill appeared to be making little headway. At this point the League resolved to assert once more the right of public meeting in Hyde Park. The Government banned the meeting and concentrated troops in and around the park. It mobilised thousands of special constables. Men were employed on overtime making batons. Police officers descended on the offices of the Reform League threatening the direst consequences if the authority of the Government was challenged. There were rumours that artillery was being brought into London from Aldershot. Beales, under heavy pressure from his own left wing, refused to be intimidated.

On the evening of May 6, 1867, the Reform League called the Tory bluff. A vast army of Reformers marched triumphantly through the gates and occupied the park. Whereas in July 1866 the Government had been unable to maintain order without the League, in May 1867 the orders of the League prevailed over those of the Government.

The middle-class press could not conceal its anguish. The "roughs" had triumphed over respectable society. It was evident that the Reform question would have to be brought to a conclusion as soon as possible. The Prime Minister himself was forced to acknowledge that his Administration had "suffered some slight humiliation in the public mind". He offered up his luckless Home Secretary, Spencer Walpole, as a sacrifice. The victory of the Reform League on May 6, 1867, had revenged the humiliation of the Chartists on April 10, 1848. The League was henceforth a power. It exchanged messages with Bismarck and enrolled Garibaldi among its members. Its class pride was enormously enhanced. It adopted a sharp and censorious tone in its dealing with those bourgeois patrons to whom it had hitherto tended to defer.

Gladstone had advised the League against a confrontation with the Government. He now moved sharply to the left. Disraeli had already privately revealed his own motives: he sought, he explained, "to destroy the present agitation and to extinguish Gladstone and Co." He could only hope to attain the second of these objectives to the extent that he was able to convince Parliament that it was imperative to achieve the first. The "destruction" of the agitation was only possible through far-reaching concessions to its demands: concessions which went far beyond anything which Disraeli, Gladstone, Bright or any other Parliamentarian had wanted or imagined. Dizzy had, at all costs, to avoid appearing to accept dictation from his great rival. Under the circumstances he could only do so by accepting amendments still more radical than those favoured by the Liberal leader.

Disraeli had little interest or knowledge of the details of the Bill. He was probably tiddly for a good deal of the time. He asked his colleagues to come and speak on key clauses explaining that he did not care whether they spoke for or against so long as they spoke. But behind a pleasant alcoholic haze, the mind was clear: he was going to stay on the horse's back even if he could not pretend to determine just how far the horse was going to go. And it did not go all that far: before Reform one adult male in five had the vote: after Reform the proportion was still only one in three.

When the Government surrendered to the League on May 6, it exchanged the associations of Peterloo for those of Hyde Park. Henceforth Hyde Park acquired its distinctive significance within the British political tradition. It stood for the triumph of popular rights over aristocratic enthusiasm before those "occult and unacknowledged forces that are not dependent upon any legislative machinery". The limitations of the right that had been established are as evident as the right itself.

As with the park, so with Reform. The workers were encroaching on established power and simultaneously being involved more deeply in the *status quo*. The very advance that they made diminished their own sense of identity upon which further advance depended. Within the framework of the liberal democratic state it was to prove difficult to recover the spirit of "the Democracy" —the rule of all the poor and all the oppressed. The workers had to master a new kind of politics once "good will" had been tried and was answering.

ROYDEN HARRISON   *Before the Socialists: Studies in Labour and Politics in England, 1861–1881* (1965) The present article derives from the third chapter of this book.

HENRY KATZ   *Anglia U Progu Demarkracji (England on the Threshold of Democracy)*, (Warsaw, 1965) This scholarly and important work badly needs to find an English translation; the same applies to Dr Katz's monograph history of the Reform League.

F B SMITH   *The Making of the Second Reform Bill* (Cambridge, 1966) The best general history available, sound, balanced and reliable if not inspired.

MAURICE COWLING   *1867, Disraeli, Gladstone and Revolution* (Cambridge, 1967), pp. 450. Originally a polemical attack on the chapter referred to above in Harrison: written from the standpoint of "pure" and "high" politics.

GERTRUDE HIMMELFARB   *Victorian Minds* (1968) The last chapter is a furious assault on Whig, Marxist and the new left dogs barking in the gutter. More entertaining but perhaps less responsible than Cowling.

F M LEVENTHAL   *Respectable Radical* (1971). A careful biography of George Howell, the Secretary of the Reform League.

David Tribe
Charles Bradlaugh

DAVID TRIBE *was born in Sydney in 1939. He is an author, critic, journalist, broadcaster and poet. His published works include* WHY ARE WE HERE? *(1965),* 100 YEARS OF FREETHOUGHT *(1967),* PRESIDENT CHARLES BRADLAUGH MP *(1971),* NUCLEOETHICS: ETHICS IN MODERN SOCIETY *(1972) and numerous pamphlets. While in England he was editor and later chairman of the* FREETHINKER, *president of the National Secular Society and a member of the executive of the National Council for Civil Liberties.*

Though only 57 when he died Charles Bradlaugh left a record of work and achievement that only the Victorians, for all their faults, seemed capable of. Plunged into radical causes as a boy and toiling away at correspondence and parliamentary and editorial duties on his death-bed, he had no sparkling childhood or golden retirement, and little private life in between.

While he was an individualist in basic philosophy and personality, no man more submerged himself in popular causes and the concerns of others; and, though the details of his life were unique, the pattern of it was typical of nineteenth-century radicalism.

A self-made man of shrewd East End origins, he acquired in turn a reputation for skilled agitation, a weekly paper, the leadership of a viable national movement and some others that were more transient, the accolade of regular prosecution, a seat in the Commons, belated recognition and posthumous "canonisation". Each step in this advance just happened to be more colourful than with most of his contemporaries.

During his lifetime (1833–91) all the great intellectual and political movements of the twentieth century passed through their formative stages. Bradlaugh was never far from the centre of them. Omnivorous reading and attention to detail gave most of his writings a powerful topicality that soon dates.

But if he is less read today than authors who went in for the windy generalities that are more "timeless", the causes that he took up have an uncanny modernity. Those that have been achieved and most of those that have not are now seen to be more important than was generally recognised at the time. Even those that are dismissed as "dead letters" seem simply to have been overtaken by circumstances and not to be, in retrospect, period pieces or historical curios.

In all his exertions he put people before ideology. Poverty he saw as a curable social disease. It is difficult to say which of his many campaigns was the most significant. Ultimately, I think, his fight for family planning (neo-Malthusianism, as it was then called) will gain the laurels. Together with that remarkable woman Annie Besant, he republished a birth control pamphlet, Charles Knowlton's *Fruits of Philosophy*, which had been withdrawn after legal action against its regular publisher, and invited a new prosecution.

For this encouragement of "wickedness, lewdness and debauchery" both publishers were sentenced to six months' imprisonment and a £200 fine; but with that legal acumen which was the envy and fury of Britain's leading professional lawyers, Bradlaugh got the sentence quashed on a technicality. From that time (1877) the large Victorian family with its attendant sickness and poverty began to diminish, but greater longevity and industrialisation have kept the population problem in the forefront of attention.

An example of his compassion and his style can be seen in this statement, made to the jury during the birth-control trial.

"Put yourself in the position of the agricultural labourers. They have not the training and education that you have, and sometimes mere sexual gratification is the only pleasure of their lives. They cannot read Virgil; they cannot read Dante. They cannot listen to Beethoven; they cannot listen to Handel. They cannot go to a musical réunion; and they cannot visit a sculpture gallery. They have no time occasionally to run across the Alps. They have no opportunity of finding recreation in the Pyrenees. They cannot yacht in the North Sea. They cannot fish for salmon at New Brunswick or St John's. They are limited to their narrow parish bound, and their bound is only the work, the home, the beerhouse, the poorhouse, and the grave. We want to make them more comfortable; and you tell us we are immoral. We want to prevent them bringing into the world little children to suck death, instead of life, at the breasts of their mother; and you tell us we are immoral. I should not say that, perhaps, for you, gentlemen, may judge things differently from myself; but I know the poor. I belong to them. I was born amongst them. Among them are the earliest associations of my life. Such little ability as I possess to-day has come to me in the hard struggle of life. I have had no University to polish my tongue; no Alma Mater to give to me any eloquence by which to move you. I plead here simply for the class to which I belong, and for the right to tell them what may redeem their poverty and alleviate their misery."

Bradlaugh's legal genius figured in other important controversies. In 1868 his paper, *The National Reformer* (the *Tribune* of the Victorian age), was prosecuted by Disraeli for defying the Security Laws requiring a recognisance and sureties against the appearance of "blasphemous and seditious libels".

Since only a lunatic would put his money into almost weekly jeopardy, Bradlaugh decided to defy the prosecution. The case lapsed, but to everyone's amazement Gladstone restored it. In a fight which was described as "the most valuable personal contribution ever made to the liberty of the press", Bradlaugh gained such sympathy that the Security Laws were repealed before the case was decided.

The legal action—or tangled web of actions—which most captured the public's imagination and gave him a place in constitutional history (his importance in social history has not been appreciated to this day) was over his struggle to enter Parliament.

In 1880, after 12 years of nursing the constituency, he was elected one of the two members for Northampton. In the light of his reputation as probably the most notorious iconoclast in the realm ("Iconoclast" was the pseudonym he adopted during his youthful career) this achievement was remarkable enough in it-self. It turned out to be the beginning, not the end, of his struggles. One by one the requirements of the oath, which had for centuries been used to try to secure religious and political "reliability", were relaxed in favour of Quakers, Moravians, Separatists, Roman Catholics and Jews, either by allowing affirmation instead or by altering the terms of the oath.

In 1869 and 1870 following the manifest injustice resulting from a civil action brought by Bradlaugh, where he was unable to give evidence and a friend unable to go bail, two Acts were passed allowing atheists to affirm in courts of law and similar tribunals. Debate persisted over whether this provision extended to Parliamentary oaths.

Advised that it did, Bradlaugh sought to affirm before taking his seat. When this right was challenged the Speaker declined to give a personal ruling and a select committee was set up to decide the issue. It reported that he was ineligible to affirm but could, if he liked, take the oath. Bradlaugh cheerfully agreed, but this was challenged with greater indignation and another select committee appointed. Citing his own arguments in favour of affirming, it decided that he was disqualified from taking the oath but should be allowed to affirm at his legal peril. And peril it was. At the first court decision against him he lost his seat.

Then there began a saga of court actions and counter-actions to try to bypass the basic ideological difficulty, impassioned speeches at the Bar of the House, self-submission of the oath in surprise sallies, three by-elections which he won against every personal and public libel which the civil and ecclesiastical establishment could think up, the last imprisonment of a Member in the Clock Tower, physical ejection from the House in a state of collapse, nation-wide demonstrations and counter-demonstrations, debts amounting to thousands of pounds. It lasted for the entire life of the 1880–5 Parliament.

In the new Parliament a new Speaker allowed him to take the oath, and in 1888 he piloted through an Oaths Act which made affirmation legal in every situation where an oath might be required.

As an MP he earned the respect of both sides of the House, becoming known as the "Member for India", and was promised office in the next Gladstone administration (probably as Under-Secretary of State for India). Had he lived, the history of that troubled subcontinent might have been very different.

He ferreted out not only abuses of modern capitalism but singular survivals of the feudal system like market rights and tolls, which kept food prices high. He was an indefatigable asker of awkward questions about foreign and imperial policy and served on or advised royal commissions and committees of enquiry into a number of complex issues. But he was allowed only a handful of years in the House and it is an extra-parliamentary figure that he is best remembered.

In the early 1870's many thought that he would overthrow the constitution itself. The people had grown tired of constant rearguard actions by the Lords against reform, and the successful republican movement in France and retirement of Queen Victoria to Windsor stimulated discontent with the monarchy.

As leader of England's most widely based republican movement and writer of the best-selling *Impeachment of the House of Brunswick*, Bradlaugh was most likely to emerge at the head of any upheaval. Had he been prepared to sanction an armed uprising it is just possible that a republic would have come about. But the republicans were divided by class, sectarian and ideological differences, and the British ruling class bent in the wind until the gales of popular discontent blew themselves out. By the time they raged again in the late 1880's, Victoria was a national monument, Bradlaugh a sober MP. By this time, too, Marxist influence was sufficiently strong to have diverted public wrath from the aristocracy to the bourgeoise, without apparently noticing that the power of the nobility, who had the best of both worlds, derived from their land rather than their "capital".

As president of the Land Law Reform League, Bradlaugh was in the nineteenth-century radical tradition which saw the basis of English class society as a system of "laws which make pheasants more valuable than peasants". Stopping just short of land nationalisation, on the grounds that the cost of compensation would be prohibitive, he advocated a land tax and a wealth tax. His successors in the popular movement turned to trendier things so that today, after a spot of nationalisation in this industry and part of that, society is as unequal as ever it was, and land speculation has been the chief maintainer of this inequality.

"Iconoclast" was rather more successful as president of the National Secular Society. In those days, the chastisement of error was deemed worthy in itself (truth had not yet become "what works") and Bradlaugh was something of a biblical scholar in the original languages. It cannot be denied that his bible-smashing activities gave him intellectual satisfaction. But they also had a social purpose.

Though recognising that Catholic was more outlandish than Anglican theology, he directed his major blasts against the Church of England and biblical fundamentalism. For he saw what reverent agnostics could not, or would not, see: that the Church was indeed the Tory Party at prayer and, particularly in country areas, the clergy dominated the social, cultural and intellectual life of the people in the interests of the ruling class, while Church rates, tithes, rents and other dues were a continual drain on the poor. Biblical texts were repeatedly quoted to obstruct science and social progress, and would continue to be so used till the authority of the bible had itself been undermined.

If the NSS never attracted a vast membership, its rationalist and reforming work exerted an enormous impact and can perhaps best be seen within the Church. (The same may be said of the House of Leeds, even before the introduction of life peers as Bradlaugh advocated.) In the NSS Bradlaugh also had a far-flung instrument which, at a touch of his finger, could raise protest notes throughout the country. He was a *maestro* at orchestrating perfectly disciplined demonstrations, with the concerted action of meetings, marches and petitions, from which today's revolutionaries could learn a lot.

The breadth of his interests can best be shown by listing some of the causes he fought for: temperance; disestablishment; universal suffrage (in opposition to the "intelligence franchise" which a number of other radicals of the day were toying with); female emancipation; colonial freedom within a multi-racial Commonwealth; Home Rule for Ireland, whose Fenian Manifesto of 1867 he assisted in drafting, as part of a federation of the United Kingdom which would give some self-government to Wales and Scotland too; penal reform, with the abolition of the birch and the noose; industrial arbitration; co-operative societies; proportional representation; the abolition of all penalties on opinion; a Channel tunnel; world disarmament; disengagement from the Suez Canal, where he was one of the first to recognise the danger of Britain's shareholding; sex instruction; free, secular and compulsory education; international arbitration. But all his activities had one thing in common, which he put succinctly and movingly in a speech to the Indian National Congress in 1889: "For whom should I work if not for the people? Born of the people, trusted by the people, I hope to die of the people. And I know no geographic or race limitations to this word 'people'."

In his later years he was accused by the socialists and the "new unionists" of having sold out on the people to feather his own nest. It was rather ironical, as he died in debt and in the midst of reforming work, while many of them passed on to the comforts of theosophy, literature and social respectability.

The rows of the 1880's were to some extent linguistic. Bradlaugh advocated certain policies that no "socialist" government has dared to touch. It is true that he had some rather naive views on the degree to which savings bank accounts made people "property owners" and he shared the general Victorian misgiving that the welfare state would vitiate the principles of self-help and community-help. Suspicious of big government, which he regarded as a necessary consequence of socialism, he stressed the importance of free bargaining between employers and employees. As a man of affairs he rejected utopianist schemes and as a lover of peace shrank from Red revolution whose consequences could not be predicted.

Rightly or wrongly he thought 100 per cent socialism incompatible with personal freedom, and no socialist country has yet proved him wrong. He believed he could make the Liberal Party a national radical party, avoiding class bitterness. If that aspiration seems unrealistic today, it was a view shared by many union leaders of the period.

To the Durham miners, who invited him a record number of times to their annual gala, the shoemakers and the many craft unions to whom he freely gave legal advice and other help, he remained a popular idol whatever the "red-raggers" might say. For he had one quality the people instinctively recognised: he was incorruptible.

CHARLES BRADLAUGH   *The Impeachment of the House of Brunswick* (1871)

CHARLES BRADLAUGH   *The Autobiography of C Bradlaugh* (1873)

(Court transcript)   *The Queen v. Charles Bradlaugh and Annie Besant* (1877)

ADOLPHE S HEADINGLEY   *The Biography of Charles Bradlaugh* (1880)

HYPATIA BRADLAUGH BONNER & J M ROBERTSON   *Charles Bradlaugh: A Record of His Life and Work, with an Account of His Parliamentary Struggle, Politics and Teaching*, 2 vols (1895)

Bradlaugh and Today, Speeches at Centenary Celebration (1933)

Champion of Liberty: Charles Bradlaugh, Centenary Volume (1933)

ARTHUR H NETHERCOT   *The First Five Lives of Annie Besant* (1961)

WALTER L ARNSTEIN   *The Bradlaugh Case, A Study in Late Victorian Opinion and Politics* (Oxford 1965)

DAVID TRIBE   *President Charles Bradlaugh, MP* (1971)

Toiling peasants in the Luttrell Psalter

John Lilburne

Thomas Paine

William Cobbett

William Hone's sarcastic
comment on Peterloo in his
Facetiae and Miscellanies

Drawing by
George Cruikshank

VICTORY OF PETERLOO.

A MONUMENT is proposed to be erected in commemoration of the achievements of the MANCHESTER YEOMANRY CA-VALRY, on the 16th *August*, 1819, against THE MANCHESTER MEETING of Petitioners for Redress of Wrongs and Grievances, and Reform in Parliament. It has been called a *battle*, but erroneously; for, the multitude was *unarmed*, and made no resistance to the heroes *armed*; there was no contest—it was a *victory*; and has accordingly been celebrated in triumph. This event, more important in its consequences than the Battle of Waterloo, will be recorded on the monument, by simply stating the names of the officers and privates successfully engaged, on the one side; and on the other, the names of the persons killed, and of the six hundred maimed and wounded in the attack and pursuit; also the names of the captured, who are still prisoners in His Majesty's goals; with the letter of thanks, addressed to the victors, by His Majesty's Command.

The Home of the Rick-Burner

Robert Owen in 1829

MR. BRADLAUGH AND THE OATH OF ALLEGIANCE—CAPTAIN GOSSET, SERGEANT-AT-ARMS, ARRESTING MR. BRADLAUGH UPON THE SPEAKER'S WARRANT

Bradlaugh fails to gain admittance to Parliament in 1880

from Hyndman's autobiography Vol I (1911)

Hulton

H M Hyndman

William Morris

Hulton

Annie Besant

Trafalgar Square in 1886

Mrs Pankhurst & Christabel Pankhurst

Hulton

Keir Hardie addressing a peace demonstration in 1914

Hulton

Ben Tillett

UNDER WHICH FLAG?

Punch's comment on the General Strike was reprinted in the British Gazette, the government propaganda sheet and got the reply at right in Lansbury's *Labour Weekly*

"Tackling the First Giant" by Whitelaw (Daily Herald)

Asa Briggs
H M Hyndman

ASA BRIGGS *was born in 1921. He has been professor of history at the University of Sussex since 1961 and vice-chancellor since 1967. He was the first chairman and then the president of the Society for the Study of Labour History, until 1971. He is the author of a large number of books on nineteenth- and twentieth-century British history including* VICTORIAN PEOPLE *(1954),* THE AGE OF IMPROVEMENT *(1959) and* VICTORIAN CITIES *(1963). In the field of labour history he is the editor of* CHARTIST STUDIES *(1959) and, with John Saville, of two volumes of* ESSAYS IN LABOUR HISTORY *(1960 and 1971).*

So many influences shaped the making of the Labour movement in late nineteenth-century Britain that it is difficult to separate them out. Hope and fear, pride and guilt, collective solidarity and individual rebellion were all part of the intricate pattern.

At first sight, there should have been one example of simplicity in the midst of complexity. The Social Democratic Federation, which acquired its name in 1884, was Marxist in style and in message, revolutionary in ethos, and basically proletarian in composition. It proclaimed "scientific Socialism" and sought to evolve independent tactics grounded in its science. From the 1880's until 1920, when it contributed the biggest single block of supporters to the newly-founded Communist Party, it continuously advocated class warfare and a complete transformation of the social system. Its guiding ideas were too extreme for it ever to win large-scale support, but it recognised clearly that it could not become a mass political party. It had more in common with continental Socialism than characteristically eclectic British bodies like the Independent Labour Party, founded a decade later, or the Fabian Socialists, who expressed, not least in their compromises, much of the continuity of English history.

Yet there is a paradox. For most of its history the Social Democratic Federation was led by a man who combined in himself more incongruities than most of the rival organisations which claimed the support of British Socialists. Many of his incongruities were quite specifically and distinctively English. He dressed immaculately in frock-coat and top hat. He had been educated first by a private tutor and later at Cambridge. He played cricket for Sussex, and once had the mortification of seeing W G Grace dropped off his bowling (by a future peer) and go on to score 276. He prided himself on his friendship with Meredith, his understanding of Disraeli and his feeling for Clemenceau, "the most brilliant man I ever knew". He had substantial private income from investments, and he knew from experience what it meant to be a speculator.

Born in 1842, Hyndman did not become a Socialist until he had travelled round the world and met a surprisingly mixed group of well-known people. He "read hard at Marx" in Salt Lake City of all places, but it was not until 1881 that he began to appreciate clearly that he was living in what he aptly called "the dawn of a revolutionary epoch". By the mid-1880's all his social and political views were formed, and he had established his position, in Kautsky's phrase, as "the most energetic embodiment of the British section of Marxism". Again there was a paradox. He did this in face of the unconcealed suspicion of Marx, who called him a "weak vessel", and the open hostility of Engels, whom he never met formally.

The last ten years of his life were among the oddest. He had always warned his fellow-countrymen against "German militarism"—there was a prophetic note in his writings even when he was not discussing Socialism—and when war broke out in 1914 he supported the struggle. There had already been many splits and deviations in the pre-war history of his party, along with changes of name, but in 1916 there was a particularly bitter and decisive break. Most of his keenest disciples stayed with him in the tiny National Socialist Party. He had told an American journalist in 1914 that if he had not been 72 years old he would have "gone out to fight" himself : this was the kind of remark that made his political opponents brand him as a militarist himself. There was an equally sharp division on the significance of the Russian Revolution of 1917. Hyndman was so little in sympathy with it that Bernard Shaw could accuse him of seeking "to out-Churchill Churchill".

Yet Hyndman never abandoned his Socialism, and continued to believe that it should be of a comprehensive kind, dealing in revolutionary change and not in "palliatives". "No hope but in the Labour Party, and not much in that" was his caustic comment on the political scene in 1920. The tragedy for him was that he had always held that Britain had been especially favoured to become the centre of world Socialism, and even when all personal hopes had long been dashed he could still maintain just before his death in 1921 that "we Englishmen, owing to our geographical, social, economic, and political situation, are nearer to the realisation of Social Democracy and the Co-operative Commonwealth than any other people in the world". He had always fancied himself as Prime Minister of such a Commonwealth, and a number of his contemporaries—seriously or satirically—had encouraged him to indulge in his fancies.

Eric Hobsbawm has rightly pointed out that the Social Democratic Federation was always something more than Hyndman, and that one element in it survived Hyndman's withdrawal as coherently as the party as a whole had survived many other sectarian withdrawals during its often stormy history. Many Social Democrats never fully accepted Hyndman's views on foreign affairs : many of them were aggressively proletarian, representing a tradition of working-class secularism and militant theorising which goes back to the eighteenth century, particularly in London, where the SDF was relatively strong. At the same time, Hobsbawm does not seek to probe Hyndman's motives or to examine his inadequate conception of leadership : he is content with the verdict that "superior leadership would have produced better results".

Another indispensable work on Hyndman, the Japanese Chushichi Tsuzuki's *H M Hyndman and British Socialism*, is more concerned with chronicling Hyndman's career and the

development of the SDF as an organisation than with painting a
personal picture. It is itself paradoxical that the most authorita-
tive book on a man who thought of himself as the most English
of Marxist Socialists should be written by a Japanese scholar,
who, as E P Thompson has noted in a perceptive review (in the
Labour History *Bulletin*, No. 3, 1961), appears to be very little
surprised at the eccentricities of his subject. An earlier book,
F J Gould's *Hyndman, Prophet of Socialism*, expresses the mood
of Hyndman's most loyal supporters, the people who remained
with him through thick and thin. Their influence has never completely disappeared within the Labour movement.

The best starting point for a contemporary study of Hyndman
remains his published works. *The Record of an Adventurous Life*
(1911) really is the record of an adventurous life, vigorously
written and deliberately frank and provocative. It was so successful as a book that Hyndman followed it up immediately with
Further Reminiscences (1912). Among his other writings *England for All* (1881) is a valuable historical document, preceding
as it did the Liberal split of 1886 which is usually said to have
given "the gospel of Socialism" its chance; it is also of significance
in that it alienated Marx, who objected to being referred to
anonymously in the preface as "a great thinker and original writer" whose work "will, I trust, shortly be made accessible to the
majority of my countrymen". Hyndman was adept in his two
volumes of autobiography in generously conceding the greatness
of erstwhile opponents—Morris stands out in this respect as well
as Marx—while at the time he had been a master at losing friends
and failing to influence people. Moreover *England for All* as
early as 1881 set a kind of hectic now-or-never note which was
bound to make people feel that if Hyndman's prophecies did not
come true, there was something wrong about his doctrines. It was
easy for a shrewd political journalist in pre-war London to dismiss Hyndman as "that sturdy squire of Socialism, who used to
predict the imminence of the Socialist Revolution much as Old
Moore foretold fogs for London in November and troubles in the
Balkans in Spring".

Hyndman himself was referred to as late as 1891, in a general
book about contemporary Socialism, not as a Socialist leader, but
as "a journalist of standing and ability". His articles in *Justice*

are still worthwhile reading, although he came to believe that 'invaluable service as the paper has rendered at times, we should have done far better to have expended our money and enthusiasm in other directions". He never liked to be thought of as a "mere" propagandist any more than Marx liked to be thought of as a mere "great thinker and original writer", even though it was through his persistent and often persuasive Marxist propaganda in a non-Marxist labour movement that Hyndman guaranteed his place in British labour history. The fact that his Marxism was of a closed and bigoted variety provides yet another complication.

Three of his other works reflect his range of interests and the characteristic form of his analysis. *The Historical Basis of Socialism in England* (1883) is a weighty attempt to give a theoretical extension to his political thinking. *Commercial Crises of the Nineteenth Century* (1892) was reprinted as late as 1932 when a bigger crisis had hit the world. It had a preface from J A Hobson, whose under-consumptionist thesis was never taken up by Hyndman. Both these books reflect Hyndman's interest in history which pre-disposed him to Marxism and made him an acute and sympathetic student of Chartism. *Commercial Crises* also expresses Hyndman's considered view, still relevant, that although Britain "owing to its economical development, its commercial and financial position, its preponderance of great cities, and its geographical situation, must inevitably take the lead in any important social transformation", nonetheless international economic factors could always qualify this. "For England, more than any other nation, is dependent upon foreign countries so largely, and in some cases so exclusively, for her supplies of food and the raw materials of her manufactures, that nothing can be done without touching exterior interests at some point."

The Awakening of Asia (1919) shows that Hyndman's prophetic powers ranged widely over the world and not simply over Britain or Europe. It also demonstrates that though he supported the war effort between 1914 and 1918, he was by no means a *persona grata* with the powers that be. The book was held up by the censor for more than two years. Anyone who believes that Hyndman was an imperialist—and there are many writers who have dismissed him in this way—should re-read *The Awakening of Asia.* It states categorically that "Asia owes to Europe little or nothing"; it forecasts a new period when Asian affairs will dominate the headlines; it urges Indian independence and warns against Japanese militarism; and it demands categorically "the frank abandonment of the fallacious policy of Imperialism". "We are turning over a new page in the history of the human race", Hyndman concludes. "What will be written upon it depends on the men and women of the rising generation. If in international relations, the old race and colour prejudices are maintained, if trade and commerce, interest and profit continue to be the principle objects of our statesmanship, then troubles may easily ensue beside which even the World War may take second place."

Hyndman had always been interested in foreign affairs and in the affairs of India. This, indeed, was what first pushed him into politics. He liked to be "in the know", and although he realised the danger in David Urquhart's bizarre and conspiratorial approach to problems of foreign policy, there was a link between what he advocated and what Urquhart, who influenced Marx (and, after Urquhart, Joseph Cowen, who directly influenced Hyndman) had advocated before. Home affairs perhaps came second in his mind, and there are some signs that he returned to this balance of preoccupations in the last period of his life. It is important to bear in mind in seeking to understand him that both in relation to home affairs and to foreign affairs, he started with a strong anti-Liberal bias. Unlike most Labour leaders, although there were some who shared his views, particularly in London and in Lancashire, he held that "the only hope of rapid improvement" in the way of social "palliatives" lay through the actions of the Conservative Party. Emotion entered into this verdict, although he usually stated it in the most realistic terms. "Measures of this kind [palliatives] if introduced by the Conservative Party could not be opposed by the Liberals without imperilling their cohesion as a political organisation; whereas, if the Liberals introduced Bills in favour of such beneficial social changes, the more reactionary Conservatives would be sure to revolt and to find a factious backing in the country."

The same kind of "realism" comes to the surface in his dismissal of the battle between Liberals and Conservatives as a "sham fight", yet when he passes from the general to the particular he reserves his most cutting criticism for the Liberals. "Liberal mendacity" was one of his favourite expressions. Salisbury as well as Disraeli got a very good word from him, but Gladstone is lambasted for his "verbose rhetorical periods and dexterous casuistry" and for what Marx called his "oleaginous hypocrisy".

As for Lloyd George, he was "the most unscrupulous and treacherous political adventurer that has been seen in our time", and his famous Budget of 1909 was "the biggest fraud". There was a sense in which Hyndman really was a "squire", a man of strong and often unattractive prejudices which remained more or less the same before and after he became a Socialist. It is important to bear in mind that when he burst into politics during the Near Eastern crisis of the late 1870's, he did so on the opposite side to William Morris. He disliked Liberal policies in relation to Russia, Turkey and India, and lamented the fall of Disraeli's government in 1880.

Of course, Hyndman attacked the blindness of Conservatives who would not see the light and move with him or towards him, and he was unimpressed by both Balfour and Chamberlain. Yet he retained an almost Tory attitude towards the "masses", and this affected his conception of "leadership". He writes of "taunting a working-class audience with their apathy, indifference and ignorance", of "holding forth at length upon their contemptible lack of capacity to understand their own power", of dealing in *Justice* "with questions that the mass of mankind did not wish to have thrust upon them". Trade unionism was always a strange and somewhat uncongenial subject for him. Only in education, which he spoke of in very general terms, far more general than the terms employed by Morris, did he believe that the working classes could be redeemed.

His top hat and frock-coat must surely have been obvious symbols of difference, class-bound symbols of difference, more obvious than Edward Carpenter's sandals in a society of clogs. He sometimes gives himself away not only in his statements about policy but in what he says about his social dealings with the working classes, on the need to humour them and not to press them too hard, almost as if he thought that the huge, variegated British working class were just like an audience in Hyde Park. He also gives himself away in what he says (favourably) about salons and (unfavourably) about whelks. He and Henry George once passed a whelk stall in Great Portland Street. George wanted to eat some whelks on the spot. "Expostulation was useless . . . George consumed his whelks from the barrow while I, got up in the high hat and frock-coat of non-whelk-eating-at-the-corner-civilisation, stood by and saw him do it." He adds with engaging frankness first, that he had not then "cleared myself of old class prejudices even to the extent I have today" and second, that "I never see a whelk stall at a street corner to this day but I feel inclined to bolt off in another direction".

Whelks should not be the last word. To appreciate how genuine Hyndman's Socialist convictions really were, much the best passage of his writings to read is Chapter 3 in his *Further Reminiscences* which deals with his election fights at Burnley, where he spent more time than in any place in Britain except London. After explaining why, in his view, Marxist Socialists had to be prepared to fight elections but not to join "ministries of the governing class", he describes his first visit to Burnley in the 1880's. He had been told that he should not expect Burnley workers to be poor or depressed people. "They earned, I was told, about the best wages of any Lancashire folk, they had fine Co-operative Stores, large sums of money in the Savings Banks, took a solid holiday at midsummer extending over a full fortnight, for which period they heartily enjoyed themselves at Blackpool or some other pleasure resort, had good food, good clothing, and good housing, and altogether, being besides shrewd and fairly well educated, I should find them to be quite different from the working men and working women whom I had encountered in the South of England and even in other parts of Lancashire."

Hyndman goes on to paint the picture of Burnley and of working men in Burnley as he really saw it. He does so vividly, powerfully, and with a profound sense of humanity. He also goes on to delineate some of his general views on the nature of nineteenth-century liberalism in a very specific Lancashire setting. He ends by reaching the same conclusions about working-class apathy which seemed so patronising in a more general context. "In spite of all our efforts and the steady work of enthusiastic comrades, the people were not educated enough to understand the crucial importance of Socialism to themselves and their children in their daily life."

Whether Hyndman learned all the right lessons from his "adventurous" life—even at Burnley—can be a matter of argument. He could seldom keep out of adventure. Unusually knowledgeable about "the establishment"—he has much of interest to say about this—he deliberately made himself unusually knowledgeable about the working classes. This was not enough, however, to make him into a really effective working-class leader. He was blind to almost every new dynamic force that did not fit his formulae. Nor could he see as clearly as Morris, for all his gift of prophecy, what twentieth-century society would be like. Paradoxically enough, and this must be the last of the paradoxes, he is often more illuminating when talking about palliatives, in which he refused to put his trust, than in talking about strategies. What he says about working-class housing would provide a study in itself. To understand what made him think and act as he did, it is necessary to look not only at the history of the Labour movement but at the more comprehensive and complex history of British society of which this is only one strand. There was nothing simple about Hyndman.

A bibliographical note on Hyndman follows the next article.

Chushichi Tsuzuki
Hyndman & the Social Democratic Federation

CHUSHICHI TSUZUKI *was born in Japan in 1926. He studied at Hitotsubashi (Tokyo), Wisconsin and Oxford. He was a research fellow at St Antony's College Oxford, a visiting professor at Sheffield University and is now professor of social thought at Hitotsubashi University. He is the author of* H M HYNDMAN AND BRITISH SOCIALISM *(1961) and* THE LIFE OF ELEANOR MARX *(1967) and is now working on the life of Edward Carpenter.*

It must have been a curious, even bizarre, sight : a middle-aged Englishman, on board a Cunarder and at his hotel in a Western mining town, tackling a copy of the French edition of Marx's *Capital*. It was the summer of 1880, and H M Hyndman was on his last, apparently unsuccessful, business trip to America. He had just made Marx's acquaintance, and shortly after his return to England put to him the idea of reviving Chartism. He soon announced "the Dawn of a Revolutionary Epoch" and set out to form a "New Party" the object of which he defined as "the direct representation of labour".

The man who was thus to become the first of the pioneers in the revival of socialism and Chartism in the 1880's and 1890's, was, however, a puzzle to his contemporaries and at one time considered unreliable by his associates. He was the son of a wealthy West India merchant, having strong family ties with the Empire, and was equipped with the social advantages of a university education. Thus Hyndman combined an incorruptible faith in socialism with advocacy of the benefits of the Empire and consequently of a big navy; a fierce attack upon class-ridden capitalist society with an obstinate attachment to the symbols of his own class, an immaculate frock-coat and top hat.

A city man speculating in stocks and shares and company promotion at the time of the "Great Depression", he knew the weakness of capitalism from the inside and, almost as an act of vengeance, he determined on its destruction, seeking to finance his socialist agitation with the fruits of his business activities. A true adventurer, he would delight in a political crisis and even in a catastrophe, though he was genuinely seeking orderly change.

The opportunity for Hyndman to launch his own party, the Democratic Federation, as it was called, was provided in 1881 by the Radical protest against Gladstone's Coercion policy in Ireland. He wrote to Marx at the time: "Revolution is possible: since the recent foolish action of our Government in many directions I had almost put probable. But what I mean is I do not wish to push men on to what must be violence when they might easily attain their object by peaceful action in common."

Here is the keynote of his subsequent campaign through all its vicissitudes. His *England for All*, a booklet distributed at the inaugural conference in June 1881, already contained a fair summary of the Marxian theory of surplus value. Nevertheless, it was characteristic of the socialist revival which took place under his leadership that he himself was disavowed by Marx, who felt that his own theory was "altogether out of place" in a party led by a man still regarded in some quarters as an "ultra-Jingo".

Acceptance of Marxian socialism was greatly facilitated when Henry George, the American land reformer, conducted a campaign in 1882 for a single-tax solution of the problem of poverty which stirred the public mind to examine the social question and to reconsider political economy. There was a new intellectual awakening, which carried over into the Federation with the influx of new recruits, many of them students of George, of Marx or both; prominent among them were H H Champion, a former artillery officer, William Morris, the poet and artist, E Belfort Bax, a journalist and Edward Aveling, a secularist leader. The last-named united in free-love with Marx's youngest daughter Eleanor (after Marx's death), and she brought some of her father's moral and intellectual stamp and international links to the Federation which had already committed itself to a socialist

programme (adopted in June 1883) which included the nationalisation of the means of production and distribution. At the annual conference held in August 1884 it changed its name to the
Social Democratic Federation, and was thereafter known as the
SDF.

Thus the revival of socialism in the early 1880's emerged first
of all as a movement of ideas. From the start, however, the Federation sought contact with the masses. Its weekly organ, *Justice*,
while explaining to the educated classes that socialism had a scientific basis, tried to stir up discontent among the workers. This
proved to be an arduous task. The English working class, in the
words of Marx, had gone so low as to constitute "the tail of the
great Liberal Party of Capitalists". Even the "Great Depression",
with its recurring slumps, only slightly affected the "aristocracy
of labour", though the distress among the "fringe of labour", as
Hyndman called it, became acute.

It was mainly to agitation among this "fringe" that the SDF
devoted itself, and in fact it grew more rapidly in periods of serious unemployment. Yet the working-class membership of the
SDF was very mixed. Apart from a few old Chartists who had
survived the period of apathy there were unskilled workers like
Jack Williams, a dock labourer, and Harry Quelch, a packer in
a warehouse, on the one hand and skilled engineers such as John
Burns, Tom Mann, and J L Mahon on the other. The bulk of its
support came from the skilled artisans, and this, together with the
continued existence of the middle-class leadership, explains the
predominance of London, from which it drew half of its strength.

In its attempt to win the working-class masses over to socialism,
the SDF groped its way. It broke with Radicalism, which seemed
to establish the working class in the system of the capitalist *status
quo*. It was thus significant that the SDF got up a separate demonstration in favour of socialism in Hyde Park on July 21,
1884, the day on which a great franchise rally of Radical working
men and trade unionists was held in the park to protest against
the blocking by the House of Lords of the Third Reform Act
(which was to increase the electorate by 66 per cent).

Unlike the franchise demonstration 18 years before, the crowd
demanding the County Franchise, "the franchise of every working man" and "Government by the People", was "orderly and

good-humoured", and the police were in "excellent temper". Penny portraits of Gladstone were on sale, and *The Times* endorsed Joseph Chamberlain's argument for "the supremacy of popular rights and representative institutions over personal authority and hereditary privileges".

As a fierce popular campaign stirred up the country for the franchise reforms, the socialists quarrelled among themselves over the question of political action and other relevant issues. In spite of his revolutionary vehemence Hyndman had not altered his view that the British workers would not accept "the subversionary doctrine of the Continental agitator" so long as constitutional means were open to them. Morris objected to parliamentary compromises, believing that socialism could be achieved only by "general revolt against the tyranny of commercial war", and he had certain Anarchist allies. According to his critics, Hyndman's view entailed elements of "chauvinism", and it is true that his opposition to British imperialism was not as thorough and consistent as might be expected from an international socialist.

Indeed, Hyndman's response to the ending of British monopoly in the world market and the rise of New Imperialism was more complex than that of an artistic mind like Morris or Aveling. Moreover, the dispute had its personal side in the animosity between Hyndman and Engels, or rather Engels' protégé Aveling. A split became inevitable, and it emphasised an extreme position in each of the opposing factions. The Socialist League which was set up at the end of 1884, by Morris and his followers, and which committed itself to "Revolutionary International Socialism," gradually fell into the hands of the Anarchists.

Hyndman's SDF, on the other hand, decided to take political action "in whatever way circumstances may suggest," and the odour of political opportunism, though not necessarily that of the "Tory Gold" that the Federation accepted to finance its two metropolitan candidates at the general election of 1885, caused another split in its ranks. The middle-class leadership was largely discredited in the eyes of the working-class members who remained. In an effort to free itself from this awkward situation, the SDF intensified agitation among the unemployed workers, taking advantage of a sharp increase in their number in the slump of 1885–6.

As a result the famous "West End Riot" took place on February 8, 1886. The story of the riot has been told many times, notably by David Rubinstein in an article in this book. Although the Socialist leaders, as it turned out, were acquitted of sedition. the struggle for speech in public places had not been won.

In November 1887 the Metropolitan Police, after clashes with unemployed demonstrators, prohibited the holding of all public meetings in Trafalgar Square, the "Forum of London Democracy" as Hyndman called it. On November 13—later to be known as "Bloody Sunday"—when the Metropolitan Radical Association sought to hold a "test meeting" (an anti-Coercion demonstration) in conjunction with the SDF and Morris's Socialist League, all the processions heading for the square were broken up by the police, and the demonstrators who made a determined attempt to break through a thick police cordon encircling the square were repulsed after a hand-to-hand tussle, leaving behind two captives, Cunninghame Graham, the Radical MP, and John Burns, who were later sent to prison.

A surging mass of people around the square was finally dispersed by police on foot and on horseback. Over 100 casualties were reported on that day; Eleanor Marx, who was said to have been "the Attacker" as well as "the Attacked," thought that the brutality of the police was worse than in Germany or Austria. Morris, who was also involved in the mêlée, felt that he had seen "the true face of reaction," and this discovery led him to abandon hopes for a successful revolutionary uprising under the existing circumstances.

Hyndman's SDF, on the other hand, did not abandon the militancy that it had acquired through agitation among the unemployed, and committed itself as ever to "vehement social agitation," even when a recovery in trade as well as the example of "Bloody Sunday" made such agitation appear almost impracticable. This was all the more unfortunate as attempts were then being made by several socialists to make contact with the working-class masses.

First in the field were Aveling and Eleanor Marx, who started a campaign to attract the Radical workers in the East End of London with a view to setting up "an English Labour Party with an independent class programme" as Engels remarked. Then there was J L Mahon, who organised a North of England Socialist Federation among the miners and ironworkers around Newcastle which he hoped would put pressure upon the squabbling London leaders to unite in pllitical action. Inside the SDF, Champion led a revolt against Hyndman, hoping to organise a "Labour Party" with a broad basis (such as the Labour Electoral Committee of the TUC might provide) and a programme of practical reform.

It is true that these attempts had no immediate results of great importance, but each in its own way assisted the tremendous awakening of working-class consciousness after 1889. Even the SDF's "vehement agitation" contributed to this. Although the Championite split deprived the SDF of its fair claim to much of the credit for the success of the great dockers' strike, Hyndman could take pride in his activities at the dock gates, where he and other SDF leaders spoke one after another from an orange box to hundreds of dockers at five o'clock in the morning, day after day for weeks before the strike.

Under the auspicious circumstances of the rise of New Unionism, the Avelings made a further attempt to form a mass labour party recruited from the new unions with the backing of the Second International which had also come into existence in 1889. In accordance with the resolutions adopted at the Paris Congress of the International, the first May Day demonstration demanding a legal eight-hour day was held at Hyde Park on May 4, 1890 (the first Sunday in the month). There assembled a vast crowd of 250,000–300,000, and from a platform Eleanor Marx declared that "the unemployed both at the top and at the bottom of society would be got rid of".

Engels, who was present as an observer, wrote to Eleanor's sister: "I can assure you I looked a couple of inches taller when I got down from that old lumbering waggon that served as a platform—after having heard again, for the first time since 40 years, the unmistakable voice of the English proletariat." He believed that a mass socialist movement was born on that day. Indeed, Aveling managed to form his own party, the Legal Eight Hours and International Labour League, but it failed to obtain mass support, and was even repudiated by the newly formed Independent Labour Party, which embodied a new type of working-class politics in the line of "labour alliance".

Meanwhile, Hyndman remained singularly inactive. This may be explained by his financial losses during the Barings Crisis in 1890, which crippled his parliamentary ambitions for some time. He fought Burnley unsuccessfully at the general election of 1895, though it was around this time that organised socialism in Britain was at the highest point it ever reached in the nineteenth century. Thereafter, the Labour movement as a whole stood on the defensive. Imperialism grew and brought fresh discord in the socialist ranks.

The SDF joined the Labour Representation Committee when it was formed in 1900. In the following year, however, when it failed for the second time to carry a class war resolution, it withdrew. At the same time, Hyndman temporarily retired from the active leadership of his party. The movement for which he had fought with "magnificent tenacity" was apparently at the end of an epoch. He despaired even of parliamentary action, and looked round to see what steps could be taken to control the "old worn-out system" of administration "when the break-down we anticipate occurs". Yet he returned to political action, and the SDF to the Labour Party, and the SDF's revolutionary tradition was carried on by the new generation of those socialists who became increasingly dissatisfied with the "old Adam of Jingoism" in Hyndman when the country went through the Great War and the impact of the Russian Revolution.

Engels often vilified the SDF as a sect which turned Marxism into a rigid dogma, but the rival organisations he patronised failed even more dismally to develop from sects into parties. In fact, the SDF remained a party of middle-class intellectuals and working-class élite, whose paying membership stood at 2,500 towards the end of the century. It was a party of the vanguard and also a movement of ideas; and it never became a mass party. Yet in its attempt to win the masses over to socialism, it greatly encouraged the political independence of the working class. Even its effort to organise discontent—a series of popular demonstrations, particularly of the unemployed—pointed in the same direction. At a local level, its influence helped to undermine the grip of the older parties.

Hyndman himself freely mixed millenarianism, a constant prediction of an imminent revolution, with reformism, as in, for example, one of the earliest programmes of municipal socialism he wrote for London. His party combined revolution romanticism and reformist realism, just as he did, and herein lay its weakness as well as its strength.

H M HYNDMAN   *England for All: The Text-Book of Democracy* (1881)

JOHN RAE   *Contemporary Socialism* (1884, 2nd ed. 1891)

H M HYNDMAN   *The Record of an Adventurous Life* (1911)

H M HYNDMAN   *Further Reminiscences* (1912)

ROSALIND TRAVERS HYNDMAN   *The Last Years of H M Hyndman* (1923)

F J GOULD   *Hyndman:Prophet of Socialism* (1928)

H W LEE & E ARCHBOLD   *Social-Democracy in Britain* (1935)

E J HOBSBAWM   *Labouring Men* (1964), ch. 12

C TSUZUKI   *H M Hyndman and British Socialism* (1961)

HENRY COLLINS   "The Marxism of the Social Democratic Federation" in *Essays in Labour History 1886–1923*, eds. Asa Briggs & John Saville (1971)

Anthony Arblaster
William Morris: Art & Revolution

If the name of William Morris means anything to the English middle class it probably suggests first wallpaper designs, and secondly a highly self-conscious attempt to revive handicrafts and "get back to the middle ages". To most workers he means nothing at all. Morris, when he is not totally neglected, is still widely misunderstood. (He was born in 1834 and died in 1896.)

This is unfair, not only to Morris, but also to ourselves; for Morris's understanding of capitalism—and, not least important, of capitalism's immense capacity to disarm and neutralise its potential opponents, the working class—was profound and farsighted. It was Morris, for example, who saw that the great extensions of government intervention into social and economic life in the nineteenth century did not *necessarily* constitute so many steps in the direction of socialism, as many of the Fabians thought. They provided only "a *machinery* of Socialism", and Morris saw that that "machinery" could all too easily be put to other than socialist uses. He predicted that "the Society of Inequality might . . . accept the quasi-Socialist machinery above mentioned, and work it for the purpose of *upholding* that society, in a somewhat shorn condition, maybe, but a safe one" (my italics). It was he who foresaw :

"instead of the useless classes being swept away by the useful,
the useless gaining some of the usefulness of the workers, and
so safeguarding their privilege. The workers better treated,
better organized, helping to govern themselves, but with
no more pretence to equality with the rich, nor with any more
hope for it than they have now. But if this be possible, it

will only be so on the grounds that the working people
have ceased to desire real socialism and are contented with
some outward show of it joined to an increase in prosperity
enough to satisfy the cravings of men who do not know what
the pleasures of life might be if they treated their own capacities
and the resources of nature reasonably with the intention
and expectation of being happy." (*Communism*, 1893)

It is worth reading that passage carefully. It is the best short summary of the subsequent development of "affluent", "welfare" capitalism that I know. And it was written in 1893. There is much
that Morris wrote besides this passage which has gained rather
than lost relevance with the passage of time. No one, for example,
has been more profoundly aware than Morris of the damage
which industrial capitalism does to both the man-made and the
natural environment. Eighty years later middle-class opinion is
just beginning to catch up with him.

But if we are to come to appreciate Morris at his true worth, we
shall have first to destroy the false image of him which I mentioned above. Misconceptions about Morris are not merely widespread. They have been actively propagated by many eminent
people who ought to have known better.

The most persistent of these misconceptions is the belief that
Morris was inspired, above all, by a hatred of machinery, and
with it of modern civilisation as a whole, and that his response to
industrialism was a completely futile and impractical attempt to
revive handicrafts and drag the world back towards a highly
idealised conception of the middle ages—the epoch which had
been sentimentally celebrated in the paintings of the Pre-Raphael-
ites and in the poems of Tennyson and of Morris himself. Thus
C P Snow, in his notorious lecture on *The Two Cultures and the
Scientific Revolution* (1959), asserted that "intellectuals, particularly literary intellectuals, are natural Luddites", who "have
never tried, wanted, or been able to understand the industrial
revolution, much less accept it". He particularly derided the reaction to industrialism of Morris and others : "some, like Ruskin
and William Morris and Thoreau and Emerson and Lawrence,
tried various kinds of fancies which were not in effect more than
screams of horror". To anyone who has actually read the relevant writings of Ruskin, or Morris or D H Lawrence, it will be

clear that this is a total travesty of their response, which could only have been based on sheer ignorance.

It is not, however, very different from the comments of some other writers who were obviously better informed about Morris than was Snow. Thus Nikolaus Pevsner, in his book *Pioneers of Modern Design* (1960), informs us that "the machine was Morris's arch-enemy", and speaks of "Morris's attitude of hatred towards modern methods of production".* Graham Hough, in *The Last Romantics* (1949), echoes this view: "Modern technology was at least as much his enemy as modern social organisation." For good measure he also dismisses Morris's socialism as "a brief and transitory phase of the Socialist movement". Morris was "the prophet of a kind of Socialism that is no longer active". If these writers were to be believed, Morris's life and writings would be only of historical interest, and that of a very limited kind. Posterity is not usually very curious about failed Luddites.

Yet, as Raymond Williams has pointed out, there is something very odd about the reiteration of this view that Morris was making a wholly unrealistic attack on industrialism as such. For there is so little evidence to support it. It is as if people were unwilling to face the fact that Morris's target is not industry as such, not the machine as such, but what capitalism does with them. And his alternative is not pseudo-medieval arty-craftiness, but the reconstruction of society according to socialist principles.

It is true that Morris once wrote that "apart from the desire to produce beautiful things, the leading passion of my life has been and is hatred of modern civilisation". But it is hard to see how this can be misconstrued when in the very next sentence he goes on to speak of "its supplanting by Socialism", and when the whole passage appears in his essay "How I became a Socialist". As for the vexed question of machinery, on this too Morris spoke clearly; and *against* those "cultivated" people who condemned machinery as such:

"I have spoken of machinery being used freely for releasing people from the more mechanical and repulsive part of necessary labour: and I know that to some cultivated people, people of the artistic turn of mind, machinery is particularly

* Elsewhere, however, Pevsner has been more accurate in explaining Morris's views on machinery.

distasteful, and they will be apt to say you will never get
your surroundings pleasant so long as you are surrounded by
machinery. I don't quite admit that; it is the allowing machines
to be our masters and not our servants that so injures the
beauty of life nowadays."

(*How we Live and How we Might Live*, 1888).

It was the misuses to which machinery was put, and the distortion
of the proper relationship between human beings and machines,
between man and the man-made, which he condemned:

"We should be the masters of our machines and not their slaves,
as we are now. It is not this or that tangible steel or brass
machine which we want to get rid of, but the great intangible
machine of commercial tyranny."

So much, then, for the "natural Luddite" of Lord Snow's damaging fantasy.

There is, nevertheless, a sense in which the question of machinery *was* near the centre of Morris's preoccupations. For in his
critique of capitalism the question of work occupied a most prominent position. For Morris *any* economic and social system
which imposed on the majority of people forms of work not merely
directed to the production of useless or even harmful goods but
also in themselves forms of drudgery, devoid of joy or satisfaction,
was morally and humanly unacceptable. Morris never endorsed
that common distinction between work and leisure which serves
the function of disguising the fact that for most men and women
real living is confined to their "free" leisure time, while work is
only undertaken to earn that "living". He believed in work, not
because of some warped Protestant conviction of the virtue of
misery and toil, but because work as he knew it was essentially
creative and the source of the deepest satisfaction he could find.
He could not accept that for the vast majority of his fellow creatures it should connote only boredom and dreariness. And he
saw that this dreariness was produced not only by work which
was inherently undemanding and repetitive, but also by the futility of the purposes of that work. Like Ruskin before him he
opposed production for the sake of production. Only those things
which were worth making, which brought real human benefit,
should be made: "labour, to be attractive, must be directed towards some obviously useful end ..."

This in itself, however, would not be enough to remove the drudgery from work. Morris looked to machinery to eliminate some of the most degrading kinds of work; and he believed, too, that there should be an end to the division of labour whereby at any state of life a man is confined to one job only :

"To compel a man to do day after day the same task, without any hope of escape or change, means nothing short of turning his life into a prison-torment. Nothing but the tyranny of profit-grinding makes this necessary."

And it followed from this that education should equip people to make the best use of all their various faculties, rather than training them for one particular type of job :

"At present all education is directed towards the end of fitting people to take their places in the hierarchy of commerce— these as masters, those as workmen. The education of the masters is more ornamental than that of the workmen, but it is commercial still; and even at the ancient universities learning is but little regarded, unless it can in the long run be made to *pay*. Due education is a totally different thing from this, and concerns itself in finding out what different people are fit for, and helping them along the road which they are inclined to take."

It is, once again, an indication of the radicalism (that is, root-and-branch character) of his analysis of capitalism that, despite the abolition of some of most blatant cruelties of the work system, this account of work under capitalism is still wholly relevant. The essay from which these last quotations come, "Useful Work versus Useless Toil" (1885), is one of Morris's most important, and needs to be read as a whole. But its themes are constantly appearing in Morris's writings. For him the question of work was a vital test of the human, or inhuman, character of any civilisation :

"Nothing should be made by man's labour which is not worth making; or which must be made by labour degrading to the makers. . . . Simple as that proposition is . . . it is a direct challenge to the death to the present system of labour in civilized countries."

That difficult word "civilized", so often used to denote little more than the drinking of wine and comfortable armchairs, brings us to the question of the relation between Morris the artist and Morris the socialist. Yet in a sense there is no "question" because there is no disjunction here. For it was through his concern with art that Morris, like John Ruskin, came to develop a fiercely radical critique of nineteenth-century capitalism. It seemed to Morris, as to Ruskin from whom, as he confessed, he learnt so much, that the "civilisation" which surrounded them was simply incapable of producing anything worth calling art. "Shoddy is king", said Morris, and this was not surprising, for "art is the expression of man's pleasure in labour", and it was abundantly obvious that it was next to impossible to obtain pleasure from labour as it was in the nineteenth century. Thus for Morris the question of work and the question of art were closely linked. Unless the whole culture was fundamentally healthy there could not be any really healthy art. Morris firmly rejected the common conceptions of art as a mere decoration of reality, or as a compensation for a basically wretched existence, and he hated the élite character of established culture :

"I don't want art for a few, any more than education for a few, or freedom for a few."

And he was convinced that the touchstone of art must be its usefulness, not in any narrowly economic or moralistic sense, but in the broadest human terms :

". . . nothing can be a work of art which is not useful; that is to say, which does not minister to the body when well under the command of the mind, or which does not amuse, soothe, or elevate the mind in a health state."

But, contrary again to some common misconceptions, Morris did not overestimate the importance of art :

"Surely anyone who professes to think that the question of art and cultivation must go before that of the knife and fork (and there are some who do propose that) does not understand what art means, or how its root must have a soil of a thriving and unanxious life."

He had his priorities right. But he did not make the mistake of those modern social democrats who suppose that the achievement of general prosperity is *all* that socialists can be concerned about, and that art, in one form or another, is simply to be left as one more consumer good which an affluent working class may or may not choose to enjoy. Wealth, he knew, was no final test of the quality of a social system. It was the character of its whole collective life that mattered in the end.

But how was capitalism to be changed, or, rather, replaced? As we saw at the beginning, Morris was not a facile optimist. He did not usually under-rate the power of capitalism to survive. And he knew too that what socialists were faced with was not a social and economic system which only required a few minor and marginal reforms to be "humanised", but one which was wrong at the very roots. Exploitation and the class structure and the drive for profit—these, he knew, were not fringe defects of capitalism, but constituted the very core of the system. And it was because he saw this system *as* a system, and as one which was by its very nature inhuman and oppressive, that he was a revolutionary socialist.

> "The word Revolution, which we Socialists are so often forced
> to use, has a terrible sound in most people's ears, even when
> we have explained to them that it does not necessarily mean a
> change accompanied by riot and all kinds of violence, and
> cannot mean a change made mechanically and in the teeth of
> opinion by a group of men who have somehow managed
> to seize on the executive power for a moment. Even when
> we explain that we use the word revolution in its etymological
> sense, and mean by it a change in the basis of society, people
> are scared at the idea of such a vast change, and beg that
> you will speak of reform and not revolution . . . it may
> frighten people, but . . . also it may encourage some people,
> and will mean to them at least not a fear, but a hope."
> (*How we Live and How we Might Live*)

Morris was convinced that this revolution could only come about through class struggle, through the activity of the working class as a class. He did not think, as he explained to a friend, that "*individuals* of good will belonging to all classes" could do it:

> ". . . the antagonism of classes, which the system has bred, is
> the natural and necessary instrument of its destruction".

He was clear, too, that "meritocracy" and the career open to talent were no substitute for the emancipation of the working class as a whole; quite the opposite, in fact:

> ". . . much as I want to see workmen escape from their slavish
> position, I don't at all want to see a few individuals more

creep out of their class into the middle class; this will only
make the poor poorer still : . . . the really desirable thing that
being still workmen they should rise in culture and refinement
they can *only* attain to by their whole class rising".

This was the firm, but not rigid, Marxist foundation on which
Morris's involvement in practical politics was based. He was far
from being a writer with no experience of what he talked about.
On the contrary, he acted according to his principles, and he
learnt from his practical experience. The thought and the life
were one. That is not to say that he was a very successful "politician", nor that he was free from the kind of personal defects
which can play a large part in the success or failure of small political groups. But, looking back, we can see that the 1880's and
1890's were inevitably a period of ferment and uncertainty for
English socialists. The Labour Party, which was to act as the focus
for much socialist activity in Britain after 1900, had not yet been
formed. The future lay open and big with promise. Naturally
the various small groups of socialists which came into being at
this time jostled for position, for a stake in that hopeful future.

It is too facile to write of Morris's part in that ferment as a
political failure. One reason for this is that it is a matter of at-
tested historical fact that the influence of his writings in creating
a socialist consciousness in Britain has been very great. G D H
Cole was one among many who was converted to socialism by
reading Morris's utopian fable, *News from Nowhere* (1890).
Morris has inspired generations of socialists, and more has been
and continues to be written about him than about any other
pioneer of British socialism.

The other reason is more topical. The reformism of the Labour
Party has lately fallen into deep and perhaps lasting discredit
among British socialists, not only on account of the party's performance in office, but also because events have exposed the shal-
lowness of the optimistic analysis of latter-day capitalism on which
that performance was partly based. Socialists today are more likely
to respond to Morris's understanding of capitalism than they
would have been fifteen or twenty years ago. And we seem to
have entered another period of ferment and uncertainty similar
to that in which Morris lived and worked. Once again there is
talk of revolution, and there are, too, revolutionary groups, at

odds with each other as they were in the 1880's. It is no easier for
the honest and independent-minded socialist to see the way forward now than it was for Morris nearly a hundred years ago. So
far from his representing a "transitory phase" of no lasting relevance, we find ourselves in much the same situation. It would be
strange if his life and work had nothing to teach us. It would be a
tragic arrogance if we refused to learn.

Two collections of Morris's writings available in many libraries
are :
G D H COLE (ed.)   *William Morris, Prose, Verse, Lectures and
        Essays* (first published 1934)
ASA BRIGGS (ed.)   *William Morris: Selected Writings and De-
        signs* (1962, reprinted 1973)
to which may be added :
PHILIP HENDERSON (ed.)   *The Letters of William Morris to his
        Family and Friends* (1950)
Among the many biographies of Morris may be cited :
J W MACKAIL   *The Life of William Morris* (first published
        1899). This remains the standard biography.
A CLUTTON-BROCK   *William Morris* (first published 1914). This
        draws heavily on Mackail; it is a much shorter, useful
        summary.
E P THOMPSON   *William Morris, Romantic to Revolutionary*
        (1955). The most ambitious and comprehensive modern
        biography.
PHILIP HENDERSON   *William Morris* (1967)
PAUL THOMPSON   *The Work of William Morris* (1967)
These are the most recent full-scale biographies. Finally :
RAYMOND WILLIAMS   *Culture and Society, 1780–1850* (1958)
        connects Morris with John Ruskin and a tradition of nine-
        teenth-century social criticism.

David Rubinstein
The Sack of the West End 1886

DAVID RUBINSTEIN *taught history in London comprehensive schools from 1956 until 1965. Since 1965 he has been a lecturer in social history at the University of Hull. Among his publications are* SCHOOL ATTENDANCE IN LONDON, 1870–1904: A SOCIAL HISTORY *(1969),* EDUCATION FOR DEMOCRACY *(co-editor with Colin Stoneman, 1970) and* THE EVOLUTION OF THE COMPREHENSIVE SCHOOL, 1926–1972 *(co-author with Brian Simon, 1973). He has written and reviewed for* TRIBUNE *for many years. He is the vice-chairman of the Ramblers' Association and has spoken and written widely on access to the countryside and related matters.*

The mid 1880's were marked by a number of demonstrations, some of which ended in violence. One of the most famous was the riot sometimes called "Black Monday", 8 February 1886. At this time the young socialist movement was struggling out of its initial obscurity. Its struggles were adversely affected by the split in the principal socialist body, the Social Democratic Federation, and by the charges of "Tory Gold" in 1885 to which Chushichi Tsuzuki has already referred above. A more favourable period began early in 1886 when a sharp rise in unemployment caused considerable agitation. The SDF led demonstrations in London which reached a peak on 8 February.

The Fair Trade League had called a meeting on that day in Trafalgar Square. This organisation, several of whose leaders were strike breakers of unsavoury reputation, was subsidised by certain wealthy Conservatives who were alleged to pay large sums to secure good attendances at their meetings and break up those of reformers and socialists. Its appeal to the working class was based on the claim that higher tariffs would end unemployment. The

SDF seized the opportunity to hold a meeting of its own at the same time and place. It was addressed by its leader, H M Hyndman, John Burns, then a fiery young socialist but later a Liberal Cabinet Minister, and others.

Like much else that happened that day the exact words of the speakers were variously reported. Burns was alleged to have cried: "Unless we get bread, they must have lead!" What was generally agreed is that Burns asked: "When we give the word for a rising, will you join us?" "To which", *The Times* reported, "a large number of the audience replied that they would, and almost as large a number declared that they would not." The SDF paper *Justice*, on the other hand, claimed that "a great shout of assent went up. Contrary to the statements in the capitalist press, we are bound to say that no one in the crowd expressed their dissent."

At this point Burns and Hyndman, among others, led the crowd up Pall Mall and to Hyde Park, their intention being either to avoid a fight with the Fair Trade group or, after a march, to hold a second meeting in the Park. Burns was a notable figure with his black beard and a red flag. While there had been police in Trafalgar Square, including the Chief Commisioner, Sir Edmund Hamilton, there were none in Pall Mall. Sir Edmund, soon to be dismissed for his incompetence in this affair, sent a message for 100 waiting police reinforcements to hurry to Pall Mall, but through a mistaken message they went to the Mall instead. "Accordingly", as Bernard Shaw wrote, "they were shivering in St James's Park whilst the unemployed were passing through the street of rich men's clubs."

It was at this stage that violence began. This was agreed, but the causes of the violence were not. Quite unprovoked, the respectable press said, the mob began to throw stones (conveniently available due to road-mending operations) at club windows. Shortly afterwards a member of the Carlton Club asserted: 'No member of the Carlton would think of jeering at a crowd of unemployed."

This, however, was not how the socialists saw it. *Justice* had commented in menacing tones only two days earlier on the practice in some clubs of mocking at the unemployed and socialist demonstrators in Pall Mall. It now claimed that the crowd stopped peacefully, outside the Reform and Carlton Clubs while

Burns and others addressed them. Then the provocation began. As Bernard Shaw wrote : "Dives, not noticing the absence of the police, mocked Lazarus. Lazarus thereupon broke Dives's windows." *Justice* continued : "The inmates of the Clubs standing behind the windows grinning and mocking the misery which they themselves had created" were the cause of the stone-throwing. "This foolish exhibition of contempt and mockery roused the ire of the yet peaceful crowd and the GRINNING PROFITMONGERS received a volley of stones which caused them to grin on 'the other side of their faces', and beat a hasty retreat."

Among the clubs subjected to this treatment was the New University, which, as *The Times* grimly pointed out, was "the very club from which Mr Hyndman was expelled some time ago" for making too ardent socialist speeches.

Upon arriving at Hyde Park the socialist orators again addressed the crowd, urging them in conclusion to return home peacefully. This, however, was not to be. Blood was up, much pillaging and destruction took place and, as all sides claimed, a significant criminal element was present; both socialists and the capitalist press denied that looting and overturning carriages were the work of respectable English working men. William Morris's own art shop narrowly escaped plundering—"by about $\frac{1}{2}$ a minute", he wrote later. *Justice* commented that "high hats were regarded as the distinguishing marks of aristocracy and unemployed hatters will probably derive benefits from yesterday's proceedings". By 14 February claims for compensation had reached £11,000.

Respectable London was horrified by these events. *The Times* gave the riot many columns of coverage, and demanded severe punishments for Burns, Hyndman and the other leaders. (If any of the rioters read *The Times*'s account on the 9th they might also have seen two advertisements; one for the sale of a gentleman's bay mare for 180 guineas, the other wanting a cook in a London home for a wage of £18 to £20 a year.) Letters poured in to the paper supporting the strongest measures against potential rioters, among them fire hydrants, mounted police, and signal rockets which, an old army officer claimed, were an "infallible" method of "putting to flight any mob". One correspondent looked back longingly to 1848, when he had been a special constable against the Chartists. Another letter was from a man of 70 who had been mishandled by the mob and who said that his contributions to charities would cease. 'I have always advocated the cause of the people. I shall do so no more." Still another writer explained that his tailor had visited him to apologise for the fact that a suit had not been finished as promised. "The man who was giving it the finishing touch gave up working at 2 o'clock to join the demonstration of the unemployed."

The Times said that the riot was more alarming than the Chartist demonstrations of 1848, and its view was widely shared. For several days shops remained partly or wholly shut while rumours of more and greater riots multiplied. On both the 10th and 11th February panic was reported all over London, and on the latter day "from the heart of the City to the far-off suburbs preparations were made to meet bands of ruffians stated to be on the march".

Parliament too was outraged. Lord Midleton felt that the Government's Irish Home Rule policy was partly to blame. His view was: "Now that London abounded with large halls, where the utmost freedom of speech could be indulged in, there was really no occasion for out-door demonstrations." Lord Fitzgerald said that troops should have been used, advice followed on "Bloody Sunday" the following year. Earl Fortescue claimed that the riots would accelerate the departure of capital from England to foreign countries. Lord Lamington could not believe that Hyndman was really a "gentleman". He thought that "unless the matter was taken in hand the end would be a social and terrible revolution". He was at one with Queen Victoria, who could not "sufficiently express her *indignation* at the monstrous riot" and denounced the "*momentary* triumph of socialism and disgrace to the capital".

Following "Black Monday" a new attitude was apparent towards the poor. Joseph Chamberlain, President of the Local Government Board and a noted radical, denounced the riot, saying in words familiar to our own day that "constitutional methods" should have been used and that violence was only legitimate against a tyrannical government. Nevertheless, he urged immediate increased Poor Law assistance for the unemployed and on the 15th of March issued a circular to local authorities urging them to provide work at wages for the unemployed without having to submit to the indignities of the poor law. *The Times*, though deploring the events of the 8th, added that unemployment formed "a very serious and a very real difficulty and hardship". It urged that at least a few public works should be undertaken and praised the "labour register" then being pioneered by N L Cohen in Egham, Surrey, one of the earliest labour exchanges. This form of assistance, the paper thought, 'might well be copied in every town in the country".

Another form of relief which *The Times* thought might be used with some caution was the Lord Mayor's fund for relief of distress. This fund had been started immediately before 8 February. It now rose with astonishing speed. By the 16th of February it stood at £32,000, and the Lord Mayor commented somewhat bemusedly that he had never heard of so much money being collected so rapidly. By the 24th it had reached over £62,000. Relief works were provided all over the country, including work for 895 unemployed men in Glasgow in a single day. As Belfort Bax wrote in the Socialist League's journal *Commonweal*: "Verily the rattle of plate-glass windows speaks more eloquently to the capitalist heart than any sentimental appeal. A sop must be thrown to Cerberus at all hazards, even though we damn him the while."

Socialism now received a prominence hardly dreamed of before the riot. Hyndman, Burns and two other SDF leaders were tried for sedition and their trial and acquittal in April gave them ample opportunity to publicise their cause. John Burns' memorable speech in his own defence was reprinted by the SDF as *The Man with the Red Flag*, and made an effective socialist document.

"We are not responsible for the riots", he declared. "It is Society that is responsible, and instead of the Attorney-General drawing up indictments against us, he should be drawing up indictments against Society, which is responsible for neglecting the means at its command. . . . Well-fed men never revolt. Poverty-stricken men have all to gain, and nothing to lose, by riot and revolution."

Even Morris, who deprecated "aimless" rioting and wanted "Education towards Revolution", wrote that the riot "does look like the first skirmish of the Revolution". The Social Democratic

Federation was triumphant. Hyndman wrote that the riot was the natural results of unemployment and of extreme contrasts between wealth and poverty. He added: "The State Prosecution of the Social Democrats for trying to rouse the people from their apathy is the beginning of the great English Revolution of the Nineteenth Century."

The predictions of revolution were disapppointed, and neither the League nor the Federation was to be the main instrument of British socialism. But socialism as an organised force had come to stay; not for the last time violence had been the only means of making the English ruling classes listen to the demands of the underprivileged.

Bibliographical Note

The "Black Monday" riot has a prominent place in labour movement history, both in the accounts of participants and in secondary sources. An early account was given in a letter dated 25 March 1886 by William Morris, who was not in fact present. This is reproduced in *The Letters of William Morris* (ed. Philip Henderson, 1950). Bernard Shaw, also not present, wrote his account in *The Fabian Society: its early history* (Fabian Tract 41, 1892). H M Hyndman wrote from the point of view of a participant in his *The Record of An Adventurous Life* (1911) and H W Lee, nearly fifty years after the event, also wrote as a participant in *Social-Democracy in Britain* (H W Lee and E Archbold, 1935). Joseph Burgess, in *John Burns: The Rise and Progress of a Right Honourable* (1911) gave a lengthy account of the riot, including interviews with participants and extracts from their trial. The most interesting modern accounts are by E P Thompson in *William Morris* (1955), Chushichi Tsuzuki in *H M Hyndman and British Socialism* (1961), Bentley Gilbert in *The Evolution of National Insurance in Great Britain* (1966) and Gareth Stedman Jones in *Outcast London* (Oxford, 1971). All of the modern sources and a number of the earlier ones lay stress on the latent fears of revolution amongst the wealthy and the realisation that concessions were needed to avert it.

David Rubinstein
Annie Besant

Annie Besant was the outstanding political and social leader among women of her day. Her career was dazzling, her disappearance from political life sudden and total and the last half of her life was absorbed in fields remote from British political and social controversy. It is a relatively brief period, between 1874 and 1889, which made her such a striking name in social history.

Born Annie Wood in 1847, she had a happy but sheltered upbringing, and "innocent on all questions of sex" she married the Rev. Frank Besant at the age of 20. The marriage quickly proved a failure and in 1873, after two children had been born, a legal separation was arranged. The Rev Frank was, as regarded his wife, a typical mid-Victorian; and "a woman of strong dominant will" with "strength that panted for expression", as Annie later described herself, was no wife for him.

Her early religious faith was already leaving her, and after hearing the famous atheist Charles Bradlaugh speak in 1874 she joined his National Secular Society. She became a travelling secularist lecturer, almost the first woman to engage in this kind of activity. The hazards of this lecturing are illustrated by an incident typical of many others. At a meeting Mrs Besant was sitting on the platform, she wrote in her autobiography, when she "received a rather heavy blow on the back of the head from a stone thrown by some one in the room. We had a mile and a half to walk from the hall to the house, and were accompanied all the way by a stone-throwing crowd, who sang hymns at the tops of their voices, with interludes of curses and foul words."

Malcolm Quin, a contemporary observer, wrote of the young Annie Besant of the 1870's in his autobiography fifty years later. This was perhaps the best account of Mrs Besant in her youth, at the height of her beauty and effectiveness. (As photographs show, however, she long remained a dynamic and attractive figure.) Quin, despite the many women speakers he had heard in the intervening years, found Annie Besant "incomparable". Her appearance and her voice had an immediate effect on her audience. "She was facing a hostile world on behalf of liberty and truth; and we young men, who had the passion of these things in our souls, responded readily to the passion with which she pleaded for them. We were carried away." (*Memoirs of a Positivist*, 1924) (also discussed above by David Tribe.)

In 1877 she was involved with Bradlaugh in a celebrated case involving the publication of birth-control literature. She and Bradlaugh reprinted a forty-five-year-old American pamphlet by Charles Knowlton which described various methods of contraception. The reprint, published in March 1877, was specifically aimed at the working class, and the publishers' preface stated: 'We think it more moral to prevent the conception of children, than, after they are born, to murder them by want of food, air, and clothing. We advocate scientific checks to population, because, so long as poor men have large families, pauperism is a necessity, and from pauperism grow crime and disease.'

The trial came at a fortunate time for the birth-control movement. The absurdity of bringing to trial the publishers of a pamphlet which had freely circulated for forty-five years was obvious. *The Fruits of Philosophy*, as it was quaintly called, had sold some 700 copies annually, but the tremendous publicity which the decision to prosecute aroused led to 125,000 copies being sold in the ensuing three months. In addition, many of the upper classes and the better off working classes were already beginning to limit their families. (The birth rate in fact reached its height in 1876 and dropped by over a third by 1914.) The subject was becoming topical.

The Solicitor-General, Sir Hardinge Gifford, acting as prosecutor for unnamed patrons, dwelled on the fact that the pamphlet sold at only sixpence so that almost anyone could purchase it. Moreover, he asserted, the pamphlet tended towards the grossest immorality. Its object was "to enable persons to have sexual intercourse, and not to have that which in the order of Providence is the natural result of that sexual intercourse . . . Is not that calculated to deprave and destroy the morals of the persons among whom it may be circulated? . . . Here are the means by which the unmarried female may gratify her passions."

In their defence Mrs Besant and Bradlaugh pointed out that many other works, most of them much more expensive, were readily available to the public. As already shown by David Tribe, much of their case rested on the burdened lives of the poor. Mrs Besant spoke in her opening statement of "the fathers, who see their wage ever reducing, and prices ever rising . . . the mothers worn out with over-frequent child-bearing . . . the little ones half starved because there is food enough for two but not enough for twelve".

The jury found the defendants guilty but exonerated them from corrupt motives in publishing. Later they were freed on a technicality. The case gave an immense stimulus to the birth-control movement, as did Mrs Besant's own *The Law of Population*, published later in 1877. It sold some 175,000 sixpenny copies by 1891, when, after her conversion to theosophy, she withdrew it from sale. It was dedicated "to the poor in great cities and agricultural districts, dwellers in stifling court or crowded hovel, in the hope that it may point out a path from poverty, and may make easier the life of British mothers".

Mrs Besant's courage had won her much publicity not only for her views but, like Bradlaugh, for daring to represent herself in court without counsel. The case also won her an important place in the history of family limitation, but the short-term cost was severe. In 1878 her husband sued in the Court of Chancery for the custody of his eight-year-old daughter Mabel, whose guardian Annie Besant had been since the separation in 1873. On the grounds of her atheism and her support of contraception her child was taken away from her, the judge (the Master of the Rolls, Sir George Jessel) openly expressing full support of the Rev. Frank Besant.

It was in 1885 that Mrs Besant was converted to socialism, becoming the first prominent public figure to join the Fabian Society. Gradually she moved further to the left, joining the

Marxist Social Democratic Federation in 1888 without breaking with the Fabians. In these years she was involved in most of the important socialist activities in London, including the celebrated "Bloody Sunday" riot in Trafalgar Square in November 1887. When the lectures were given in 1888 later made famous as *Fabian Essays in Socialism* Annie Besant was the only well-known person among the seven lecturers. (The authors were all to become famous in varying degree; two of them were Sidney Webb and Bernard Shaw.)

It was in the summer of 1888 that her advocacy of the cause of the underpaid match girls employed by Bryant and May in Bromley by Bow, East London, won Annie Besant her greatest fame and influence. In February 1888 she began a short-lived weekly journal, the *Link*, devoted to working for radical and socialist causes. (She edited also a more literary journal entitled *Our Corner*, which appeared monthly from 1883 until 1888.) Following a meeting of the Fabian Society on women's work and investigations of her own Mrs Besant published an article in the *Link* on 23rd June 1888 under the title "White Slavery in London". It was this article which led to the strike of the match girls, one of the crucial events in the revolt of the unskilled and underpaid workers known as the New Unionism.

The previous year, she pointed out, Bryant and May had paid a dividend of 23 per cent. How was the money made to pay such dividends? The summer working day of the girls and women was $11\frac{1}{2}$ hours, with an hour and a half off for meals. Many fines were imposed, for such misdemeanours as talking, having dirty feet or leaving the floor untidy under workbenches. The wages of girls, large numbers of whom were employed, were often only 4s 6d, to 5s od, a week and only four women earned as much as thirteen shillings. Wages had been stopped to raise money for a statue of Gladstone. "But who cares", the article asked, "for the fate of these white wage slaves? Born in slums, driven to work while still children, under-sized because underfed, oppressed because helpless, flung aside as soon as worked out, who cares if they die or go on the streets, provided only that the Bryant and May shareholders get their 23 per cent, and Mr Theodore Bryant can erect statues and buy parks?"

After the original article appeared and throughout the strike the directors of Bryant and May steadfastly denied most of the allegations made by Mrs Besant and the strikers. They asserted that the average wage of adult women was 11s 2d, that fines were rare and almost all of the workpeople fully satisfied. At this distance in time it is impossible to know the exact degree of truth of each of the charges. However, there is no doubt that at a time when Charles Booth was discovering that 35 per cent of the population of East London was living in poverty, most of the girls employed by Bryant and May were among "the poor." (Booth's investigator, Clara Collet, later one of the first women factory inspectors, lent credence to a number of Mrs Besant's allegations, but showed that the conditions of matchworkers were no worse than those of many other women workers in East London. Their social status, however, was exceptionally low.) Moreover, investigations carried out by four East London social workers went far to support Mrs Besant's charges. One of them, H Llewellyn Smith, was an assistant of Booth's and in later years a leading civil servant and social scientist.

In a series of letters to *The Times* the four presented the case for both sides and concluded that Bryant and May's wages were scandalously low and their dividends scandalously high. "It will indeed be difficult", they pointed out, "to prove that contentment reigns in a factory in which—to take the version of the directors themselves—the appearance of an article in an obscure print has proved sufficient to break up the connexion of so many years." Strikes by unskilled workers, after all, were rare. Strikes by women were almost unheard of.

The company threatened to sue Mrs Besant but did not. After the dismissal of a girl for insubordination (allegedly for refusing to sign a paper saying that the girls were well treated and contented) the strike broke out on July 5th. At its height some 1,400 girls and women took part. Annie Besant, presented with the strike, quickly assumed its leadership and was assisted by a number of other socialists, especially Herbert Burrows.

Apart from the socialist and radical weeklies, few newspapers gave support to the match girls. The conservative *Morning Post* ignored the strike altogether. The *Church Times*, the *Illustrated London News* and *The Times* blamed the state of the market for low wages and said that employers were unable to alter prevailing conditions. Indeed, the *Church Times* suggested that without Bryant and May the matchworkers might well have been unemployed. In a splenetic leader on 14 July *The Times* blamed the strike on agitators and asserted: "No effort has been spared by those pests of the modern industrial world, the Social Democrats, to bring the quarrel to a head."

A number of other papers gave spasmodic support to the strikers, of which the most surprising was the *Financial World*. Although a paper of finance and investment it described the Bryant and May dividend as "Blood Money" and blamed the shareholders, whom it accused of caring for nothing but the size of their dividends. "The idea of that money being produced under conditions little short of slavery never enters their mind. Yet such is the case." Finally, warm and consistent support came from the two London radical dailies, the *Star* and the *Pall Mall Gazette*.

Mrs Besant carried on a strenuous campaign, virtually turning the *Link*'s four pages into a strike sheet. She discovered that among the shareholders of Bryant and May were to be found three MPs and 55 clergymen. Bitterly remembering that her own clerical husband had taken her daughter from her Mrs Besant reminded the "country clergyman with shares in Bryant and May's" that his own daughter's "silky, clustering curls" contrasted horribly with the partial baldness of the 15-year-old match girls who carried boxes on their heads.

She opened a subscription fund which received widespread support, mainly from the London labour and socialist movement. Among the subscribers were Sidney Webb, William Morris and his daughters Jenny and May, Edward Carpenter, Margaret Harkness, the socialist novelist, and a number of radical and Liberal MPs. Quintin Hogg, founder of the Regent Street Polytechnic and grandfather of the Conservative politician and Lord Chancellor, was also among the subscribers. Over £400 was collected and two distributions were made to over 650 of the strikers, of between four and six shillings each. Through the pages of the *Star* we have a glimpse of a harassed Bernard Shaw, paymaster: 'Mr G B Shaw counted the four-and-sixpences, and was observed to be labouring under a sense of little freedom and great responsibility."

After nearly a fortnight the mediation of the London Trades

Council brought the strike to a close with the match girls victorious. Fines and deductions were to be abolished, a trade union was to be formed by the workers, and a separate room was to be provided for girls to eat their lunch. (The girls had been accustomed to eating their food in their working rooms so that they were imbibing phosphorus from the matches with their food: "They eat disease as seasoning to their bread" was Mrs Besant's comment.*) Finally, there was to be no victimisation. Blustering letters to the press from Bryant and May directors did not disguise the extent of the victory which had been won.

The *Pall Mall Gazette*, acclaiming "A Great and Noble Victory" commented: "Of all women in London to-day, Mrs BESANT has most reason to feel proud." The *Star* said that public opinion had for the first time asserted itself in a strike of this kind. Now that it had been won it was necessary to turn from the older fight for "the political emancipation of the toilers" to "achieving their social salvation".

The aftermath of the strike was mixed. On the one hand at a meeting of Bryant and May shareholders at the end of July 1888, a spokesman claimed: "Everything was going on exactly as it was before the strike took place." The *Financial World* reported: "The shareholders accepted their fifteen per cent dividend gratefully, and no doubt are doing their best to forget all about the disagreeable incidents of the past month." Bryant and May shares, in fact, had risen in value during the strike itself. Women's conditions continued to be abysmal in many factories and shops. Fines and deductions, whose legality was dubious in 1888, continued and were firmly legalised by an Act of 1896. Very few women were members of trade unions even after 1900.

On the other hand a union of matchmakers was established on 27th July and the following day 468 members were enrolled. On 8th September the *Link* reported over 600 members, with Annie Besant as secretary. By 1889 the number had risen to nearly 800. In 1893 an investigator reported that the Matchmakers' Union was still the strongest women's trade union in London, though its numbers had decreased markedly. The impact of the strike and the union may explain the fact that wages of women and girl

---

* Necrosis, the dreaded "phossy jaw", had, however, declined in the match industry through greater cleanliness and a reduction in the use of phosphorus.

matchworkers were significantly higher in September 1888 than in September 1887.

As for Annie Besant, she undertook her last great campaign in November 1888, standing in the Tower Hamlets as a socialist candidate for the London School Board with radical and Liberal support. "Plump for Annie Besant, the people's friend", her posters declared. Her programme emphasised the need for free schools, free meals for the children and payment of the trade union rate of wages in Board contracts. In one of her final election speeches she declared : "All over the world your verdict will go, for there is not one civilised country where my name as a Socialist is not known, and there is not one country, whether at home, in the Colonies or abroad, where your vote will not echo either as an encouragement or as a discouragement to the democratic party."

She was returned triumphantly, at the top of the poll. Though she remained a School Board member for only three years, her influence was remarkable in view of the Board's conservative and clerical majority. Free schools, free meals and trade union wages were adopted or supported in varying measure and under her stimulus the Board made a prophetic declaration in 1889 : "The Board are of opinion that there is considerable advantage in having children of all classes attending the same schools."

It was in 1889 that Annie Besant met Madame Helena Blavatsky and became absorbed in the doctrine of theosophy. She quickly dropped both secularism and socialism, did not stand for re-election to the London School Board and until the end of her long life in 1933 devoted herself to theosophy. Though she was a leader of the movement for home rule for India before 1919, her British political influence was at an end.

She remained popular with her old comrades for many years, even when renouncing her former beliefs. Only 42 when she turned to theosophy, she achieved in fifteen years as much as many leaders of the labour movement in a lifetime. The cause of working women has had its heroines; the labour movement has had its leaders and its martyrs. Few of them possessed such magnetism and few had greater influence than Annie Besant.

Bibliographical Note

Annie Besant's life has been extensively chronicled, from a variety of points of view. She herself wrote two accounts of her life, *Autobiographical Sketches* (1885) and *An Autobiography* (1893). Many other biographies have been written of her, of which it is pertinent to mention here Gertrude Williams *The Passionate Pilgrim, A Life of Annie Besant* (n.d., 1932), not because of its intrinsic worth but because of its list of her publications to 1927 and books about her and her interests. The fullest biography of Annie Besant is *The First Five Lives of Annie Besant* (1961) and *The Last Four Lives of Annie Besant* (1963), by Arthur Nethercot. Nethercot's biography, however, is not entirely satisfactory and there is no really definitive life of Annie Besant. Her secularist activities are described by Hypatia Bradlaugh Bonner and J M Robertson in *Charles Bradlaugh* (2 vols, 1895), by Warren Sylvester Smith in *The London Heretics, 1870–1914* (1967) and by David Tribe in *President Charles Bradlaugh MP* (1971). Ann Stafford has given a vivid account of the matchgirls' strike in *A Match to Fire the Thames* (1961) and I have described her election to the London School Board and her meteoric career there in "Annie Besant and Stewart Headlam: The London School Board Election of 1888", *East London Papers*, vol. 13, no. 1, Summer 1970, and *School Attendance in London, 1870–1904, A Social History* (Hull, 1969). Almost all books dealing with the radical and socialist movements of the 1870's and 1880's write at some length about Annie Besant.

John Lovell
The New Unionism & the Dock Strike of 1889

JOHN LOVELL *was born in Bath and read history at* Hull University *from 1958 until 1961. He then went to the* London School of Economics *where he obtained his PhD. He is the author of* A SHORT HISTORY OF THE TUC *(with B C Roberts, 1968) and of* STEVEDORES AND DOCKERS: A STUDY OF TRADE UNIONISM IN THE PORT OF LONDON, 1870–1914 *(1969). He is currently a lecturer in economic and social history at the University of Kent at Canterbury.*

The London dock strike of 1889 is certainly one of the most famous industrial disputes in British labour history. The reason for its fame lies not in its size (the miners' lock out of 1893 lasted four times as long and cost thirty times as many working days) but in the extraordinary degree of interest which it aroused at the time. This interest sprang largely out of a general concern with the problem of poverty, a concern which had become increasingly marked in British society of the 1880's. Whenever poverty was discussed the condition of the dockers nearly always received attention. Of all occupational groups their plight seemed to be the most desperate. The dock labour market operated on a purely casual basis, dockers in consequence were chronically under-employed and many lived in acute poverty. Furthermore the status of the occupation was at rock bottom, for it was believed that the waterside labour force was recruited from the failures and unfortunates of industry generally. One London docker, formerly a skilled craftsman, lamented in 1889: 'Only a dock rat, that's what I've been called ever since I lost my place, and became a docker.'

The 1889 strike was, therefore, no ordinary industrial dispute. It was a revolt of the most downtrodden and despised members of society, men who normally fought against each other every morning in the scramble for work at the calling-on stands, men universally regarded as being utterly demoralised. Yet these men came out in their thousands in August 1889, brought the world's largest port to a standstill, and remained out until they had won. It was an event which gave a tremendous stimulus to trade union organisation amongst less skilled workers throughout the country. After over a decade of stagnation, the British trade union movement doubled its membership between 1889 and 1892. The movement became known as the New Unionism.

In reality this upsurge of activity amongst the unskilled and semi-skilled sections of the population was not as 'new' as it seemed. Even on the London waterfront trade unionism and industrial action were by no means new phenomena. In the early 1870's there had been widespread strike activity, and at this time there even existed a trade union of dock and wharf workers. For a variety of reasons, however, the movement of the early 1870's did not attract the same attention as that of 1889. So far as the London dockers were concerned, this was perhaps largely because gains were achieved in the earlier period in piecemeal fashion, by picking off employers one by one. There was no spectacular port wide confrontation such as occurred in 1889, and there was also no revived socialist movement to provide the dockers with an able and flamboyant leadership. Thus, even if in reality the events of 1889 were not entirely new, they seemed to be so.

The 1889 dock strike had its origins in a dispute over the method of piece work payment at the South West India dock. The men's spokesman was Ben Tillett, an ex-sailor who worked in a tea warehouse. Tillett ran the tiny Tea Operatives and General Labourers' Association which had a few members at the dock. In view of the weakness of his union, he was not inclined to call a strike, but his hand was forced by another group of waterside workers who were anxious to emulate the spectacular success won by the gas stokers in their claim for an eight-hour day. The gasworkers' leader, socialist Will Thorne, even came down to the dock gates himself to exhort the men to take strike action. Following his lead the dockers at this centre came out, and by August 14th work there was at a standstill. The dock company, however, refused to negotiate, and introduced blacklegs into the dock to take over the work. This might well have been the end of the matter had it not been for the action of the stevedores—the relatively skilled group of workers who loaded vessels. These men normally worked alongside the dockers, and when blacklegs were introduced they began to come out in sympathy. Almost alone of London port workers the stevedors had maintained their trade union organisation intact from the early 1870's, and on Saturday, 17th August, their union called an official strike in support of the dockers: "we feel", the union proclaimed, "our duty is to support our poorer brothers".

The decision of the Stevedores Union was critical. Not only did it keep the strike in the India docks alive, it also made it almost certain that the stoppage would spread to other parts of the port, for the stevedores brought prestige and organising ability to the movement. Other factors favourable to the dockers were the strong upswing in trade, which greatly enhanced their bargaining power, and the stimulus provided by the earlier victory of the gasworkers. On the Monday following the stevedores' entry into the dispute the strike was indeed greatly extended, and by Thursday, 22nd August, it had become port-wide in scope. By this time it was an enormously complex affair, embracing dockers, stevedores, lightermen, wharf and warehouse workers, comporters and many other waterfront groups. The direction of a stoppage on this scale raised enormous problems, for only a mere fraction of the workers involved were in unions. Direction was undertaken by a central strike committee which met at the Wades Arms in Poplar—the headquarters of the Stevedores Union. The stevedores of course played a vital role on the committee, but important also were leaders thrown up by the dockers themselves, and various others brought in from outside. Of the dockers' own leaders Ben Tillett was far and away the most important. He was to become the great orator of the waterfront, and having overcome his hesitancy at the outset of the dispute he quickly assumed a key position in the leadership. It was Tillett who formulated a general programme of demands on the dockers' behalf. His programme comprised not simply a minimum rate of sixpence per hour ("the full round orb of the docker's tanner"), but the abolition of the existing systems of subcontracting and piecework, and the introduction of various measures aimed at reducing the purely casual nature of dock employment. Tillett had also, from the very beginning, brought in outsiders whom he felt could help the cause. Chief amongst these latter were two socialist engineering workers who had been active in the Social Democratic Federation—Tom Mann and John Burns. Numerous other socialists, such as H H Champion and Eleanor Marx-Aveling, gave valuable assistance to the dockers as they had done earlier to the gasworkers.

The united front of strikers faced an uneasy alliance of port employers—dock companies, shipowners, wharfingers, stevedoring and lighterage firms. Relations between the various employers were not good, but for the moment the alliance held and employers generally followed the intransigent lead given by the dock companies. The latter were led by the redoubtable Mr Norwood, of whom the *Star* newspaper remarked: "He is in appearance and manner the very embodiment of the insolence of capitalism. He is stout, well-fed, and arrogant." To win, the strike committee had to maintain the stoppage intact until the frail alliance of employers split up. But to do this required two things. Firstly, the strikers had to be fed and their morale maintained. Secondly, an elaborate system of picketing had to be organised to prevent the employers breaking the strike with imported labour.

So far as the first was concerned, the principal tactic employed was the public demonstration. Great processions of strikers were organised and led by John Burns, and they marched into the heart of the City of London. These enormous and well disciplined processions maintained morale, and, much more important, attracted the favourable attention of the general public. Public sympathy was crucial to the dockers' cause, since the strikers had no funds of their own and were therefore forced to rely on outside contributions. Because of the general sympathy with the dockers' plight funds were indeed forthcoming; the general public subscribing almost £14,000. The response from the established British trade unions was, however, disappointing—less than £4,500. For a while the flow of funds enabled the strikers to be fed fairly adequately, but as the dispute dragged on the position became serious. The crisis was reached at the end of August. The strike committee decided it would try to force the issue by extending the stoppage beyond the waterfront, and it drew up a manifesto calling on the various trades in London to strike in support of the port workers; a desperate remedy for a desperate situation. The manifesto was issued on August 30th, but it was withdrawn almost immediately. It had been rendered unnecessary by a quite extraordinary turn of events. News of the strike had spread to Australia, where there existed strong unions on the waterfront and elsewhere. At the very end of August funds began to arrive from this quarter, and in all the Australians sent £30,000. Thus the first problem was solved : the spectre of defeat through hunger had been banished.

The changed situation enabled the strike committee to switch its tactics. The processions into the City were abandoned, and efforts were now concentrated on the picket lines, where the organising ability of Tom Mann was of crucial importance. Several thousand blacklegs were working in the docks, but some of these were persuaded to leave, and by mobilising as many as 3,000 pickets the strike leaders were able to reduce the movement of shipping to a minimum. This in turn brought increasing strain to the employers' alliance, as the shipowners began to press the dock companies to reach a settlement. Victory was in sight, but in so far as it was made possible by effective picketing, it is clear that the attitude of the police had been vital. The Home Secretary and Commissioner of Police kept the police on the sidelines, leaving the pickets free to tighten their hold on the port. Such restraint by those in authority was exceptional, and it was not to be repeated in the years that followed. On September 4th a settlement favourable to the men was reached with the wharfingers— the employers' alliance was breaking up. On the following day the Lord Mayor intervened and set up the Mansion House Committee, composed of prominent Londoners. The Committee's job was conciliation, and after a protracted series of negotiations it was finally able to achieve a settlement that covered all the various parties to the dispute. The agreement signed on September 14th embodied the main points of Tillett's programme, but the dockers were forced to make some concessions. Cardinal Manning, a member of the Committee, made the major contribution in bringing the two sides together, and his influence over the dockers, many of whom were Catholics, was of particular significance.

To many at the time, the most important outcome of the strike seemed to be the establishment of a dockers' trade union. Tillett's tiny Tea Operatives Association had grown from a few hundred members at the commencement of the stoppage to 18,000 at its close. In mid September it was reorganised as the Dock, Wharf, Riverside and General Labourers' Union, and it soon began to expand rapidly into the provinces. People felt that in this trade union, rather than in the immediate improvements won in the strike, lay the hope for the future; it would restore to the workers their dignity and self-respect, it would end the purely casual system of employment, it would achieve a decent standard of living for its members. But it was not to be. To describe the dockers' victory in the 1889 strike as a fluke would be to exaggerate, but it was nonetheless made possible only by a very fortunate conjunction of circumstances. The trade boom, the Australian windfall, the attitude of the police, the sympathetic public, the divided employers, these were the things that enabled the strike to be won and the Dockers' Union to emerge in strength. For a while after the strike the union was recognised by the employers and all seemed well, but when the latter counter-attacked the union immediately began to crumble. The exceptional advantages enjoyed during the strike were no longer there, and in one sector of the port after another the union lost influence and membership melted away. Finally in 1900, after an unsuccessful stoppage in the union's one remaining metropolitan stronghold, the Dockers' Union to all intents and purposes vanished from the London waterfront for a decade. In the provinces too there were reverses, most dramatically at Hull in 1893, but many provincial districts did manage to cling on until more fortunate times, so that all was not lost.

The 1889 strike was a memorable victory, and its impact on trade union organisation was very great, not only on the waterfront but throughout society. But great too was the employer reaction against this advance of labour. So great in fact that the battles of 1889 had to be fought over again in 1911–12, and even then union organisation was still not securely established in the ports and in many other sectors. It was indeed a protracted struggle.

H LLEWELLYN SMITH & V NASH   *The Story of the Dockers'*
      Strike (1889) (n.d., 1889)
SIDNEY & BEATRICE WEBB   *The History of Trade Unionism*
      (1894)
BEN TILLETT   *Memories and Reflections* (1931)
FRANCIS WILLIAMS   *Magnificent Journey* (1954)
ANN STAFFORD   *A Match to Fire the Thames* (1961)
HENRY PELLING   *A History of British Trade Unionism* (1936)
H A CLEGG, A FOX & A F THOMPSON   *A History of British Trade
      Unions since 1889*, vol. I (Oxford 1964)
E J HOBSBAWM   *Labouring Men* (1964)
PAUL THOMPSON   *Socialists, Liberals and Labour* (1967)
JOHN LOVELL   *Stevedores and Dockers* (1969)
DAVID F WILSON   *Dockers* (1972)

Fred Reid

Keir Hardie & the Origins of the Labour Party

FRED REID *is lecturer in history at the University of Warwick. He was educated at the Royal Blind School, Edinburgh, and subsequently at Edinburgh University and the Queen's College, Oxford. His study of Keir Hardie's early life, "Keir Hardie's Conversion to Socialism", was published in* ESSAYS IN LABOUR HISTORY *1886-1923 (eds Asa Briggs and John Saville, 1971). He is currently at work on a biography of Keir Hardie. His interests include mountaineering and politics. He is President of the National Federation of the Blind of the United Kingdom and a leading activist in the Disablement Income Group.*

James Keir Hardie's name will always be linked inseparably with the origins of the Labour Party. To many men and women of the Labour and socialist movement, he is still the legendary "first Labour MP", eclipsing the reputations of Alexander Macdonald and Thomas Burt, the two miners' leaders returned to Parliament in 1874, nearly 20 years before Hardie. His "cloth cap"— it was really a deerstalker—which he wore on his first appearance in the House of Commons in 1892, has become the mythical symbol of the class-consciousness of British Labour, cherished by friends, ridiculed by critics.

Keir Hardie the legend is well known. Keir Hardie the man has long remained a mystery. Works of hagiography have dwelt lovingly on the heroic moments of his long crusade to establish Labour as an independent political force such as his first parliamentary contest in the by-election at Mid-Lanark in 1888, and the "scenes" he made as "Member for the unemployed" in Parliament from 1892 to 1895, and the guttering flames of his stop-the-war agitation of 1914.

Hardie the agitator is well-documented. What has hardly yet received sufficient attention from historians and biographers is Hardie the politician, who was always ready to concede and to compromise and whose willingness to do so was conditioned by a deep-rooted belief that the British working class could win reforms and achieve Socialism only by co-operating closely with people of goodwill in all classes. His career could be summed up as expressing defiance in the teeth of class oppression but deference to the managerial classes, whom he saw as making a useful contribution to society, when they acknowledged the grievances of the working man.

Born in Lanarkshire, Scotland, in 1856, Hardie was the illegitimate son of a farm-servant, Mary Keir. In 1859 she married David Hardie, a ship's carpenter, who took her and the boy to live in Glasgow, beside the shipyards where he worked.

Mary Hardie struggled hard to give her family the life of decent respectability to which the skilled men in the British working class aspired in the 1860's, but, when Hardie was about ten years old, adversity struck the family a series of reeling blows. His stepfather suffered frequent unemployment, due to bad trade in the shipbuilding industry, and his mother had a series of pregnancies which must have kept her from contributing to the family income. Household possessions had to be sold or pawned and Mary Hardie, forced to give up her ambition of having James apprenticed to a good trade, sent him out, instead, to drift from one casual job to the next in order to eke out the family earnings.

It was while working thus as a baker's errand boy that Hardie was peremptorily dismissed and fined a week's wages for being late on three successive mornings, when his brother was at death's door with fever and his mother was nearing the end of another wearying pregnancy. The boy, however, was given no opportunity to explain these mitigating circumstances. Shortly after this episode David Hardie went to sea in search of the steady work that had eluded him ashore and Mary took the children to live in the mining village of Quarter, near Hamilton, where James started working in the coal mines as a trapper.

The miners of the west of Scotland were, at this time, thought by almost everyone to be beyond the pale of respectable working-class life, dirty, drunken and morally degraded. Mary Keir, who had wanted so much a decent chance for her son that she had herself taught him to read when she could no longer pay to keep him at school, must have seen the life of the mining villages as a setback to her striving.

But something of her spirit had entered into James. As he grew to manhood and became a skilled face-worker in the pits, he began to join some of the self-improvement societies in Hamilton. He had taught himself to write by scratching with a pin on a stone blackened with the smoke of his pit-lamp and, in 1878, he joined the Evangelical Union, a Scottish Christian sect which had, on the one hand, affinities with the fashionable Scottish Congregational Church and, on the other hand, a considerable working-class following, especially in the mining districts.

The influence of the Union on Hardie was formative because it stressed that the Christian gospel was for the poor as well as for the rich and because it rejected theological disputes, especially about election and pre-destination, and boldly asserted what it took to be the simple truth : that Christ's atonement was for all who would believe in him.

The Union encouraged teetotalism and Hardie "took the pledge", joining the Independent Order of Good Templars, a sort of Masonic organisation which campaigned for state-prohibition of the drink trade. Both these organisations campaigned vigorously among the working class and made much of working men who joined their ranks and set a good example to their brethren. They satisfied, therefore, Hardie's deep-seated longing to be valued.

So eager was he to conform to respectable standards at this time that he bought a frock coat and top hat in which to go about his religious activities. He accepted the view of the Evangelical Union that men of Christian goodwill in all classes were united in a war against selfishness and sin. Hardie had too many bitter memories from his childhood, however, to think that working men would get goodwill from employers merely for the asking. As a miner himself, he could see how the big ironmasters and coalmasters cheated the men of the fruits of their labour by short-weighing, fines and even by the truck system, long thought to have been suppressed by Act of Parliament. When he himself tried to organise the miners around Hamilton into a union, he was dismissed and blacklisted throughout the district. He stuck to his guns, however, and continued to organise the men in the two counties of Lanarkshire and Ayrshire.

In thus defying the employers, however, he was not declaring war upon employers as a class. He believed that the real interests of employers and workmen were the same. They were partners in a productive enterprise who, given goodwill, could "meet together under one roof-tree to smoke the pipe of peace" and so dispel "all the feelings of discord that ever existed between those twin brothers, whose best interests are inseparable". In practice, he believed that the best method of securing this harmony in industrial relations was to establish the sliding scale, by which miners' wages moved upwards or downwards with the selling-price of coal. He praised the small minority of coalmasters who had shown themselves ready to adopt the sliding scale and he attacked his fellow-miners for not being willing to accept the discipline of the market. He remarked that those who cheered loudest when wages went up were the first to denounce their union leaders when they went down with prices.

Hardie believed that the men were too selfish, too addicted to strong drink, to be ready to work within a framework of agreed bargaining. He led them when they went on strike only because he also believed that most of the coalmasters were too selfish to allow the men to organise and that they really wanted the men to submit to industrial slavery.

In reality, however, it seems that the miners knew better than Hardie that the sliding scale would do nothing to keep their wages up to a decent level when the market was falling and that the policy which he advocated for this purpose, restriction of each man's output, was unworkable. Not surprisingly, while Hardie advocated these policies, he found it difficult to keep the men from deserting the unions he organised.

The intransigence of the coalmasters and the indifference of the bulk of the miners forced Hardie to rethink his policy. If the men would not or could not restrict their output by their own volition, then the state must make it easier for them to do so.

In this frame of mind, he took up in 1883, an older miners'

demand, which had been submerged in the pro-*laissez faire* mood of the trade union leadership in the 1870's, the demand for a legally fixed eight-hour working day underground. By the time the next wave of unionisation gathered force among the miners, in 1886, he was ready to write this demand into their policy.

For a time, he believed that the Liberal Party could be brought to carry an Eight Hours Bill if only the Radicals and the miners' leaders co-operated to force it upon the Right-wing "Whig" section, and he threw himself into the work of organising the newly enfranchised miners to vote Liberal in the general elections of 1885 and 1886.

Two events in 1887, however, disenchanted him with this policy. One was the strike of Lanarkshire miners, which was broken by troops and police escorting blacklegs to work through the pickets, and which the Scottish Liberal press condemned as having been fomented by socialist agitators. The second was the failure of the Liberal Opposition in Parliament to support the Scottish miners' "eight hours" amendment to the Mines Regulation Bill.

By the end of the year, it seemed to Hardie that the time had come to put Liberal professions of goodwill towards working men to the test. He kicked up a row about the actions of the "Labour" MPs at the Trades Union Congress in 1887 and published his own Labour programme which, though saying nothing about socialism, supported some of the socialists' demands, as well as the miners' eight-hour day.

In 1888, he had himself nominated as the miners' and Home Rule candidate in the by-election at Mid-Lanark. The Liberal Party managers tried to buy him off with fair promises of safe seats and the like, but he had the support of the local miners' leaders and of a well-heeled socialist journalist, H H Champion. He polled only 617 votes, but went on audaciously to form a Scottish Labour Party.

This was Hardie in his defiant mood. The Liberals, he believed, had shown themselves unresponsive to the claims of Labour and now they must be forced to make way for a Labour Party in Parliament which would subordinate the Labour programme to no other political consideration. This view brought him very close to socialists like Friedrich Engels and Eleanor Marx, with whom he kept in close touch at this time and who brought him to the foundation conference of the Second International in Paris in 1889.

Once again, however, we have to note that, while Engels and his followers were aiming at the dictatorship of the proletariat, Hardie had no thought of uncompromising class-war against the Liberal Party. Hardie saw his party as a union of the respectable men in the working class with men of goodwill in the middle class to enforce just laws upon selfish men in all classes. Socialism was to come about, not from any intensification of the class-struggle, but as a result of the growth of this mutual deference and the weakening of the power of selfishness.

Writing explicitly on this point at a later date (1904), he commented : "Socialism makes war upon a system, not upon a class . . . I can imagine one reform after another being won until, in the end, socialism itself causes no more excitement than the extinction of landlordism in Ireland a year ago."

Hardie does not seem to have grasped, or may have chosen to ignore, the point made by some of his socialist critics at the time, that reforms, beneficial in themselves to the working class, may be supported by middle-class people as part of an ideological strategy to defend the capitalist system and the individualist system of ethics which rests upon it.

This tendency to give place to educated middle-class opinion and to accept an interest in social reform as tantamount to a desire for socialism owed much to the formative influences of Hardie's early Scottish background. It led him to reject the intransigent "class-war" language of H M Hyndman and the Social Democratic Federation and to associate himself with the movement that led to the formation of the Independent Labour Party in 1893.

Although the ILP had a socialist objective written into its constitution, its propaganda tended to be wrapped up in a sentimental longing for a utopian commonwealth of love. It was extremely weak on issues of socialist theory and, even from the beginning, its rules permitted local alliances between its own people and Liberal candidates for Parliament. Hardie's combination of defiance and deference, then receiving maximum publicity from his campaign in Parliament on behalf of the unemployed, suited it

very well and he quickly became its chairman and leading propagandist. His contempt for doctrinal disputation, also acquired
from his early Scottish training, led him to insist that arguments
about the desirability or otherwise of socialism were irrelevant.
He always thought more in terms of specific, practical steps
and worked to bring into one alliance all those who would support them. Foremost among these steps was that the trade unions
should back the creation of a Labour Party separate in organisation from the Liberal Party.

By 1900, thanks to a worsening climate of industrial relations
in Britain, he had succeeded in persuading some of the unions
to join with the socialist societies in the formation of the Labour
Representation Committee which, in 1906, became the Labour
Party. In order to bring this about, the Socialists, including Hardie, had to acquiesce in a party which was committed neither
to achieving socialism nor even to a programme of specific reforms, but Hardie congratulated himself that he had secured one
of the aims of his career since 1887, the creation of a separate
political organisation for the Labour movement.

He hoped that the threat implied in this step would persuade
the Liberals to show more goodwill towards the working class
by proceeding as rapidly as possible to enact such reforms as old
age pensions and unemployment provision, which were among
the first fruits of the "New Liberalism" at the turn of the century.

In practice, however, the Labour Party's performance before
the outbreak of the first world war was disappointing. Its first
secretary and later chairman, James Ramsay MacDonald, led it
in close alliance with the Liberals, with whom he had made a
secret electoral truce in 1903. Especially after the Osborne Judgment (1909), which prevented the trade unions from contributing
to the party's finances, he had no means of putting electoral
pressure on the Liberal Party.

At a time when the working-class standard of living was falling,
Labour seemed once again to have become the tail of the Liberal
Party—a situation which led to a great deal of working-class un-
rest and to campaigns against the leadership within the ILP.

Hardie, who began to age rapidly around 1907, found himself
a prisoner of the Labour alliance which he had helped to create.
He seems to have been searching in the years that followed for an

issue that would reunite the Labour and socialist movements in a campaign against the Liberal Party. Those in which he really had his heart, however, like women's suffrage, served only to divide. Really, the only likely issue was the defence of strikers who, in 1910–11, had to face the combined opposition of employers, troops and police.

Hardie had always been good on this kind of issue, but to press it now meant supporting working men who were themselves critical of the outcome of the Labour alliance and Hardie had never been good at admitting that his own leadership had been wrong and that the rank and file were right. So he contented himself as best he could with attacking the Government for using troops against the strikers, while rounding upon the Left-wing socialists and "syndicalists" for condemning the Labour Party.

For a brief moment, the outbreak of war in August 1914 seemed to unite all sections of the Labour and socialist movements against the Government and Hardie was prominent at a huge "Stop the War" rally in Trafalgar Square. But the moment passed. With the invasion of Belgium, the trade unions and the working class generally rallied to the flag. A hundred years of Liberal propaganda that British foreign policy was designed to oppose the rise of tyranny and single-power domination of the continent weighed more heavily than 30 years of the socialist message that only the capitalist class benefited from the war. Tired and dispirited, Hardie died at his Ayrshire home in September 1915. This ending, together with his gloriously defiant record as an agitator, ensures Hardie's legend a long life, as it ensured him, during his own lifetime, the deep loyalty of the ILP and the respect even of its Socialist critics. But his career, like the history of the Labour Party itself, will always be a frustrating one for socialists to evaluate.

Great in defence of fundamental working-class rights, he was too complacently assured that the recognition of these rights was evidence of progress by the middle classes in a socialist direction and that the passing of social reforms was the same thing as the passage to socialism.

W STEWART   *Keir Hardie* (1921)

H PELLING   *The Origins of the Labour Party, 1880–1900* (1954)

E HUGHES   *Keir Hardie* (1956)

F BEALEY & H PELLING   *Labour and Politics, 1900–1906* (1958)

H PELLING   *A Short History of the Labour Party* (1961)

K O FOX   "Labour and Merthyr's Khaki Election of 1900", *Welsh History Review* (vol. 2, no. 4, 1965)

J G KELLAS   "The Mid-Lanark By-Election (1888) and the Scottish Labour Party (1888–94)", *Parliamentary Affairs* (vol. XVIII, no. 3, Summer 1965)

K O MORGAN   *Keir Hardie* (1967)

F REID   "Keir Hardie's Conversion to Socialism" in A Briggs and J Saville (eds) *Essays in Labour History 1886–1923* (1971)

Laurence Thompson
Gentlemen of the Socialist Press

LAURENCE THOMPSON *(1914–72) was the son of Alexander Thompson, for many years the colleague of Robert Blatchford of the* CLARION. *He was a lifelong journalist and writer, who worked for a number of journals, including* REYNOLDS NEWS, TRIBUNE, NEWS CHRONICLE *and the* OBSERVER, *and both the BBC and independent television. Among his books dealing with a variety of subjects were* ROBERT BLATCHFORD: PORTRAIT OF AN ENGLISHMAN *(1951),* PORTRAIT OF ENGLAND *(1952),* A TIME TO LAUGH *(a novel, 1953),* NINETEEN-FORTY, YEAR OF LEGEND, YEAR OF HISTORY *(1966),* THE GREATEST TREASON *(a study of the Munich crisis 1968) and* THE ENTHUSIASTS *(a biography of the pioneer socialists John and Katharine Bruce Glasier, 1971). At the time of his death Laurence Thompson was writing a history of the Labour Party.*

On a winter's day in 1884, a ruddy-cheeked, burly man with curly hair and beard, dressed in light blue soft shirt and dark blue serge suit, and looking like a retired sea captain, stood outside the Law Courts in the Strand, shouting, "Justice! Twopence!'

This was the greatest of British socialists, William Morris, and the justice he sold so markedly more cheaply than that purveyed inside the courts was the new journal of the Democratic Federation started on a gift of £300 from Edward Carpenter.

The ancestry of socialism in Britain can be traced back at least to the middle ages; but it is a fair claim that the modern mass movement began with the Democratic Federation's *Justice.* and its propagation of a popularised Marxism through the writings of Hyndman, Belfort Bax, Harry Quelch and others.

THE SOCIALIST PRESS 171

The paper's circulation was tiny, and it was kept going in its early days only through substantial subsidies from Morris's own pocket which, he recorded, "crippled" him. But *Justice* was the slender thread linking the handful of eccentrics who, in places as far apart as Bristol and Glasgow, were beginning to call themselves socialists, with a distinctive body of doctrine based, however remotely and however many of them struggled to get away from it, on Marx's teachings.

Control of the party press has always been a key-point in any struggle for political power, and the control of *Justice* was one of the causes of the celebrated quarrel between Morris and Hyndman. Engels, a great meddler—always, of course, from high political principle, never because he enjoyed it—tried to get control of *Justice* through Eleanor Marx and Edward Aveling, with whom she lived in a "free association".

It is almost impossible to be unfair to the nasty little Irish adventurer, Aveling, outrageously sentimentalised by Shaw as Dubedat in *The Doctor's Dilemma*, but I will do my best. Aveling was expelled from almost every organisation he ever joined, either for seducing the members' wives and daughters, pocketing the petty cash, or both; and he murdered Eleanor Marx as surely as if he had put arsenic in her soup.*

Hyndman, of an explosive and dictatorial temperament, would have resisted any attempt to get the editorship of *Justice* away from him even if it had been in favour of an archangel; but, unlike Engels, Morris and many others, he was too much a man of the world to be taken in by a crook. "I shall be quite ready", he wrote to Morris at the end of 1884, "to hand over the editorship to any man in whose competence *and honesty* we all have the fullest confidence."

Morris, of an equally explosive temperament, was by then on his high horse, and led the schismatics out of the Social Democratic Federation to form the Socialist League, with its own paper, *The Commonweal*, of which Aveling became sub-editor. He did not last long.

Morris took great pains to make *The Commonweal* typo-

* He may, in fact, have done something not very different. See Chushichi Tsuzuki's *Eleanor Marx* (1967, Ch. XIII). See also Tsuzuki's article in the present book for further material on Eleanor Marx and Edward Aveling. —Editor.

graphically pleasing—though even he, I regret to say, occasionally called it by the horrible jargon name of *The Weal*—and it is
impossible to turn its pages today without experiencing some of
the excitement which must have been felt by lonely young men
witnessing for their socialist faith in Leeds, Glasgow, Oldham and
such squalid places, as they read for the first time :
> "He rose, thickset and short, and dressed in shabby blue,
> And even as he began it seemed as though I knew
> The thing he was going to say, though I never heard it before.
> He spoke, were it well, were it ill, as though a message he bore,
> A word that he could not refrain from many a million of
>   men.
> Nor aught seemed the sordid room and the few that were
>   listening then
> Save the hall of the labouring earth and the world which was
>   to be.
> Bitter to many the message, but sweet indeed unto me,
> Of man without a master, and earth without a strife.
> And every soul rejoicing in the sweet and bitter of life."
>   (from *The Pilgrims of Hope*, 1885–6)

Into *The Commonweal* Morris poured without stint his riches :
A Dream of John Ball and *News from Nowhere*, as well as *The
Pilgrims of Hope* and many of the *Chants for Socialists*. Unfor-
tunately, the readers did not reciprocate.

"Here are the hard facts", he wrote to the secretary of the Glasgow branch of the League in the late 1880's. "With the present
circulation of say about 2,800 we are losing £4 per week, suppos-
ing the numbers sold are all paid for : there are moneys owing
to us of about £40 but about half that must be written off as *bad* :
owing to a bad habit that both branches and individuals have got
into of not sending us the money for the sales they made and so
accumulating a debt which now they *cannot* pay." Even after
the editorship had been taken away from him by what he rightly
described as "a majority of stupid hobbledehoys who call themselves anarchists and *are* fools", Morris continued to subsidise the
paper at a rate of £500 a year.

There has never been anything quite like *The Commonweal*
in socialist journalism, and until there is another Morris there
probably never will be; but its influence persisted through two

of Morris's disciples, Robert Blatchford of *The Clarion*, and John Bruce Glasier, who, conveniently forgetting Morris's revolutionary communism, set himself up as a kind of mini-Morris and became an influential editor of the ILP's *Labour Leader*.

The ILP itself owed its existence to a substantial shove from yet another of the socialist and Labour papers which sprang up in the 1890's. Most, with no Morris to sustain them, had a life of gnat-like brevity, but Joseph Burgess and *The Workman's Times* have a claim to be better remembered than they are.

Burgess began work as a child half-timer in a Lancashire cotton-mill, drifted into journalism, and used his position as editor of *The Workman's Times* to conduct a campaign throughout 1892 for the formation of a national Independent Labour Party.

His principal allies were members of the provincial Fabian Societies, in revolt against the London Fabian policy of permeating the two existing parties, and Beatrice Webb, with her infallible instinct for backing the wrong horse, saw no future for them and their rackety little party.

If that future had been left to Joe Burgess, she would have been right, since he had the political finesse of a five-footed rhinoceros. There he stands in the photograph of the party's original council, bearded, curly-headed, lowering napoleonically into his left middle-distance like the man of destiny he believed himself to be—and might have been with greater opportunities of birth and education.

He lived on to old age, becoming increasingly dotty in a rather splendid way. In 1928, he was receiving the assistance of spirits in writing a 100,000-word book, *From Napoleon to Lincoln: The History of a Lancashire Weaver-Family*. He became addicted to the cinema, and his grandson, Wilfred Fienburgh, wrote some sketches of the old man which were both touching and hilarious. But Burgess had a moment of true glory at the Bradford Labour Institute on January 13 and 14, 1893, and for this he should be gratefully remembered.

In the autumn of 1891, the star contributor to Edward Hulton's *Sunday Chronicle* got ideas above his station, and walked out after a series of quarrels with Hulton about socialism and other matters. With three of his colleagues, and a capital of £500, he founded a weekly paper of his own with which he hoped to emulate Hulton as a newspaper proprietor. The suggested name of the new paper was *The Champion*, which one of the partners misheard as *The Clarion*, and *The Clarion* it became, though known to its staff and many of its readers as *The Perisher*.

Robert Blatchford, son of travelling actors, of partly Italian ancestry, ran away from a brush-making apprenticeship in Halifax, joined the Dublin Fusiliers, left the army with the rank of sergeant, and became a clerk with the Weaver Navigation Company until propelled into journalism as a hard-working general reporter on the sporting and dramatic paper, *Bell's Life in London*.

"He can write anything from a comic song to a bishop's sermon", said his delighted proprietor. To this varied equipment Blatchford presently added a sentimental socialism based on the woeful state of the Manchester slums, to which his attention had been pointedly directed by an unemployed member of the SDF, and Marx *à la* Hyndman and Morris.

Blatchford found his *métier* at the exact moment of the socialist ferment of the 1890's, and until the turn of the century his influence, both direct and indirect, was immense. One of his *Sunday Chronicle* converts was the eccentric Derby solicitor, Henry Hutchinson, who financed the Fabian travelling lecturers, and, when he blew his brains out, left the money with which the London School of Economics was founded.

In March 1893 Blatchford began publishing in *The Clarion* a series of letters on the Labour Problem, addressed to John Smith of Oldham, A Hard-headed Workman Fond of Facts. Thus began probably the most widely-read of socialist tracts, of which the *Manchester Guardian* wrote that for every British convert to socialism made by *Das Kapital* there were a hundred made by *Merrie England*. Blatchford asked:

"Are the best men of to-day the best paid? Are the most useful men the best paid? Are the most industrious men the wealthiest? Do the noblest and the cleverest men work for gain? Do they get rich? Do the great mass of the labouring classes work for gain? Do *they* get rich? . . . During an election there are Tory and Liberal Capitalists, and all of them are friends of the workers. During a strike there are no Tories and no Liberals amongst the employers. They are all Capitalists and enemies of the workers.

Is there any logic in you, John Smith? Is there any perception in you? Is there any *sense* in you?"

But Blatchford had neither the patience nor the inclination for sustained political effort, and his bohemianism, combativeness and vanity—he had, as Shaw remarked, something to be vain about—outraged the puritans of the ILP almost as much as his support of the Boer War.

The Clarion's rival for influence and circulation was Keir Hardie's *Labour Leader*, which began life in 1887 as *The Miner*. Hardie, who was quite as vain as Blatchford, esteemed himself to be many things, among them a journalist and businessman, but when the ILP began negotiations in 1902 to buy *The Labour Leader* from him, the circulation stood at not much more than 10,000 and Bruce Glasier described the paper as "rubbish . . . not worth a penny, and but for Hardie's toil and the risk of his competing against us, I would advise starting a new one".

One of Hardie's stipulations was that he should remain editor, but this was refused, and the post was offered first to MacDonald, then to Snowden. Both declined, and the third choice was Glasier, who had served an apprenticeship to journalism as a contributor to *The Commonweal*.

He was at once over-conscientious as an editor, and inattentive to detail—items tended to get printed twice, and a packet of "copy" for the printers in Manchester was quite likely to be addressed to Sheffield—but it was Glasier who gave the *Leader* its slightly peevish tone of mystical socialism which was as distinctively ILP as the stentorian acerbities of Harry Quelch, the self-educated ex-labourer who became a very good editor of *Justice*, were distinctively SDF.

Under Glasier, the circulation of the paper rose to over 40,000 a week, and he was as much responsible as any man for holding together through its early days the uneasy ILP-trade union alliance which created the Labour Party. But he was not a robust character, and he resigned the editorship in dudgeon under the slings and arrows of left-wing criticism of his support for the alliance. For those concerned about ruthless exploitation of the workers, the ILP paid Glasier two guineas a week as sub-editor. When Fenner Brockway joined the *Leader* in 1911 as sub-editor, he was paid £2 15s a week and when he became editor a year or two later, his salary was somewhat grudgingly raised to £3 10s.

Even so, and with unpaid contributors, the paper ran a deficit of between £4 and £5 a week, much of which was found from his own pocket by the ILP treasurer, T D Benson, a well-to-do estate agent. When Benson tried to bridge the gap with advertising and the front page of the *Leader* was taken up by a eulogy of Dr Tibbles' Cocoa, the editor, Glasier, protested so vehemently that poor Benson preferred to go on making up the deficit himself rather than risk another such explosion.

In spite of the consistent failure of socialist periodicals to pay their way, Hardie in 1911 began trying to raise money to start a daily newspaper. He calculated that it could be done for £10,000, and he planned to publish two editions: one, containing the morning news, for delivery in Scotland and Wales at teatime; and an evening edition for circulation within a 50-mile radius of the publishing area. He did succeed in raising a small sum of money, but his financial dealings were always eccentric, and Benson suspected that the money had melted away in speculation in some other venture that had gone wrong. In any event, he was soon jockeyed out of control by MacDonald, who was able to tap large trade union funds.

Glasier, representing the ILP on the joint board of directors, recorded in his diary a lively account of a board meeting on the eve of the paper's launching: "Then came the question of the policy of the paper, and MacDonald asked us to read the front page article in the trial *Citizen* and say what we thought of it. The article I knew had been written by MacDonald himself—though none of us were supposed to know it. MacDonald himself drew attention to the chief points.

"Pease [of The Fabian Society] opened the ball by asking rather casually if we should not decide first of all whether the word socialism should not be included. (It was not once mentioned in the article!) I then said quite bluntly that the article was enough to damn the paper at the start . . . It was tamer than many moderate Liberal papers would have put out."

In these not very promising circumstances, *The Daily Citizen*, first official organ of the Labour Party, was launched on October 8, 1912. Its make-up resembled that of *The Morning Post*, though its politics were a little to the left of that newspaper, and almost the only thing memorable about it was that a young man named Tom Webster drew the political cartoons.

By March of the following year it was in dire financial straits, and when the board sought to remedy the situation by publishing betting news and tips, Arthur Henderson, the Methodist lay preacher, resigned. The paper limped along on trade union subsidies until 1915, when it quietly gave up the ghost.

Its jaunty and highly unofficial rival, *The Daily Herald*, began as a strike sheet in January 1911, and was revived a year later as a daily. with a capital of £300. and Ben Tillett as the dynamite behind George Lansbury on the editorial board. A Miss Rebecca West contributed to the woman's page, and it almost, but not quite, had Frank Harris as its second editor. He would no doubt have saved Hugh Cudlipp the trouble and expense of having to kill the paper half a century later. Will Dyson's vivid and striking cartoons often occupied the front page, and a sample of the *Herald's* style is contained in this leader of 30 November 1912: "Leaders and followers, we all need more ideas, more spirit, more militancy. We ought to be clearer as to the extent and nature of our rights, as to the revolution we are out to make, the sort of country and civilisation we want to substitute for the present chaos and injustice; and we ought to be much more militant, insistently and steadily militant, in our procedure."

No one in Britain has grown fat out of socialist journalism. With empty columns gaping to be filled, its practitioners wrote too much, too quickly. Glasier's record was 17 columns, about 11,000 words, in a week. Blatchford wrote 10,000 words of *Merrie England*, three short stories and a number of articles in five days, working almost round the clock. They were a quarrelsome lot, and tended to take the easy way out of column-filling by launching attacks on each other. Few of them, except Joe Burgess, could point to any concrete result of their labours other than the steady growth of the movement they tried to serve.

Blatchford defined his own conception of his function thus: "The masses are inarticulate. I am a writer and I have the opportunity of doing the masses a good turn, I try to use that opportunity; and I think I do a little good. Because, although I offend many people and make many enemies, and although my work may seem harsh and blunt and deficient in graces of style, yet it serves its purpose. My readers may kick and prance and throw verbal bouquets; but they do not generally go to sleep."

I hope some, at least, of my readers are still awake.

Bibliographical Note

Laurence Thompson, himself a distinguished socialist journalist, made the history of the socialist press very much his own subject. There is some discussion of *Justice* and *Commonweal* in H M Hyndman, *The Record of an Adventurous Life* (1911), in H W Lee and E Archbold, *Social-Democracy in Britain* (1935) and in the various biographies and published letters of William Morris. The standard secondary histories of the labour and socialist movement also give some attention to socialist journalism in the 1880's. For the later journals the following sources may be consulted :

A NEIL LYONS   *Robert Blatchford* (1910)
GEORGE LANSBURY   *The Miracle of Fleet Street* (1925)
GEORGE LANSBURY   *My Life* (1928)
ALEXANDER THOMPSON   *Here I Lie* (1937)
FENNER BROCKWAY   *Inside the Left* (1942)
LAURENCE THOMPSON   *Robert Blatchford* (1950)
RAYMOND POSTGATE   *George Lansbury* (1951)
WILFRED FIENBURGH   "The Greatness of Grandfather", *New Statesman*, vol. 49, 18 June, 1955
LAURENCE THOMPSON   *The Enthusiasts* (1971)

Janet Blackman
The First Women's Liberation Movement

JANET BLACKMAN *lectures in economic and social history in the University of Hull. She is particularly interested in social consequences of industrialisation, and is making a study of the history of food and diet in this country. As national chairman of the United Nations Association's Annual Conference, she has looked at similar problems in developing countries. Her contributions to the women's liberation movement have been mainly in Hull, and she has written for the* TRADE UNION REGISTER *(1971, 1972) on equal pay.*

In 1970 the Equal Pay Act was passed, over eighty years after the Trades Union Congress first declared its support for this cause. In 1867 John Stuart Mill had proposed to admit women to the Parliamentary vote, but it was not until 1918, fifty years later, that the first woman gained the right to vote and sit in the House of Commons. The fight for women to have the right to vote remains one of the most significant single issue campaigns in our history. It was uncomplicated and uncompromising.

As a political movement the campaign led by the Pankhursts inevitably had its internal dissensions, debates about broadening the issues and crises of leadership, but it was and remains unique as a movement. Dominated by one family, mother and daughters, the Pankhursts' name is still linked with militancy and direct action. It was their style which was so different, not their aim. And yet their movement must be set in its period, a time of increasing violence in Ireland, in labour relations and elsewhere. Reviled, decried and laughed at at the time, commentators still attempt to denigrate their work, to label the suffragettes as lesbians, psychopathic, racialist, hysterical, politically naive, and worse of all, militant. Annie Kenney, the Lancashire cotton worker, moves in and out of the picture as the working-class origins of the movement are sought or denied. It was, and remains, a movement which arouses strong passions which are poor substitutes for analysis.

Never really a social reform movement, the aim was women's political emancipation; its style a resourceful campaign of political agitation. Why should it cause so much concern?

The extension of the franchise in parliamentary elections to women had long been sought by men and women. The suffragists, the non-militants as they appeared in comparison with the suffragettes, were forced into a position in the decade prior to the First World War of comparing tactics, and claiming success for their more peaceful forms of pressure.

There will always be this type of tactical controversy in any campaign; in this way the issues themselves become clear, and so should the nature of the opposition. For this reason, from one campaign to the next the controversy is never quite the same, and is never purely a question of tactics. But the debate about tactics has been allowed to obscure the nature of the opposition.

In her Preface to her daughter Sylvia's book, *The Suffragette* (1911), Emmeline Pankhurst wrote:

"The men and women of the coming time will, I am persuaded, be filled with admiration for the patient work of the early pioneers and the heroic determination and persistence in spite of coercion, repression, misrepresentation, and insult of those who fought the later militant fight."

To concentrate on the tactics sometimes seems to be our way of shrinking from an assessment of the nature of the struggle. After all this was the nearest the world has been to a war between the sexes. There were similar movements overseas, especially in America.

Of course there were men on the side of the women suffragettes, but this had to be essentially a women's movement, and it had to be against men and their entrenched power. The persistence and vitality of the campaign upset all the established beliefs about women. Where was their lack of organisational ability, willing-

ness to work together with other women, the docility and deference?

Annie Kenney was a born tactician, saw the opportunities
the Lancashire Wakes' weeks gave to her and her friends to get
their message across to the holiday crowds, full of working women.
A visit to the House of Commons to listen to the hoped-for
introduction of the Women's Enfranchisement Bill in 1904
quickly revealed the tactics MPs were taking, and the women
were just as quick to develop their own tactics.

The Bill was talked out by prolonging the previous debate on a
fore and aft light for cars at night. The campaign for the vote,
and the reaction it provoked now became raw, aggressive, even
savage. There was violence on both sides. The women's may have
been born of frustration, reflecting their lack of direct access to
power in any other way. The direct action and disruptive tactics
were largely aimed at the Liberal Government starting with its
election campaign and landslide victory in 1906. What is perhaps
more disturbing is the reaction of this radical party of reform.
Why did the Liberal Government retaliate so aggressively?

Perhaps they were in unfamiliar territory, the issue too clear-
cut. There was no possible compromise or palliative. There was
only a choice of two responses—support the campaign and give
the women the vote, or destroy their movement. It is an interesting comment on leading Liberal opinion of the day that the
latter was attempted until the eve of the world war.

In October 1903 Mrs Pankhurst formed the Women's Social
and Political Union, building to some extent on the work she had
done for women's suffrage with her husband when he was alive
some 20 years earlier.

Mrs Pankhurst had assisted her husband, Dr Richard Marsden
Pankhurst, with his public work in Manchester. He was a much
respected figure in a wide field of social causes, including women's
political rights. He had been one of the founders of the Manchester Women's Suffrage Committee, and had drafted a bill on this
subject, which was introduced in the Commons by Jacob Bright
in 1870.

His interests in such a subject must have meant that Mrs Pankhurst had been used to controversy and being a controversial figure throughout her married life. Much younger than her hus-

band, she devoted a great deal of her time after his death to bring-
ing up their family, took a position as Registrar of Births and
Deaths to make ends meet, and continued as an Independent
Labour Party member of the Manchester School Board.

It was the increasing interest of her daughters in career prospects and their disabilities as women which rekindled Mrs Pankhurst's enthusiasm for women's suffrage.

She quite deliberately formed a separate women's organisation,
conscious as she was that the Tories and Liberals were hostile and
unlikely to take up the question of women's political freedom
and rights. She had watched the growth of the Labour movement,
had joined the Independent Labour Party in 1894, and had
tried to interest the trade union branches locally in women's
suffrage.

What appeared essential at that stage was a single-purpose
movement with a precise goal, a women's movement in which
they could work out their own ideas and salvation.

Emma Paterson had already started a trade union movement
for women workers which became the Women's Trade Union
League in 1891. Under the leadership of Mary MacArthur this
body campaigned for legislative control of the sweated trades
which employed so many women in book-binding, box-making,
shirt and dress-making, etc. The Co-operative Women's Guilds
began to look after the interests of women in the home.

The better-known leaders of the suffragettes may have been
drawn from the higher income groups, as were Paterson and Mac-
Arthur, and political rights a middle-class demand. But they
gained the support, sometimes active, sometimes tacit, of thousands of unnamed women with or without money and education.
The campaign for the vote crystallised a deep-seated sense of injustice which probably cut across class barriers. The meetings and
demonstrations often drew large crowds, many of whom had come
to listen and join in. Hannah Mitchell, a working-class girl who
devoted her life to the women's movement and to local politics in
Manchester, knew she could count on the support of many of
her neighbours, sometimes shown only as a warning whistle to
their sons to go to the aid of Hannah and her friends who were
being manhandled by hostile crowds.

As women their conduct in daring to ask questions about

women's political rights at public meetings could in those days
be so easily condemned as unseemly. The treatment they received
during the Liberal campaign before the 1906 general election
revealed no lack of militant suppression by their denouncers.
The violence of the reaction to their public questioning still
leaves a nasty taste in the mouth. The subsequent forced feeding,
physical ejection from meetings, assaults, the pushing, shoving,
jibes and threats turned this into a militant campaign as soon as
it began. The women responded.

The Government replied with the notorious "Cat and Mouse"
Act whereby a hunger striker could be released from prison to
recuperate and then be rearrested when well enough to resume
her sentence. As Mrs Pankhurst made this Act work again and
again against herself in 1913, Christabel Pankhurst stepped up
the militant campaign outside prison directing it from Paris
where she had fled in 1912.

These last few years of the militant suffragettes' campaign were
the most controversial and perhaps the most misunderstood. It
is only too easy to emphasise the sexual aspect of this sex war, to
explain it in terms of the sexual repression of the women themselves who were leading the campaign, or even its lesbian over-
tones.

Christabel, in the paper *The Suffragette*, castigated the dual
standard of morality which made women the sex slaves of men,
and advocated "chastity for men" as well as votes for women as
a solution to the spread of venereal disease to innocent women
and children.

She and her mother had no intention of attacking established
values, but of strengthening them, urging men to live up to them.
In this sense they were following the conventional Victorian moral
code at its most naive. It can be argued that it was this attitude
which split the movement and split the Pankhurst family.

On the other hand it was the way in which their agitation
evolved in the last few years before the first world war which began to push the discussion and the pressure in other directions
than the original single purpose of the movement for the political
freedom of women through the right to vote.

After 1918 the non-militant suffragists may have come into
their own to continue the fight for the vote on the same terms as

men. This was achieved in 1928. But the militant suffragettes were already caught up in the next fundamental stage of the discussion on the emancipation of women—the role of the female sex in society.

Are women simply the guardians of morals, of the integrity of the family, and therefore the superior sex in this sense, dragging men unwillingly for the most part up to our standards? Or were women by demanding the right to vote, establishing themselves as one half of the human race engaged in a dialogue with the other half on the way we should live together for our mutual benefit now and in the future?

Sylvia Pankhurst and her younger sister, Adela, began to work out this argument in political terms; Marie Stopes led the sexual debate which had to accompany the discussion on political and economic freedom. This is the dialogue in which we are still engaged.

Mrs Pankhurst's "votes for women" was one stage, a vital step which had to be taken in the evolution of the British style of parliamentary democracy. But this could only be the first step. The right to vote established women's political identity, enabling them to engage on equal terms, if they want to, in the struggle for the development of democracy in this country and elsewhere. The next step—the achievement of economic and social freedom—is much more difficult and involves a less clear-cut discussion and campaign in which the economic and social responsibilities of women and men have to be worked out in a larger freedom for both.

This has come directly out of the Pankhursts' own campaign. In this sense their campaign was one of outstanding importance.

E SYLVIA PANKHURST   *The Suffragette* (1911)
RAY STRACHEY   *The Cause: A Short History of the Women's Movement in Great Britain* (1928)
VIRGINIA WOOLF   *A Room of One's Own* (1929)
E SYLVIA PANKHURST   *The Suffragette Movement* (1931)
VERA BRITTAIN   *Testament of Youth* (1933)
GLADYS BOONE   *The Women's Trade Union Leagues in Great Britain and the United States of America* (New York, 1942)

VIOLA KLEIN   *The Feminine Character: History of an Ideology* (1946)

VERA BRITTAIN   *Lady into Woman* (1953)

R FULFORD   *Votes for Women* (1957)

D MITCHELL   *Monstrous Regiment* (New York, 1965)

D MITCHELL   *The Fighting Pankhursts* (1967)

G MITCHELL (ed.)   *The Hard Way Up: the Autobiography of Hannah Mitchell, Suffragette & Rebel* (1968)

W L O'NEILL   *The Woman Movement: Feminism in the United States and England* (1969)

ANTONIA RAEBURN   *The Militant Suffragettes* (1973)

Walter Kendall
Labour Unrest before the First World War

WALTER KENDALL, *born in 1926, an active trade unionist for over a quarter of a century, past member of the London District Council of the Union of Shop, Distributive and Allied Workers, is a leading contributor to the rank and file paper* VOICE OF THE UNIONS *and one of the founders of the Institute for Workers' Control. A student at Ruskin College, Oxford, in 1963–4, he later took a B Litt at St Catherine's College, Oxford. He has taught at universities in Sussex and Detroit and is currently Senior Research Fellow at Nuffield College, Oxford. He is the author of* THE REVOLUTIONARY MOVEMENT IN BRITAIN 1900–1921 *(1969) and of* LABOUR MOVEMENT IN EUROPE *(1973), His present research interests include a study of Communism in the 1920's and 1930's, the international company and the international labour movement. He was until recently chairman of the Society for the Study of Labour History.*

A slight small man with broad shoulders and the sunlit profile of a renaissance page boy stood on an improvised platform at Tower Hill in sight of the London Docks, before him a rippling sea of cloth caps and murmuring upturned faces. The whole port was out. A rancid smell of mouldering Tooley Street butter drifted across the river with the breeze. The strike was at a deadlock. The small man called for the whole vast assembly to sink to their knees. Slowly, in an irregular stumbling movement, down they went.

"I want you to pray", declared Ben Tillett, "for the success of our claim and the removal of the main obstacle to its success. May God strike Lord Davenport dead!"

In due course, the Almighty took the chairman of the Port of London Authority to his bosom although with such delay as to leave the efficacy of Tillett's injunction open to question. The strike itself brought results more quickly. Within days, on August 11, 1911, the strike was over, major concessions granted to the men almost all along the line.*

One spark for the 100,000 strong mammoth strike which closed tight the Port of London for 11 momentous days, for the first time in this century, and brought the narrow, purblind, reactionary employers to heel, had come a few brief weeks earlier from Hull, still a centre of port worker militancy today. In London mass picketing had been one means of keeping blacklegs out of the port. In Hull the level of militancy was, if anything, even higher.

"One shipowner came to me", relates the Governments' chief industrial arbitrator, Lord Askwith. "He spoke to me of it as a revolution, and so it was." The dockers had new leaders, men unknown before. "The employers did not know how to deal with them." One town councillor had been "in Paris during the Commune and had never seen anything like this". When the proposed settlement was announced to a crowd of 15,000 men, "an angry roar of 'NO' rang out." "Let's fire the Docks" came from the outskirts. The whole settlement had to be renegotiated again from the beginning.

The burning powder train that led from Hull to London, had begun in Southampton on June 14. Of all the underpaid, badly fed, undernourished, scandalously treated, evilly housed millions of the British working class in this glorious heydey of the post-Edwardian era, those at the very bottom of the pile were perhaps the merchant seamen. Ignominiously stood in line before signing on, the despised sailor was frequently abruptly ordered to "drop your trousers" and undergo a degrading VD inspection before the eyes of all his fellows.

Inspired by a spirit of rising manliness the downtrodden seamen, responding to calls by veteran seafarer organiser Havelock Wilson and stalwart Tom Mann, had with unparalleled effron-

* The scenario is correct. The date is wrong. Tillett uttered his plea to the Almighty in 1912 when the dockers lost their strike, not in 1911 when they won it. (Christians will please note)—W K.

tery stopped the White Star Line's *Olympia* on her maiden voyage. In the hard days and weeks of struggle which followed, the seamen and their union fought the masters to a standstill. The settlement, though grossly imperfect, remains a landmark in the still unclouded struggle for self-respect in maritime affairs. Racing loose through the green fields of England, over the hills through narrow mountain valleys, up rivers, along the roads and railway tracks, in great cities and small mining villages too, a new spirit was loose in the land. "The straining of the spirit of man to be free."

On August 5, 1911, while London was still strikebound, 1,000 employees of the North Eastern Railway at Liverpool stopped work in the face of the employers' adamant refusal to pay heed to their demands. The strike spread rapidly to all areas in and around the port. Tom Mann, himself a long-standing engineer and member of the Amalgamated Society of Engineers, was drafted to Merseyside to help organise the ranks. On August 14 the shipowners declared a lock-out. The strike committee, uncowed, responded with the call for a general transport strike. All Liverpool came out.

His Majesty's Liberal Government, with truly olympian impartiality, ordered two gunboats up the Mersey, doubtless to bombard workers and shipowners indifferently with high explosive. Gunboats offshore, the Scots Greys, the Warwickshire Regiment, bayonets at the ready, on shore.

A peaceful strike meeting, outside St George's Hall, in the city centre, suffers an unprovoked attack. Police assault the crowd, wielding truncheons like flails in what the *Manchester Guardian* terms "a merciless use of violence, that horrified those who saw it". The strikers stand fast—Liverpool Catholic, Liverpool Protestant together—and win.

Seamen, portworkers, a general strike in Liverpool, the fever cannot be halted now. Revolt runs out over the sleepers, out along the rails in every direction from Liverpool. On August 15 the combined executives of the railway unions, meeting in a single hall, swept along by the impetuous courage of their men, deliver an ultimatum. The companies must recognise the unions within 24 hours or face a national stoppage. There is a meeting with the Prime Minister on August 17. No result.

"Your liberty is at stake. All railwaymen must strike at once. The loyalty of each means victory for all." Two thousand telegrams rush to their destinations. On August 18 the railways are dead; 150,000 railwaymen have answered the union call. Winston Churchill calls out the troops.

From Aldershot 12,500 men are despatched to strategic centres all over Britain. London, troop encampments in the parks, is in a "state of siege".

The true leaders of this great revolt, the rank-and-file servicemen in what was above all a soldiers' war, will never be known. The lives of key figures, Noah Ablett, Marxist intellectual and South Wales Miners Agent, George Harvey, Durham pitman, and first advocate of one industrial union for the miners, remain to be written. "Rise with your class, not out of your class", they declared, stood by the text, and are cruelly forgotten as a consequence.

"A leader", wrote Ablett, "implies . . . some men who are being led . . . self-respect which comes from expressed manhood, is taken from the men and consolidated in their leader . . . the order and system he maintains is based on the suppression of the men, from being independent thinkers into being 'the men' or 'the mob' (*The Miners' Next Step*, 1912).

"A man in the workshop . . . feels every change; the workshop atmosphere is his atmosphere, the conditions under which he labours are primary . . . But let the same man get into [trade union] office. He is removed out of the workshop, he meets a fresh class of people and breathes a different atmosphere . . . He looks from a new point of view on those things which he has ceased to feel acutely . . . the result is a change of outlook . . . Government by officials . . . is steadily eroding trade union members' rights . . . real democratic practice demands that every member of an organisation shall participate actively in the conduct of business." So wrote J T Murphy, a great shop stewards' leader, some time later (*The Workers' Committee*, 1917.)

Underlying the whole giant movement was a spirit of conscious do-it-yourself.

More than any other single figure Tom Mann embodied the spirit of this age. The Industrial Syndicalist Education League founded at Manchester in November, 1910, at his instigation, excellently illustrated the free and easy, open organisational methods by which the ideals of direct action which motivated so much of the movement were propagated with such great success. "Educate, Agitate, Organise, Control" summarises Mann's campaign. It was an enormous success.

Underlying the industrial upsurge was a deep-lying and in retrospect, well-founded scepticism about classical social democracy, out of which have sprung, equally, the socialist and communist parties of the present day. Thus, wrote the Marxist socialist William Paul, "The revolutionary socialist denies that state ownership can end in anything other than a bureaucratic despotism . . . the state cannot democratically control industry. Industry can only be democratically owned and controlled by the workers electing directly from their own ranks industrial administrative committees. Socialism will be fundamentally an industrial system; its constituencies will be of an industrial character . . . when the central administrative industrial committee meets it will represent every phase of social activity. Hence the capitalist political or geographical state will be replaced by the industrial administrative committee of socialism.

"The transition from the one social system to the other will be the *social revolution*. The political state throughout history has been the government *of men* by ruling classes; the republic of socialism will be the government *of industry* administered on behalf of the whole community. The former meant the economic subjection of the many; the latter will mean the economic freedom of all; it will be, therefore, a true democracy."

(William Paul: *The State: its Origin and Function*, 1917)

Anything further removed from the Soviet-style, geographical, one-party state, as a model of socialism, it would be difficult to imagine. Anything more different from the road of talk shop Parliamentary reformism from above it would be difficult to conceive.

The great days of not so long ago point two important lessons. First, in which a world in which might is right, it pays to be strong, and to have the courage to use that strength as well. Second, the pioneers knew more of the problems of democratic socialism than we gave them credit for.

Llanelly station, August 18, 1911. Scab train steams through a cutting. Crowd throws stones and other missiles. Major Stuart, commanding the guard, orders the crowd to desist. Yells of defiance. More missiles. "Fire." Two working men die. Others are wounded. At two o'clock that afternoon a reprisal. An assault on trucks outside the station. Flames and smoke, two trucks containing detonators explode. Four men are killed. Many more are injured. Every regiment in Britain is mobilised to full strength. Every unit equipped under service conditions. And this, all this, for what? Because the companies will not recognise the unions. And in the end ... they do!

The miners, locked in the dark narrow chambers of the earth, were moving too. A struggle for the minimum wage had convulsed the Welsh coal field the year before. The Metropolitan Police (800 strong), two companies of infantry, no less than 20 00 cavalrymen were hurried into the valleys. Percy Jacobs, manager of the Tonda mine, made the opinions of the owners clear. The Metropolitan Police he declared "were sworn constables of Glamorganshire ... I ... made a special request for their services ... they were employees of mine as long as I wished ..." The sturdy pitmen held out for 12 months and lost, starved back into the ground, defeated. At least one striker was killed, 500 were wounded. Casualties among the mine-owners, judging from official records, were nil.

Taking heed from the courageous struggle in Wales miners all over Britain were now raising the standard of the national minimum wage. Over two wintry days, December 20–21, 1911, a ballot vote registered 445,800 to 115,271 in favour of a stoppage. The mine-owners returned a blunt refusal to the pitmen's claim. In February 1912 over 1,000,000 miners were out in the biggest strike the world had so far seen. At the height of the five-week stoppage, Margot Asquith, the Prime Minister's wife, invited the miners' leader, Robert Smillie, to a private *tête à tête* at the home of Sir Edward Grey, 3 Queen's Gate, London, SW1. "Even he need not know. I will just ask if he would allow me to have a private talk with a friend ..." Wisely Smillie refused and this intriguing conundrum vanishes, unsolved forever, from the corridors of history. Eventually, Asquith, Prime Minister of the most powerful empire that ever existed, attended a delegate meeting of the striking slaves of the coal owners and pleaded with them to agree to a compromise. The miners went back with major concessions in their pocket. In 1912 over 40 million working days were lost, the greatest number in any year before 1926.

The great upsurge which shook British society in the years before 1914 was denounced in its time by everyone of recognised importance. There were no more than a handful of honourable exceptions. Union strength nearly doubled between 1910 and 1914 rising to over 4 million on the eve of the first world war. In retrospect the unprecedented struggles of the years 1911–14 seem the head of a lance probing the vitals of capitalist society, demanding recognition of the labour movement's new-found strength and power. The war headed off what promised to be struggles of semi-insurrectionary proportions which reappeared with new force at its ending. Eight million strong in 1920, the modern labour movement which emerged was one which owed much of its existence to the struggles of the pre-war years.

One fact, too often ignored, has to be faced. Those foundations were not laid easily. They were not laid without suffering. They were not laid without violence. They were not laid except in the face of the employers, the state, the police and the military. They were not laid without dead and wounded in the streets. These were no gains brought Jove-like by legislation from above. Nor did they spring from consciousness brought to sheep-brained workers by sickly clever middle-class intellectuals from without. These gains were made by the workers themselves in the face of a hostile ruling class, backed and supported by the power of government and the state machine.

FRED HENDERSON *The Labour Unrest* (n.d., 1912)
Miners' Unofficial Reform Committee *The Miners' Next Step* (Tonypandy, 1912, reprinted Nottingham, 1965)
CHARLES WATNEY & JAMES LITTLE *Industrial Warfare* (1912)
G D H COLE *The World of Labour* (1913)
RAMSAY MACDONALD *The Social Unrest* (1913)
G R ASKWITH *Industrial Problems and Disputes* (1920)
GEORGE DANGERFIELD *The Strange Death of Liberal England* (New York, 1935)
R V SIRES "Labour Unrest in England, 1910–1914", *Journal of Economic History*, vol. 15, no. 3, September 1955

BRANKO PRIBICEVIC *The Shop Stewards' Movement and Workers' Control, 1910–1922* (Oxford, 1959)

HENRY PELLING *Popular Politics and Society in Late Victorian Britain* (1968), ch. 9

WALTER KENDALL *The Revolutionary Movement in Britain, 1900–1921* (1969)

ASA BRIGGS & JOHN SAVILLE (eds) *Essays in Labour History 1886–1923* (1971), chs. 4 (J E Williams) and 5 (Philip Bagwell)

STANDISH MEACHAM "The Sense of An Impending Clash", *American Historical Review*, vol. 77, no. 5, Dec 1972

There are also numerous histories of trade unions which should be consulted, notably Philip Bagwell on the railwaymen and Robin Page Arnot on the miners, as well as autobiographies of participants, including Ben Tillett, Tom Mann, Harry Gosling and Robert Smillie.

Fenner Brockway
The Left in the First World War

FENNER BROCKWAY, *born in 1888, has devoted a long lifetime to the socialist and labour movement. He is a journalist, author and politician. He worked with Keir Hardie before 1914 and was a leader of the war resistance movement in the First World War, when he was imprisoned for nearly two and a half years. He was Chairman or General Secretary of the Independent Labour Party during the 1930's, and a member of Parliament 1929–31 and 1950–64, in which year he was created a life peer. After 1945 he devoted much energy to the cause of independent Africa. Among his many books are two volumes of autobiography (*INSIDE THE LEFT*, 1942 and OUTSIDE THE RIGHT, 1963), HUNGRY ENGLAND (1932) and biographies of Fred Jowett (1946) and Alfred Salter (1949).*

The First World War, unlike the Second, came with sudden unexpectedness. I was speaking at a Sunday morning meeting in an Oldham park nine days before Britain declared war and sounded a warning. "Talk about Ireland" shouted the crowd, and certainly the threat by Carson of army rebellion against the Home Rule Bill seemed most urgent. Only those who followed European events closely saw the greater danger. A week later, but too late—the declaration of war was only a few hours off—the danger was realised.

In London there was a vast demonstration extending from Trafalgar Square to the streets around, despite continuous rain. The meeting was addressed by Keir Hardie and Arthur Henderson. Robert Smillie, President of the miners' union, had called for an international strike of coal workers. The South Wales miners resolved "not to supply the coal for the fleet". Lansbury in the *Daily Herald* appealed to the transport workers not to handle munitions. And on August 3, Ramsay MacDonald, leading in the House of Commons protested on behalf of the Labour Party against Britain's entry into the war. The next day war was declared.

The Labour Party Executive met. It adopted a forthright resolution, condemning the war, denouncing British foreign policy, repudiating the Foreign Secretary, Sir Edward Grey, for having committed Britain without the knowledge of the British people, and calling on the working class to take action to secure peace at the earliest moment on conditions which would re-establish amity between the workers of Europe.

So far unity, but in the afternoon the Parliamentary group met and turned down MacDonald's proposal that this resolution should be read to the House of Commons as a statement of Labour's policy. Instead, the majority decided to vote for the war credits and to support the war effort. For two months there was controversy within the leadership of the party, but the pressure of public opinion and the press, particularly after Germany's invasion of Belgium, swept the greater part of the movement behind the House of Commons. In October the party, with the backing of the Parliamentary Committee of the Trades Union Congress, issued a manifesto putting the entire blame on the German Government and justifying Labour support for the war by the need to save Britain and Europe from the evils of German victory. The principal Social Democratic Parties of Europe similarly supported the war once it was declared, the French, the Belgians, the Dutch, on one side, the Germans, the Austrians, the Poles, on the other. This division of the international socialist movement came as a great shock to those who had built their hopes on working-class action to resist war.

Over the years there had been many discussions at International Social Conference on the means to adopt. Keir Hardie for the ILP and Jean Jaurès, the French leader, had repeatedly urged that the mobilisation of armed forces for war should be met by an international general strike, but this was opposed both by Right and Left. The Germans opposed on the grounds that no Social Democratic Party had the strength to halt the war machine and

Lenin and Trotsky opposed on the ground that the war should be turned into revolution. Nevertheless, there was confidence that the solidarity of the socialist parties, with the support of other large sections of the public opposed to war, could prevent its outbreak.

Less than a year before the fatal August of 1914, the Socialist International had called an emergency congress at Basle (November 1913) to act against the Balkan war. It was an extraordinary occasion. Special trains brought thousands into the city. The congress itself met in the Cathedral. The speech which Jaurès delivered was described by many as the most moving they had ever heard. The delegates foresaw the danger of the Balkan conflict expanding into a European war, and adopted a manifesto detailing the action that each Socialist party should take. The parties in Germany and Britain were particularly asked to resist the mounting naval rivalry between the two countries. ("We want eight and we won't wait" was the British cry for Dreadnoughts.) The manifesto described the "artificially instigated hostility" between Britain and Germany as the greatest danger to peace and said that it would be criminal folly if a Serbo-Austrian dispute led Germany, France, and Britain into war. This was of course the immediate cause of the First World War. After this congress there was a wave of optimism throughout Europe that peace would be saved.

On July 27, 1914, the day before Austria declared war on Serbia, the Bureau of the Socialist International met at Brussels. Most of Europe's Socialist leaders were there including Jaurès, Adler, Vanderville, Kautsky, Rosa Luxemburg, and Hardie. Hope had turned to pessimism, at the best to false optimism. "There is nothing further we can do," said Victor Adler in his report. "Our Governments will not declare war", said Hardie and Jaurès. The speech which Jaurès delivered at the public meeting was his last. Two days later he was assassinated in Paris.

One of the bitterest blows we had to face in the early months of the war was the fact not merely that so many Socialists in other countries were uniting with their Governments, but that we could make no contact with the minority who were standing out. Again and again at our meetings we were met by the taunt that the German Socialists were supporting the Kaiser. We could tell of

the courageous anti-war attitude of Karl Liebknecht, Rosa Luxemburg, Clara Zetkin and others, but they seemed lost and dis-
tant voices. I was determined to make contact with them. I spent
an afternoon in October writing letters to them, making enough
copies to send through the Socialist Parties in the neutral countries—Holland, Denmark, Sweden, Norway, Switzerland, Italy,
America, and even Spain. One I hoped would get through.
Towards the end of December a bulky envelope arrived through
Sweden with their replies. I regard their letters as of historic
importance and I wish I could give them in full. These are extracts :

"I am particularly happy and proud," wrote Liebknecht,
"to send my greetings to you, to the British ILP, who, with
our Russian and Serbian comrades, have saved the honour
of Socialism amidst the madness of national slaughter.

Each Socialist Party has its enemy, the common enemy
of the International, in its own country. There it has to fight
it. The liberation of each nation must be its own work. . . .
It is the duty of every Socialist at the present time to be a
prophet of international brotherhood, realising that every
word he speaks in favour of Socialism and peace, every
action he performs for these ideals, enflames similar words
and actions in other countries, until the flames of the desire for
peace shall flare high over all Europe. . . .

In this way, even during the war, the International can
be revived and can atone for its previous mistakes. Thus it
must revive, a different International, increased not only
in numerical strength but in revolutionary fervour, in clearness
of vision and in preparedness to overcome the dangers of
capitalist dictatorship of secret diplomacy, and of capitalist
conspiracies against peace."

Rosa Luxemburg was ruthless in facing the realities of the abso-
lute collapse of the International. She did not share the view,
common in the ILP, that after the war all could be as it had been
before, and insisted on our rejecting the theory that during war
the workers must inevitably "cut each others' throats at the command of their ruling classes", and then, when the war is over,
"again exchange brotherly greetings as if nothing had happened".
With characteristic directness she wrote :

"An International which accepted the terrible downfall of the
present time as a normal occurrence for the future, and
which nevertheless pretended that it had never existed, would
be but a caricature of Socialism, a product of hypocrisy just
as much as the diplomacy of the Capitalist States with their
alliances and agreements about the 'rights of peoples'."
But still she had faith that "international Socialism is too firmly
and deeply rooted to allow this breakdown to be permanent":
"Upon the horrible ruins of civilisation which Imperialism
has created the resurrection of the International, as the only
salvation of humanity from the hell of a degenerated and
outgrown class rule, shall take place....

From this war the rank and file will return to our old flag
of International Socialism, only with a more vehement
determination not to betray it again at the next Imperialist
orgy, but to defend it unitedly against the whole Capitalist
world, against their criminal intrigues, their infamous lies,
and their miserable phrases, and to establish it victoriously
on the ruins of their bloody Imperialism."

On the initiative of the Italian Socialist party many of them
met at Zimmerwald in 1915 and Kienthal in 1916. In addition
to the Italians the Russian were there in strength, the Menshevik,
Bolshevik, and other groups, the Balkan parties, Germans,
French, Swiss, Swedes, Poles, Serbs, Americans, Argentinians.
The ILP and British Socialist Party (predecessor of the Communist Party) were refused visas by the Government. At these
conferences Lenin put forward the idea of a break with the Socialist International and the formation of a Third International, but
the majority was heavily against him. The influence of the Zimmerwald parties and sections proved of great importance before
the end of the war.

The opposition to the war of the ILP was important within
the Labour movement both because of the standing of its leaders
and the strength and service of its members. There were then no
individual members of the Labour Party and the activists were
almost entirely ILPers. Its weekly journal, the *Labour Leader*,
had a circulation of 80,000. Its leaders included Hardie, Mac-
Donald, Snowden, Jowett, Anderson, Bruce, Glasier, Wallhead,
names which all respected.

The National Council of the party met a few days after the declaration of war and adopted a stirring and challenging manifesto. I recollect the ringing tones in which W C Anderson read the words, "Out of the darkness and the depth we hail our working-class comrades of every land. Across the roar of guns, we send sympathy and greetings to the German Socialists. They are no enemies of ours, but faithful friends." One other figure at the meeting is remembered. Keir Hardie was a broken man, struck down by his disappointment with the failure of the working class to prevent war. He died the following year.

Something which few Socialists from abroad can ever understand was the relationship of the ILP to the Labour Party during the war. The two parties were in division about the decisive issue of the time. Yet the ILP not only remained affiliated but the chairman of the Labour Party in 1914 was W C Anderson, the author of the manifesto just quoted! The ILP opposed the Labour Party entering the coalition government, opposed the party recruiting for the forces, opposed conscription, was in continual conflict. But because it believed that the trade union-political alliance would be necessary after the war it stayed inside the party. The position was made easier by the tolerance which the Labour Party showed.

A major fact in opposition to the war was the refusal of 16,000 men to be conscripted into the armed forces. Through the initiative of the members of the ILP the No Conscription Fellowship was formed, recruiting Socialist and religious resisters. Six thousand members were imprisoned, many for three years. I spent twenty-eight months in prison and was not released until April 1919, nearly six months after the Armistice. Except for a postcard formally announcing our arrival, we were not permitted to write for two months. At first I was not in mental revolt against imprisonment or its conditions; I was proud to undergo it as a witness to our anti-war convictions and I accepted punishment gladly as an honour in the cause. I regarded my cell as a kind of monk's retreat in which I could meditate and, so far as was allowed, read. It inspired me to know that I was one of six hundred men who were in the prison for refusal of war service. It was a heartening experience to go out on the exercise yard and see there a hundred fellow-resisters. But later the mood of acceptance of the prison regime ended completely. My first experience of the prison technique for overcoming the silence rule was in chapel. We were singing one of the chants. Instead of the words of the Prayer Book, I heard these :

> "Welcome, Fenner boy,
> When did you get here ?
> How did you like the skilly this morn ?
> Lord have mercy upon us !"

I looked round and there was A W Haycock, a Manchester ILP member, afterwards to become Member of Parliament for one of the Salford Divisions. He continued singing without any sign of recognition.

We COs had the same treatment as all other hard labour prisoners (that is, the harshest treatment meted out in English prisons) but we had the strengthening sense of comradeship and of standing out for our convictions. Yet even for most of us imprisonment sometimes became unbearable. We were locked in our cells for eighteen out of twenty-four hours each day. We could not speak to each other without the risk of bread and water punishment. We received and wrote one censored letter a month and had one half-hour visit, always in the presence of a warder. We were treated like caged animals. without minds or personality, and were starved of all beauty. The strain of this month after month was disastrous to self-control, and the long hours of solitary confinement drove one to the verge of mental and nervous breakdown, which could be conquered only by a great effort of discipline.

This, the first major war resistance movement, has an added significance today, after American opposition to conscription in the Vietnam war and the rejection of war by youth all over the world.

One other Left contribution must be mentioned : the Union of Democratic Control. It was formed to popularise a just peace and brought together a remarkable team—E D Morel, MacDonald, H N Brailsford, C P Trevelyan and others. Their writings influenced not only Labour thinking but that of a much wider field.

So we moved to the end of the war. In March 1917 the Russian revolution took place and the Workers and Soldiers Deputies who replaced the Duma (Parliament) issued a call to "the peoples of the entire world" to end the war through a united campaign for peace, and the new government endorsed the Zimmerwald peace aims of no annexations or indemnities and self-determination. The effect in Europe was electric and determining. All the Allied Powers were shocked; Socialists almost everywhere felt liberated. For the first time even pro-war Socialists were divided from their governments. In Britain revolutionary feeling reached probably its highest point. At an astonishingly representative conference at Leeds the call went out for the establishment of workers' and soldiers' councils throughout the country.

The Scandinavian and Dutch members of the Bureau of the Socialist International responded to the new mood. They stimulated the St Petersburg Soviet to call an international Socialist conference at Stockholm. At first the Socialist parties of Britain and France rejected the invitation, but representatives who travelled to St Petersburg to convince the Russians that there should be no peace until Germany was defeated, returned instead convinced. The British representative was Arthur Henderson, a member of the Government. When he applied for a passport, he was kept on the doormat while the Cabinet decided against him. That incident contributed to the decision of the Labour Party to leave the coalition government and renew its independent struggle.

The Stockholm Conference was never held, because the Bolshevik revolution of October 1917 meant that the desire for it disappeared both on the Russian side and among Social Democrats. But the Stockholm idea did much to restore the international spirit and aims of European Socialism. We have often gone back on them; but they still live and will yet triumph.

WILLIAM GALLACHER   *Revolt on the Clyde* (1936)
JOHN GRAHAM   *Conscription and Conscience, 1916–1919* (1922)
G D H COLE & RAYMOND POSTGATE   *The Common People* (1938, many times reprinted)
MARY AGNES HAMILTON   *Arthur Henderson* (1938)
FENNER BROCKWAY   *Inside the Left* (1942)

G D H COLE   *A History of the Labour Party from 1914* (1948)

STEPHEN GRAUBARD   *British Labour and the Russian Revolution* (Cambridge, Mass., 1956)

G D H COLE   *A History of Socialist Thought, volume IV, 1914–1931* (2 vols, 1958)

DAVID BOULTON   *Objection Overruled* (1967)

JULIUS BRAUNTHAL   *History of the International, 1914–1943* (Germany, 1963; English translation John Clark, 1967)

BERTRAND RUSSELL   *The Autobiography of Bertrand Russell,* vol. II (1968)

ASA BRIGGS & JOHN SAVILLE (eds)   *Essays in Labour History, 1886–1923* (1971 See in particular chs. 7 (James Hinton), 8 (Sidney Pollard), 9 (Royden Harrison)

MARGARET COLE   *The Life of G D H Cole* (1971)

JOHN RAE   *Conscience and Politics* (1970)

MARTIN SCHWARTZ   *The Union of Democratic Control in British Politics during the First World War* (1971)

Richard Clements
Guild Socialism

RICHARD CLEMENTS *was born in 1928. He wrote for various journals before becoming editor of* TRIBUNE *in 1961. He has held this post ever since. He is the author of* GLORY WITHOUT POWER: A STUDY OF TRADE UNIONISM IN OUR PRESENT SOCIETY *(1959), and a frequent broadcaster.*

"My own opinion—which I may as well indicate at the outset —is that pure Anarchism, though it should be the ultimate ideal, to which society should continually approximate, is for the present impossible, and would not survive more than a year or two at most if it were adopted. On the other hand, both Marxian Socialism and Syndicalism, in spite of many drawbacks, seems to me calculated to give rise to a happier and better world than that in which we live. I do not, however, regard either of them as the *best* practicable system. Marxian Socialism, I fear, would give far too much power to the state, while Syndicalism, which aims at abolishing the state, would, I believe, find itself forced to reconstruct a central authority in order to put an end to the rivalries of different groups of producers. The best practicable system, to my mind, is that of Guild Socialism, which concedes what is valid both in the claims of the state Socialists and in the Syndicates' fear of the state by adopting a system of federalism among trades for reasons similar to those which have recommended federalism among nations."

Guild Socialism? "The best practicable system?" Some 55 years have elapsed since those words were written by Bertrand

Russell in his book *Roads to Freedom* (published by Allen &
Unwin in 1918 and still, I am glad to say, in print). And who
now remembers what Guild Socialism was all about? Indeed who
remembers it at all?

And yet if you want to see its monument, look about you. Guild
Socialism is enshrined in the constitution of the Union of Post
Office Workers; in a more oblique way it has had its influence
on most of Britain's major trade unions (there is hardly a constitution that does not call for the ownership by the members
themselves of the industry in which they work).

Guild Socialism as an idea sprang from the fertile minds of
three men in the Labour movement from S G Hobson, who first
put the idea of National Guilds into practical form in a series of
articles published in the *New Age*; from A R Orage, the editor
of that paper, who was such a successful campaigner in the
National Guilds League which started during the first world war;
and, in particular, from that most imaginative of minds, G D H
Cole, who, in his book *Self-Government in Industry* (published
in 1917) tailored the theory to fit the British trade union movement.

What was the theory? The best description (and indeed
the widest discussion of Guild Socialism) comes in a book published first in 1918, *The Meaning of National Guilds* by M B
Reckitt and C E Bechhofer :

"A National Guild would be a democratically self-governing
association which, consisting of all the workers engaged
in any main industry, would be responsible for carrying it
on in conjunction with the state.

For example, a National Mining Guild would be composed
of every worker of all grades—administrative, skilled and
unskilled, on the surface and underground—actively engaged
in mining. As a democratic association its members would
be associated on an equal basis, and not in the undemocratic
relationship of employers and employees.

As a self-governing body, the National Mining Guild
would have full powers, without outside interference, over
all industrial matters affecting its members, over the
administration of all the mines in the country, and over
everything that concerned methods and conditions of mining.

Ownership of the mines and of the plant and other forms
of capital used in mining would be vested in the state, but they
would be at the disposal of the Mining Guild to be worked
in the public interest."

For perhaps five years the idea took firm root in the trade union
movement. Although it had been conceived by intellectuals,
it was so sensible and practical that it appealed to the instinct of
even the most conservative of the trade unionists. It was in the
building industry in Britain that for a brief few moments the
flame of practical Guild Socialism flickered and then went out.
Following the war there was a massive shortage of working-class
housing. The "homes fit for heroes" were failing to appear and
this gave some of the most prominent Guildsmen a chance to
capture both the imagination and power of the building unions.

Two men in particular did the work. They were S G Hobson
and Malcolm Sparkes. Hobson, as I have said before, provided
the ideas, while Sparkes played the role of organiser. It was he
who had succeeded in getting the Building Trades Parliament
established in May 1918. In this "Parliament" sat both worker
and employer. It produced an amazing document—the Foster
Report (named after a prominent employer in the North West)
which said: "We have glimpsed the possibility of the whole building industry of Great Britain being welded together into one self-
governing democracy of public service . . . We believe that the
great task of our industrial council is to develop an entirely new
system of industrial control by the members of the industry itself
—the actual producers, whether by hand or brain—and to bring
them into co-operation with the state as the central representatives of the community whom they are organised to serve."

Nothing much came of the Foster Report. But the ideas ran
deep into the movement of the building workers. S G Hobson
proposed to the Operative Bricklayers' Society in Manchester that
they should solve the housing deadlock by allying their labour
monopoly to the credit of the local authority. The following an-
nouncements then appeared in the *Guildsman*, the organ of the
movement:

"BIRTH—January 1920, at Manchester, Building Trade
Unionists and the National Guilds League, of a Guild.
Parents and child doing well.

MARRIAGE—January 1920, at Manchester, a marriage
has been arranged between the Labour-power of the building
workers and the credit of the public.

DEATH—January, 1920, at Manchester, the theory of the
necessity of Capitalism passed painlessly away. No flowers
by request."

It was a brave gesture. But, in the short run anyway, the victim
proved more hardy than the offspring of the unions and the public.

A Guild was formed in Manchester. The *Manchester Guardian* of January 21, 1920, spoke of it as possibly marking "a turning point in the industrial development of the country". And the idea spread like wildfire across the country and across continents. The *Guildsman* reported the formation of new building Guilds from Ireland, America and even New Zealand.

But all was not sweetness and light. The economic boom and inducement to build at almost any cost under the Addison Act of 1919, which had so assisted the building guilds, were followed by economic slump and a much more restricted role for local authority house building. Increasingly, hostility was manifested by building employers and by the Ministry of Health. Other employers were even more hostile. For some years the Manchester Guild continued and others sprang up in London. But the odds were against them. Isolated and constantly under pressure from the suppliers of the raw materials, they staggered first into debt and finally into liquidation. As much as anything else they were the victims of the circumstances of the situation at the time. The trade union movement was not in a mood to support small experiments. This was, after all, the height of the argument between the syndicalists and the "politicals" inside the movement. Within a few years the trade unions were to be faced with a General Strike and then to opt for a course which was to take them into permanent political alignment with the growing Labour Party.

On reflection, the impact of the experiments and the argument itself about Guild Socialism, seem to have been indeed feeble; a passing phase like so many we experience in socialist movements which seem to capture the imagination and project the future. When the fire is gone these ideas are observed like the craters of burnt-out volcanoes—subjects only for the study of historians.

But Guild Socialism is, in my view, completely different. It sprang not merely from the economic and social problems of the time, but from the history of the movement. Robert Owen's New Lanark was a forerunner as surely as the occupation of the Upper Clyde Shipbuilders, fifty years later, was an echo of the idea. It is an organic part of the movement, not an abstract idea which is immediately and theoretically attractive but whose roots find no sustenance in the soil from which it is supposed to grow.

There are those who have written about Guild Socialism as a theory. One can trace its shape and identify its weaknesses. But its strength really lies in the sense that it comes directly out of the experience of working men. It was the genius of G D H Cole that he understood the British Labour movement perhaps like no man before him and no man after him. What he was able to encapsulate in an idea was the aspiration of a movement; the driving force which make men and women suffer for a cause.

It is not likely that trade unionists will go back to history books to know what to do when they face redundancy in their industry and deprivation in their community. But they know what to do. And what they do is drawn from the experience of their movement and from the ideas which generate it.

How Guild Socialism has passed the test of time can be observed from the fact that its form can be seen in the rules of the craft societies which were the forerunners of modern trade unions and that those modern trade unions have carried it into their own constitutions.

The impact of the argument was enormous. Perhaps the greatest reason why now there is such a passionate interest in all aspects of industrial democracy springs from the work which was done by men like Hobson and Cole and Sparkes. The drive towards some type of workers' control of industry is a force which is inextinguishable inside the British Labour movement. What was attractive in the idea of Guild Socialism was that it made sense in terms of the national heritage of the movement.

A J PENTY *The Restoration of the Gild System* (1906)
HILAIRE BELLOC *The Servile State* (1912)
S G HOBSON assisted by A R ORAGE *National Guilds* (1914)

G D H COLE   *Self-Government in Industry* (1917)

M B RECKITT & C E BECHHOFER   *The Meaning of National Guilds* (1918)

BERTRAND RUSSELL   *Roads to Freedom* (1918)

S F HOBSON   *Pilgrim to the Left* (1938)

G D H COLE   *A History of Socialist Thought, volume III, 1889–1914* (2 vols, 1956)

S T GLASS   *The Responsible Society, The Ideas of Guild Socialism* (1966)

ASA BRIGGS & JOHN SAVILLE (eds)   *Essays in Labour History, 1886–1923* (1971), chs. 10 (Margaret Cole), 11 (Frank Matthews), 12 (Storrington Document)

MARGARET COLE   *The Life of G D H Cole* (1971)

Tony Mason
A J Cook and the General Strike

TONY MASON *was born in Gainsborough and read history at Hull University from 1959 till 1962. His PhD thesis was on the General Strike in Northumberland and Durham. He is the author of a number of articles and of* THE GENERAL STRIKE IN THE NORTH EAST *(1970). He is currently a lecturer in social history at the University of Warwick and is writing a book on the social history of association football.*

Some times are more propitious for general strikes than others. The year 1926 did not seem to be one of them. Britain was in the throes of what economic historians now call a restructuring of British industry. The old coalfield-based, heavy industries had begun to contract in size and the new, market-oriented, consumer goods industries, though expanding, could do little to fill the gap in employment and exports which had appeared. There had been over a million workers unemployed in every year since 1921. The membership of trade unions had steadily diminished. No one seemed to know what to do.

Conservatives stressed how important and possible it was to return to the leisured prosperity of Edwardian Britain. For them, recovery was always just around the corner. They even saw it coming in 1926 until the General Strike put the tin hat on it. Labour too had hope but little else. The first Labour Government had come and gone, and the next one, eagerly awaited, could hardly arrive before 1929.

Despite this, 1926 was perhaps not so surprising after all, because in essence the General Strike was a manifestation of the organised workers at the prospect of a further decline in living standards. Stanley Baldwin was widely reported as saying that all workers would have to take wage cuts if industry was to be put on its feet, and official denials did not reassure a knowing public.

All that was required to initiate a first-class industrial crisis was for employers in a major industry to attempt to improve their competitive position by attacking wages. This was a role in which the employers in the coal industry were almost word perfect. Coal was an old-fashioned industry in the twenties. Many of the colliery companies were small and the attitude of the employers to most problems had been moulded during a nineteenth century in which the industry had continuously expanded. Productivity in the industry had been falling since before 1914 but this had been largely concealed because world demand for coal was apparently insatiable. The war demolished Britain's export trade, stimulated the search for substitutes and encouraged the opening up of new coalfields all over the world. The post-war disruption of international trade, the competition of new fuels, the increased efficiency with which coal was utilised all contributed to a slowing down in the rate of expansion, in spite of an ephemeral recovery in the industry in 1923–4.

The colliery owners had one answer to this problem : wages formed a high proportion of their total costs, therefore they must come down. But if the owners were resolute, so were the miners. They favoured nationalisation as a solution to the industry's ills and it still rankled that the Government had rejected the majority verdict of the Sankey Commission supporting nationalisation in 1919.

There were over one million miners organised in county associations which were federated in a large national union, the Miners' Federation of Great Britain (MFGB); mining communities tended to be monolithic and to ooze solidarity in the face of an enemy who was ever present and the industry was notorious for the straightforward, jackets-off method of settling industrial disputes. You fought until you dropped.

This obstinate, militant, fighting spirit was epitomised by A J Cook, General Secretary of the Miners' Federation of Great Britain from 1924 to 1931. Cook was born in Somerset in 1884 but moved to South Wales at the age of 16 where he was involved in the evangelical revivalist movement around 1900. However his experiences as a miner brought an awareness of politics and he became a member of the Independent Labour Party in 1905. He was associated with the Syndicalist Unofficial Reform Committee, which produced the famous *Miners' Next Step* in 1912. He spent a year at the Central Labour College and during the war was a pacifist. He probably became a full-time miners' agent in 1921.

By the 'twenties, most trade union leaders were beginning to have the modern stamp of bureaucratic functionary about them; they were professional negotiators with a vested interest in the expansion and stability of the organisation which had spawned them. Cook was very different. He was a miner first and last, and seemed to represent the resentment, toughness and narrow-mindedness of all those who worked at the hard and dangerous trade. It is doubtful if he was a good negotiator. He was too impatient at the sins of a system which allowed such gross iniquities to flourish.

He cannot easily be politically labelled. He often supported the position of the Communist Party and he undoubtedly benefited from the votes of the Left when elected as general secretary of the MFGB in 1924. But he had no fixed theoretical position. He saw capitalism as a monstrous thing which must be fought wherever possible and with whatever weapons were to hand. It is not too fanciful to see Cook as an embodiment of a kind of radical, practical Christianity. At any rate, he certainly spoke for the miners, however incoherent, disorganised and romantic his words.

The colliery owners made the initial moves in the summer of 1925 when they gave notice that the current wages agreement would have to be revised. It was at this time that Cook staked out the miners' position by his slogan, "Not a penny off the pay, not a minute on the day." It was a position from which they did not budge.

The confrontation of 1925 ended in Red Friday, with the transport workers' unions threatening an embargo on the movement of all coal and the Government, at the very last minute, setting up yet another Royal Commission to inquire into the future of the industry. A subsidy was to be paid so that miners' wages could remain unchanged while the Commission deliberated. Cook recognised that this was only a half-time lead, for it quickly became obvious that the Government had no intention of letting the matter rest there. The Royal Commission might fail to produce a settlement of the dispute. The Government activated its emergency services organisation so that, should the coal industry be brought to a standstill and should other trade unionists again embark on sympathetic action, they would find not merely a solid defence, but a side determined on attack.

Cook had, earlier in 1925, begun a programme of weekend speeches in mining areas throughout the United Kingdom, but tressing the solidarity of the men and warning that another fight may lie ahead. He talked, fairly vaguely, of preparations by the labour movement although the MFGB agreed with the TUC early in 1926 to shelve Walter Citrine's scheme of precautions. It was during these early months of 1926 that Cook became the bogey-man of the middle classes everywhere. Every Monday morning, or so it must have seemed, another blood-curdling quotation appeared in the newspapers. It is difficult to assess the value of his public pronouncements. He certainly encouraged the miners, although he might have misled them by his exaggerated talk of international co-operation and Co-operative Society help should there be a strike. But as well as frightening his opponents he probably solidified their determination.

What terrors would result if 1926 saw another victory for the "humble disciple of Lenin?" As Jack Lawson, a fellow-miner, wrote later, "Had the Secretary of the miners been the mildest man in the world, the miners would still have rejected the demands of the coal-owners."

The Report of the Royal Commission was rejected by both owners and men; by the former, because it advocated future reorganisation of the industry, by the latter because it laid down that wages must fall if the industry was to survive. The Government and the TUC, each in their own way, contributed to the muddle which followed. Negotiations broke down and a meeting of trade union executives agreed to support the miners by a withdrawal of labour in certain selected trades from midnight on May 3.

They were doing this in order to persuade the Government to

persuade the owners to withdraw their lock-out notices. Nothing here about fighting for Cook's slogan. It is clear that the TUC felt that there must be some downward adjustment of miners' wages but that the other side of a compromise solution must be reorganisation. The owners rejected this, believing that they only had to sit back and wait for the miners to run out of money. The Government refused to coerce the owners, feeling that industry must sort out its own problems and never really believing in the possibilities of the General Strike, stigmatised it as a threat to the Parliamentary system and ruptured the final negotiations on the strength of it.

Why did the General Strike fail? In the first place, due to Government determination plus an emergency organisation which, after all, only had to deliver the goods for nine days. Secondly because the TUC was far from convinced that a general strike was the correct policy for a respectable, constitutional trade union movement. In 1925 it had succeeded, for a variety of reasons, in bluffing the Government by threats. In 1926 it hoped to repeat the performance. When its bluff was called it did not know what to do. It could not stand on the miners' slogan because that was not "constructive" and it did not believe that it could be maintained. It could not retreat immediately because that would only further jeopardise a movement slowly losing members as it was realised that being a trade unionist was of little consequence in this depression. It was involved in a strike although it did not like it. Beneath the veneer of mass solidarity lurked inter-union differences. It was all right for the miners; no one would take their jobs. Transport workers would have to bear the brunt of the strike and might find their jobs kept by volunteers at the end of it. Perhaps everyone would have to accept wage reductions.

The respectable trade union official, who had risen from engine cleaner to Cabinet Minister via the labour movement, was reluctant to see that movement smashed by the Government. Social mobility, perhaps even socialism, was possible in time. It would be criminal to spoil that prospect by heroic but hopeless action. Even if everyone called out came out, the Government had shown it did not intend to sit back and be made redundant. If the strike proved successful, the only beneficiaries would be the communists.

This kind of reasoning negated the solidarity of the strikers in the districts and the General Strike did not really last long enough to test seriously the Government's nerve. It was just long enough to determine the trade union leadership never to have another; and the defeat in 1926 made certain that Labour movement responses to the depression would always fall short of direct action.

Cook and the miners take the prize for consistency. They take it for obstinacy and stupidity as well. There were several occasions during the six months of the miners' stoppage on which Cook appeared to favour a settlement but he could never quite push it through. Did the miners get the leaders they deserved? Was the cumbrous democracy of the MFGB an obstacle to enlightened leadership? It is difficult to escape the feeling that a more flexible, tactical approach, an acceptance of the attempted compromise known as the Samuel Memorandum for example, might have salvaged a good deal.

There is no question that Cook felt deeply the tragedy of 1926. He remains a legend in mining areas. Old men will tell you of the large crowds which gathered at his open-air meetings, and the strength which those meetings gave to every individual present. Although the words spoken were but a small part of the occasion, some impression can be gained of the man, his style and his impact by reading what he said. A speech which he made in County Durham on October 16, 1926, reflects the strained situation of the time:

"I would be a happy man if I could say that Monday would see the wheels turning and the buzzer going. I would be a happy man if I could sign an agreement which would give an honourable peace to the industry. Some people say 'fight it out'. Whoever say fight it out are not thinking men and women, but we have to fight because we cannot do anything else. No self-respecting leader could advise you to consider for one moment the proposals you have had before you. Twenty-four different agreements terminating at different times and twenty-four minimums. It is unthinkable...

"We never led you out alone, but I say here and now to those unions who decided to come into the struggle, and I say it advisedly and not in any carping spirit, that I would rather they had told us on May 1 that they did not intend to stand by us than come out and then leave us . . .

"We have brought nationalisation nearer. While we are not fighting that question in this struggle, which is for life and bread, the nation is bound to recognise, that the cost, namely £300 million, is more than will pay two years' wages to every employee in the industry. The one clear issue is that we are fighting to retain the conditions we had in April, not because we believe that they were too good, because we believe that they were too bad to be lowered. Durham has stood solid and has been an example to other counties. Other counties have broken away and it is that fact which prolongs the struggle . . .

"Peace on terms dictated by starvation is no peace. If there is to be peace in this industry, then it can only come by mutual agreements, by an agreement that is honourable, and by an agreement that can be kept."

E BURNS *The General Strike 1926: Trade Councils in Action* (1926)

K MARTIN *The British Public and the General Strike* (1926)

W H CROOK *The General Strike* (Chapel Hill, N. Carolina, 1931)

H A CLEGG *Some Consequences of the General Strike* (Manchester Statistical Society 1953/4, iii)

C L MOWAT *Britain Between the Wars* (1955, paperback 1968)

J SYMONS *The General Strike* (1957)

A BULLOCK *The Life and Times of Ernest Bevin*, vol. I (1960)

A MASON *The General Strike in the North East* (Hull, 1970)

C FARMAN *The General Strike* (1972)

Robert Skidelsky
The Labour Party & the Slump

ROBERT SKIDELSKY *was born in 1939. He was educated at Brighton College and Jesus College, Oxford. From 1965 he was a research fellow, first at Nuffield College, Oxford, and then at the British Academy. Since 1970 he has taught in the United States and at present he is Associate Professor of History, School of Advanced International Studies, Johns Hopkins University. His publications include* POLITICIANS AND THE SLUMP *(1967),* ENGLISH PROGRESSIVE SCHOOLS *(1969),* THE AGE OF AFFLUENCE, 1951–1964 *(co-editor with Vernon Bogdanor, 1970) and contributions to* ENCOUNTER *and other journals. His biography of Oswald Mosley will be published in 1974 and he has begun work on a biography of J M Keynes.*

It can scarcely be denied that the Labour Party in the inter-war years suffered a series of massive defeats. So there's no point in writing about this phase of the people's past in terms appropriate to a triumphal procession. Rather the aim should be to understand how and why these defeats occurred in a period when mass unemployment and economic dislocation seemed to provide the opportunity and the spur for radical change.

The failures of the party were not only dismaying to radicals at the time; they have been the subject of learned historical argument ever since. Theories range all the way from the "aristocratic embrace" first advanced by the Webbs in 1931 to more recent ones of working-class defeatism, which a Labour leadership merely reflected—a kind of pseudo-Marxism, with the Marxist premises stood on their head.

It's unfortunate that the question of who was to blame has become an internal party one, with the Labour Left blaming a conservative leadership, and the Labour Right emphasising the limited and defensive aspirations of the workers. For it is obvious, I think, that the two cannot be separated. A weak and lacklustre leadership may be the result of a lack of working-class reforming zeal; it also helps to limit the hopes and expectations of its clients. For example, it may be true (as W G Runciman has argued) that in the 1920's manual workers regarded unemployment as an Act of God, to be endured rather than cured. But would this conviction have been so widespread had the Labour leaders not encouraged it? For what, after all, was this Act of God other than those "facts of the situation" to which Labour leaders appealed as an excuse for not doing anything.

Despite the absence, for whatever reason, of a revolutionary zeal in the English working-class, it cannot be denied that there existed very considerable support for radical change. After all, 13 million people out of 21 million voted against Safety First in 1929. What did they think they were voting for? Merely for a change of faces in Whitehall? Surely not. Unemployment was the central issue in the election and since both Liberal and Labour Parties promised a cure, it would seem reasonable to suppose that 13 million people were voting for a more vigorous unemployment policy.

This must not be pushed too far. The experts have assured us that the way people vote has little relation to the policies put forward by the parties. Nevertheless, the evidence does not suggest a conservative electorate in the 1920's. Its attitude can best be described as permissive, prepared for experiment, potentially responsive to success, but not prepared to force a party or Government into a vigorous course of action. (There was no public outcry about mass unemployment as there would be today.)

It is true that it never gave the Labour Party a mandate for nationalisation, its main remedy. But nationalisation on its own meant very little, as the left-wing ILP realised. To take a concrete example: in 1927 the Labour Party pledged itself to nationalise the Bank of England. Let us assume that had it had a majority in 1929 it would have carried this out. Yet the mere act of nationalisation would have changed nothing unless a Labour

Government had been prepared to run the Bank in a different way—for example, by reflating instead of deflating the economy.

Similarly, nationalisation of the coalmines (another commitment) would have meant little to coalminers unless the Government had been prepared to operate a high-wage rather than a low-wage policy, or to provide unemployed miners with alternative jobs. Instead Snowden and other Labour leaders believed that even a nationalised Bank must be free from "political interference", that coalminers' wages were determined by forces outside the Government's control, and that it was not up to a Government to enter into the labour market.

With these views it was difficult to make socialism relevant to the economic problem. We have a paradoxical situation. Politically, with the rise of the Labour Party and the collapse of the Liberals, socialism became a key national issue. On the substantive level, however, it was progressively drained of content until it became that "far off Never-Never land" of MacDonald's oratory, "a Turner landscape of beautiful colours and glorious indefiniteness," as MacNeill Weir described it. And this divorce of socialism from the actual problems facing the community of course helped to breed that attitude of resignation which Runciman and others have found to be characteristic of the period.

It is important to understand how this divorce had come about. The whole of the Labour Party's gradualist philosophy of social change rested on the continued success of a British-controlled world capitalist system. Capitalism, the Webbs proclaimed in 1900, had solved the problem of production. The task of socialism was to ensure that the growing total of wealth generated by the system as a whole was distributed and organised in relation to the people's needs, rather than to the interests of a minority.

The Labour Party never expected to be faced with the problem of a breakdown in production. Hence it never imagined that it might be called upon to create a market in order to enable production to continue. It accepted, of course, the existence of the trade-cycle, during which men would be thrown out of work. But it assumed that this would be temporary only. Hence its slogan Work or Maintenance. Capitalism could normally be expected to provide work. In its periods of temporary breakdown, the

Labour Party's job above all was to provide its victims with adequate maintenance, not to take on the responsibility of finding them work.

By the 1920's this programme bore little relation to current reality. World capitalism was not healthy; there was no growing product to be redistributed. For most of the decade production was *below* what it had been in 1913, though the population had increased, and in 1930 it slumped catastrophically. The historic task of the Labour Party in the 1920's, therefore, became not one of redistributing wealth, but of stimulating production. For this task the more recent English socialist classics offered no guidance. The one section of the Labour Party that tried to relate socialism to mass unemployment was the ILP. Here the influence of the writer J A Hobson was very important. It was Hobson who insisted on the connection between unemployment and the maldistribution of wealth. The "over-saving" of the rich, in Hobson's view, led to the overproduction of commodities in relation to the consumption power of the poor, producing glut and unemployment. Redistributing wealth, therefore, was not just a matter of social justice, to be undertaken when the system could "afford" it, but a necessary measure to raise demand.

Out of these insights the ILP fashioned its *Living Wage* Proposals (1926) calling for an increase in "mass purchasing power". Oswald Mosley and John Strachey, two ex-Tory recruits to the ILP, reached similar practical conclusions via Keynes. In their *Revolution by Reason* (1925) they called not so much for redistribution as for an expansion in the money supply, to be directed towards the "necessitous areas of poverty". In both sets of proposals nationalisation was relegated to a subordinate role, as a threat to capitalists if they refused to comply, rather than as a dynamic element in the proposals.

Official Labour reaction was extremely cool. "Flashy futilities", announced MacDonald. "A combination of conceit and ignorance", wrote Beatrice Webb. In their view unemployment was caused by the dislocations of war, and the first priority of a Labour Government should be to restore the international economy to health. Hence Labour's fervent support for the Gold Standard and Free Trade at precisely the time when these things had started to stand for mass unemployment and economic stagnation.

The nemesis of 1931 is too well-known to require detailed re-capitulation. The collapse of MacDonald's government in face of the world depression was both intellectual and moral, and the second was more important. One's appreciation of a problem generally reflects what one is prepared to do about it—not the other way round, as academics like to think. The Labour Government was prepared to do very little about unemployment—it had rejected Lloyd George's and Mosley's schemes with contempt—and therefore it was forced to take the "optimistic" view as about a third of the $8\frac{1}{2}$ million people who voted for it in 1929 to save them from the dole now found themselves on the dole.

Admittedly there was an intellectual problem. The ILP tended to treat Britain as a closed system, whereas what impressed the Labour leaders was England's daunting dependence on world markets. Russia might be able to build socialism in one country; America to sustain a high-wage economy behind tariff barriers; but how could England which exported 25 per cent of its production hope to emulate either? The fact that this made the achievement of British socialism dependent on the success of international capitalism might be unfortunate, but it was one of those "facts of the situation" from which there was no escape. There was nothing for it but to sit it out, hopefully prodding the natural forces of recovery into action. Can Labour really be blamed for not anticipating that this crisis of the international order would be prolonged for 20 years or more?

This whole argument begs the question of how the Labour Party had come to saddle itself in the first place with such an *optimistic* theory of international development. It is not enough to say that it arose out of the late nineteenth century. The late nineteenth century after all was a period of acute capitalist crisis, especially for England which was starting to bear the full brunt of intensified competition from newly-emerging industrial rivals. Imperialism and tariffs threatened to cut the lines of world trade. Admittedly there was a trade recovery in the years before the First World War; but the war itself exposed the fragility of liberal international assumptions.

In other words, there was plenty of evidence for all who wanted to see it, that the international system was breaking down and that England's own position in it was steadily weakening (Joseph

Chamberlain and the Imperialists saw this very clearly). In these circumstances, to base a socialist strategy on the continuing and increasing success of this system and to persist with that belief right through the inter-war years suggests almost a wilful perversity. The truth seems to be that the Labour Party could not abandon its "optimistic" international prognostications without simultaneously abandoning its commitment to Parliamentary gradualism; its economic ideas, in other words, were functional to its political strategy. The more one unravels the tangled history of the inter-war years the more one realises the futility of looking at economic ideas in themselves. They are an expression of a theory of politics and society. For example, the notorious Treasury View of the 1920's (that all existing resources were fully employed by private industry) was no more than the economic expression of the liberal theory of Government (that Government had no role to play in the economy). Similarly Labour's obsolete economic opinions reflected a theory of politics that shrank from confrontation or struggle, and a theory of Government that shrank from the idea of a strong State.

For the doctrine that socialism could be built on the surpluses of capitalism (i.e. painlessly) removed (i) the need for the class struggle or for a "populist" style of democracy and (ii) the need to use the power of the State to attack vested interests. Ruled out of the theory of the transition to socialism was any notion of real conflict, of pain, suffering, violence. Socialism was to be achieved not through the anger of the exploited and downtrodden but through the growing consensus of men of goodwill. In this way the evolving socialist society could be squared with the practice of traditional Parliamentary politics, with its simultaneous fear of the masses and of a strong State.

The Bank of England could be both nationalised and freed from "political control" (in the sense of divisive political control); the lot of the people could be improved without the people having to be introduced as actors in the drama; industry could be organised round some generally accepted notion of the public interest. A booming society could be persuaded to accept some if not all of a socialist programme with a minimum of struggle because there was enough to go round for all. In an economically vulnerable society, on the other hand, socialism could only be achieved with struggle. That is why prosperity was a condition of the Labour Party's political strategy.

There was obviously something in this view. Why have a terrific fight if you can get progress by peaceful means? Post-1945 affluence has certainly enabled moderate social change by broad consent. There is obviously a great deal that can be said on either side of this question. My main point, though, is that such a strategy was simply not on the agenda for most of the inter-war years; indeed might never have returned to the agenda had it not been for the Second World War. For the decisive reason for the transformation of the international economy after 1945 was not the triumph of Keynesianism (America did not become Keynesian till 1963) but the triumph of American power following the war which enabled it to "manage" the "free world" economy much as Britain had managed it in the nineteenth century. The full-employment economies of the Western nations were built not on Keynesianism or socialism but on Marshall Aid, NATO, and the dollar deficit.

By contrast, in the inter-war years it had to be a national recovery programme or nothing. This would have necessitated strengthening the power of the State; which in turn would have involved the mobilisation of mass support. For in a democracy a strong State can only be built on popular support, just as a weak State rests on popular apathy. Yet the Labour Party, both in opposition and government, shrank from attempting to arm itself with that extra authority it would need to cope with vested interests entrenched behind the "rights" of private property, the rights of individuals, the rights of local authorities, the rights of everyone except those of the mass of the wage-earners. Such a strategy would have been foreign to its whole conception of Parliamentary Government, the rules of the game, and so on. As Élie Halévy summed it up after the fiasco of 1931 :

"This is the tragedy. The Labour leaders are men whose doctrine requires them to make the State stronger, and whose good British instinct is to make the State as weak as possible . . . I am afraid that rather than socialistic in spirit they are whiggish, eager to protect the individual against the State, not to make the State strong against Capitalists."

After dutifully cataloguing the failures and disasters of the inter-war years most writers on the period end up with the conventional words of praise for the resilience of our Parliamentary institutions and the "common sense" of our politicians. It is surely time that historians started weighing these virtues against the 20 years of mass unemployment and sermonising without action that accompanied them.

For this the Labour Party bears a heavy responsibility. True, it survived to fight another day, and this was in itself an achievement. We can all learn something from its harrowing experience. But that experience was bought at very considerable cost to the lives and hopes of millions of men, women and children in Britain.

EGON WERTHEIMER   *Portrait of the Labour Party* (1929)

JOHN SCANLON   *The Decline and Fall of the Labour Party* (1932)

ÉLIE HALÉVY   *The Era of Tyrannies* (Paris 1938, English translation R K Webb, New York, 1965)

RALPH MILIBAND   *Parliamentary Socialism* (1961)

W G RUNCIMAN   *Relative Deprivation and Social Justice* (1966)

R S SAYERS   *A History of Economic Change in England, 1880–1939* (1967)

R SKIDELSKY   *Politicians and the Slump* (1967, paperback 1970)

DAVID MARQUAND   "The Politics of Deprivation", *Encounter*, vol. 32, April 1969

ROYDEN HARRISON   "Labour Government: Then and Now", *Political Quarterly*, vol. 41, no. 1, Jan.–March 1970

SIDNEY POLLARD (ed.)   *The Gold Standard and Unemployment Policies* (1970)

Philip Bagwell
The Left in the 'Thirties

PHILIP BAGWELL *joined the ILP at the age of 16 in 1930 and later in the 1930's attended its summer schools as well as those of the Left Book Club. He graduated in Modern Economic History at University College, Southampton (where he was the first chairman of the Socialist Society), and gained his PhD at the LSE in 1950. He is at present professor of history at the Polytechnic of Central London.* He is author of THE RAILWAYMEN: THE HISTORY OF THE NUR *(1963)*, THE RAILWAY CLEARING HOUSE IN THE BRITISH ECONOMY 1842–1922 *(1968), and* BRITAIN AND AMERICA, 1850–1939: A STUDY OF ECONOMIC CHANGE *(co-author with G E Mingay, 1970). His essay "The Triple Industrial Alliance 1913–1922" was published in* ESSAYS IN LABOUR HISTORY 1886–1923 *(eds Asa Briggs and John Saville, 1971). From 1965–70 he was Hon Secretary of the Society for the Study of Labour History.*

To someone, like the writer, who was, in turn, schoolboy, student and young adult worker in the 1930's, the dominant political controversies of the day concerned unemployment and the threat of fascism and war. In the early years of the decade a solution of the problem of unemployment was seen as the most urgent task; in the later years the war danger overshadowed all other issues.

It is a current fashion to refer to the 1930's as years of more rapid economic growth than was experienced in any earlier period of the century. The production figures for motor cars, radios, electric cookers and council houses have convinced a number of the newer generation of historians that the standard of living of the British people was rising in the years before Munich. The picture is misleading because it has relevance only to some parts of Britain. In Greater London, the South East and parts of the East Midlands the percentage of the insured population out of work was little more than half the national average and job opportunities in the newer industries were increasing. The older industrial districts presented a bleak contrast. To suggest to an older generation miner of the Rhondda, or cotton operative of Oldham or boilermaker of Jarrow that the 1930's were prosperous would be to invite unprintable language.

The contrast between the South East and the depressed areas should not be pushed too far. London had a larger number of completely destitute persons than did South Wales or Lancashire, as family and community support for the underprivileged was stronger in the provinces than in in the capital. It was nevertheless true that many southerners had little conception of the blighted hopes and the helplessness that prolonged unemployment had brought to the shipyard towns, the coalfields and the older manufacturing districts of Britain.

The big danger was the growth of complacency. One of the most serious human aspects of the poor performance of the British economy between the wars was the existence of prolonged unemployment. In January 1932 there were 480,000 adults who had been out of work for more than a year. In 1936, when the total number of unemployed had dropped to 1,755,000, from the peak of 2,840,000 at the end of 1932, there were still as many as 205,000 persons who had been without work for over *two* years. Fatalism and apathy spread both among the long-unemployed and among the general public. To be for extended periods without work came to be regarded as the inevitable misfortune of some of the British race.

This was why writers such as George Orwell, Ellen Wilkinson and Walter Greenwood and agitators like Wal Hannington served the nation well by reminding the comfortably-off what life was really like for the less fortunate. We can forgive Orwell his jaundiced view of the Socialist intellectuals of his day because in his *Road to Wigan Pier* (1937) he stirred the conscience of his generation. He painted an unforgettable picture of pensioners driven from their families by the working of the Means Test and subsisting in dirty, inhospitable lodging houses. Those who saw Wendy Hiller as Sally Hardcastle in the dramatic version of

Walter Greenwood's *Love on the Dole* (published 1933) were reminded that "love's all right on t'Pictures, but love on the dole ain't quite the same thing".

The story of the organisation of the unemployed is indelibly linked with the name of Wal Hannington, founder of the National Unemployed Workers' Movement in 1921. Although in his *Unemployed Struggles 1919–36* (1936) and *The Problem of the Distressed Areas* (1937) he wrote a vivid record of his experiences, it was principally through the organisation of the hunger marches that he brought to the attention of the public and the National Government the plight of the unemployed. A man of unbounded energy and resourcefulness who also possessed a lively sense of humour, he was one of the great working class leaders of the 1930's. His achievement was to gain recognition for the unemployed as dignified human beings worthy of better treatment than was meted out to them under the National Government's economy measures of 1931–4. When Arthur Greenwood, Minister of Health under MacDonald's Labour Government, ordered that the hunger marchers of 1930 were to be treated in the same way as "casuals" in workhouses the movement "never accepted such treatment anywhere because, under pressure, the local authorities and Workhouse Masters gave way and broke the Minister's instruction" (*Never On Our Knees*, 1967). In June 1933 when 2,000 Scottish hunger marchers were refused overnight accommodation by the Edinburgh city authorities they slept on the pavement in Princes Street. This brought quick results. The following night they were allowed to sleep in various halls in the city.

It was alleged that the violence which accompanied demonstrations of the unemployed in Birkenhead, West Ham and elsewhere was partly due to the aggressiveness of the police and the actions of *agents provocateur*. Thus when it was planned that eighteen contingents of hunger marchers should converge on London in February 1934 a group of people met in the crypt of St Martin in the Field, Trafalgar Square, to form the National Council of Civil Liberties, with backing from such influential people as Clem Attlee, Vera Brittain and A P Herbert. A number of its members, including H G Wells, agreed to mingle with the crowd at Hyde Park when the contingent of hunger marchers

arrived. Over 100,000 persons were present to welcome representatives of the unemployed from places as far apart as Aber-
deen and Plymouth. It may be argued that the peaceful outcome
of this great demonstration was ensured through the English
drizzle dampening the ardour of the crowd: one suspects that
police knowledge of the presence of distinguished middle-class
observers in the Park also had something to do with it. It is significant that in his Budget speech a few weeks later Neville Chamberlain announced the full restoration of the cuts in unemployment benefit made in 1931.

The agitation continued throughout the decade. In 1938 unemployed demonstrators carried a black coffin inscribed with the
words "He did not get winter relief". Thereafter Hannington
was engaged in a prolonged, and often good-humoured, battle of
wits with the police to escape, not only his own arrest, but also
the "arrest" of the coffin.

The hunger marchers, by drawing attention to the seemingly
intractable nature of the unemployment problem, helped to bring
about the first major period of political activity amongst students.
There was a University Socialist Federation at Cambridge as
early as 1912 and the University Labour Federation was founded
in Oxford in 1921. These two bodies merged in 1923. But with
the exception of the days of the General Strike in 1926 there was
little political activity for more than a decade after the First World
War. The years of the great depression brought rapid change in
the Universities. Early in 1932 the avowedly Marxist October
Club was formed in Oxford and the Marxist Society began activity in the London School of Economics. In April 1933 these,
and other recently formed Socialist Societies, united in The Federation of Student Societies. When members of the October Club
marched with their banners at the head of a column of the unemployed Duff Cooper (a prominent Conservative and later a
Cabinet Minister) commented that "the University authorities
would know how to deal with stupidity of this sort". However,
the students' participation was not merely youthful bravado. Owing to a decrease in the school population of 350,000 between
1932–5 there was a substantial surplus of qualified teachers and
admissions to the universities were cut back. The theme song of
Giles Playfair and his Oxford Blazers—"Third Year Blues"—

was written round one central idea "We've no work to do". The motives of the small group of students who marched to winchester with the Southampton contingent of hunger marchers in February 1934 were mixed. Admittedly it was an exciting adventure. But in the *Student Vanguard* we had read of the poor employment prospects for graduates. It was our future as well as theirs that was at stake.

The complete failure of the second Labour Government to stem the rising tide of unemployment sprang principally from the sharp decline in world trade and other circumstances largely beyond the control of MacDonald and his Cabinet. But it was aggravated by the deadening financial orthodoxy of Philip Snowden and the inanities of J H Thomas who sought an agreement to export coal to Canda in return for large imports of unmilled wheat, in the belief that this would be a substantial contribution to the relief of unemployment. Much new thinking was needed if a debacle like that of the October 1931 general election was to be avoided in the future.

In this context the formation of the Society for Socialist Inquiry and Propaganda in the autumn of 1930 by a group of "Loyal Grousers" including G D H and Margaret Cole, Ernest Bevin, Clem Attlee, Stafford Cripps and others had considerable significance. They believed that the Labour Party was the only possible vehicle for establishing a Socialist Britain but they were also convinced that much self-education was necessary and that a new crusade to convert the public was desperately needed. In March 1931 the Coles and their friends were largely instrumental in creating the New Fabian Research Bureau, which sponsored more fundamental research work, such as the full-length study, *The Socialisation of Iron and Steel* (1936) by "Ingot" (R W B Clarke), and helped to supply the SSIP and later the Socialist League with their shot and shell. In 1939 it merged with the older Fabian Society.

Meanwhile the hitherto influential Independent Labour Party, desperately disappointed with the performance of the MacDonald government and convinced that "reformism" was a bankrupt policy, was tearing itself apart on the question of disaffiliation from the Labour Party. The special conference of the ILP at Bradford in July 1932, under the spell of James Maxton's magnetic personality and the advice of the doyen of the party, Fred Jowett, voted by 241 to 142 in favour of disaffiliation. It even ruled that trade union members should cease to pay the political levy to the Labour Party and that no member of the ILP should hold joint membership with the Labour Party. Fenner Brockway, a leading participant, records (in *Inside the Left,* 1942) that in the next two years the ILP "experimented in many directions, at one time approaching the Communist International and at another moving towards the Trotskyist position, at one stage attaching its hope to united fronts and at another reverting to purism; at one period going all out to prepare for Soviets and at another recognising again the value of Parliament". In 1934 the disaffiliation decision was at last reversed, but by then "much damage had been done". The minority, including Frank Wise, Pat Dollan and David Kirkwood, who were against disaffiliation in 1932, joined forces later that year with Cripps, Brailsford, Mellor and Laski of the SSIP to form the Socialist League, affiliated to the Labour Party. When the ex-ILP members would not accept him as leader of the new organisation, Ernest Bevin was strengthened in his conviction that the "intellectuals" of the labour movement were not to be trusted. In his autobiography (*Men and Work*, 1964) Lord (then Sir Walter) Citrine, who was general secretary of the TUC throughout the 'thirties, recorded that in 1937 G D H Cole wrote asking Bevin, as leader of Britain's largest trade union, to contribute an article to a book he was editing. In his reply, turning down the offer, Bevin wrote that he would "not have anything to do . . . with the antics of the Left Book Club, Gollancz and Laski". Citrine was equally hostile.

In the light of what was happening on the international scene the suspicion which the giants of the trade union world entertained of some of the leading socialist intellectuals greatly reduced the prospects of a widely-inclusive popular front in Britain.

The members of the Socialist League believed that if the Communists and Social Democrats in Germany had conducted a united campaign in resistance to the Nazis, instead of attacking each other, Hitler would not have come to power on 30 January, 1933. For this reason they welcomed the formation of united fronts of Socialist and Communists in France and Spain in 1934 and they saw the outcome of the Spanish general election of 16 February, 1936 and the formation of the Blum Front Populaire government of June in the same year as confirmation of their view that the onward march of Fascism could only be halted through the unity of the parties of the left in defence of collective security and social reform. On the other hand the Labour Party Executive, dominated by right wingers Bevin, Dalton and Morrison and backed at annual conferences by the block vote of the transport workers, saw infiltration of the labour movement by the Communist Party as a menace as serious as the spread of Fascism and they therefore rejected all proposals for United Fronts or Popular Fronts.

Hitler's re-militarisation of the Rhineland on 7 March, 1936, and the Franco-led rebellion of 16 July of the same year, sparking off the Spanish Civil War, were seen by the British Left as urgent danger signals that time was running out in the struggle to save the peace. One response to the events in Spain was the formation of a British Battalion of the International Brigade fighting in defence of the beleagured republic. The fact that some of Britain's most promising poets and authors, including John Cornford and Ralph Fox, gave their lives in Spain is well known : that they were greatly outnumbered by Welsh miners and other industrial workers is not so often appreciated. For sympathisers who stayed in Britain there were concerts of the Basque children to organise and protests against the farce of the Non-Intervention Agreement.

From January 1937 the campaign for a Popular Front received powerful support from the new weekly, *Tribune*, which had Stafford Cripps as its principal backer, William Mellor as its first editor and Michael Foot as "the cook's assistant and chief bottle-washer in the back room". In one of his first contributions to the paper, Nye Bevan answered those who maintained that it was inconsistent for the Left to oppose rearmament whilst at the same time advocating a policy of collective security. He warned that no collective peace policy was possible with a Tory government in power. "Under the influence of that dangerous delusion many Labour men have been seduced into playing at diplomacy with the Foreign Office. When Labour leaders substitute the role of courtier for that of agitator, they fail at both." (See *Tribune 21*.)

Giving ample evidence of the Baldwin and Chamberlain governments' pursuit of a policy of appeasement, rather than collective security, was a "small monstrosity" called *The Week*, whose editor and proprietor, Claud Cockburn, for many years one of the foremost correspondents of *The Times*, began publication on 29 March, 1933, with the aid of £40 borrowed from a friend. At 34 Victoria Street, London, he rented a small upper room from Dorothy Woodman of the Union of Democratic Control. Since *The Week* could not, for financial reasons, be made a handsome publication, it was decided to make it strikingly unlovely by cyclostyling it "on buff-coloured paper in a nasty shade of brown ink". For all its unprepossessing appearance it commanded an attention "grossly, almost absurdly, out of proportion to its own resources". (The Years of the Week, 1968)

Matching *The Week* in that it operated on a shoestring budget, though in a different medium of the arts, was Unity Theatre, St Pancras, built by the voluntary labour of London trade unionists in 1937. It was founded in the belief, expressed by Sybil Thorndike in her introduction to *Unity Theatre Handbook*, that a living theatre was not a centre for "mere pleasantness and comfortable time-passing" but a place where one was "shocked into awareness". The Theatre's star production, whose opening night came six weeks after the signing of the Munich Agreement, was Robert Mitchell's "Babes in the Wood", with Neville Chamberlain depicted as the Wicked Uncle. Despite the lampooning of the Cliveden Set *The Times* critic found the production "irresistibly funny".

Surpassing all other new political developments of the 1930's was the emergence of the Left Book Club. It was founded in March 1936 after a private meeting between Victor Gollancz, Stafford Cripps and John Strachey in a Soho restaurant. Its aim was "to help in the terribly urgent struggle for World Peace and against Fascism by giving all who are determined to play their part in this struggle such knowledge as will immeasurably increase their efficiency". The founders were well aware of the popularity of such books as G D H Cole's *Intelligent Man's Guide through World Chaos* (1932)—known in the trade as "Cole's Chaos"—and Strachey's own work *The Nature of Capitalist Crisis* (1935), but they also knew of the reluctance of many booksellers to display books written from a leftist standpoint. The distribution problem was overcome through club members undertaking to buy at the standard price of half a crown the "choice of the month" selected by Gollancz, Laski and Strachey. In terms of membership the success of the venture exceeded all expectations. The number of subscribers shot up from 5,000 to 20,000 in the course of 1936 and continued to rise until a peak of 57,000 was reached in April 1939. But the Club was much more than a convenient arrangement for the sale of books of a certain kind. In October 1936 Dr John Lewis was appointed discussion group organiser. Within a few months he was receiving reports and sending out advice to 1,500 groups. The writer of this article still carries a vivid picture in his mind's eye of John Strachey, stripped to the waist, leading a discussion on the lawn at Digswell Park, Hertfordshire, in the summer of 1938. If it is true that a distinguishing feature of the later 1930's was a great upsurge of political awareness among thousands of persons not hitherto involved in any form of political activity, this new involvement owed much to the manifold activities of the Left Book Club.

Despite Gollancz's impassioned pleas in each month's issue of *Left News* that time was running out and that more members and adherents were urgently needed the Club failed in one of its principal objectives—the preservation of world peace. One great weakness of its position throughout was that it lacked the support of the TUC and the Labour Party Executive. But its contribution to the political education of the generation of the 1930's bore fruit in 1945 when many of those who had served their political apprenticeship in its discussion groups were elected to the new parliament and even called to high office.

The 1930's were a decade of hope and frustration. For those on the Left they were above all years of excitement, hard work and enthusiasm. Their imprint remains stamped on those of us who lived through the period, and events of the 'thirties were to shape the lives of many who had never heard of Hannington and Bevin, Cole and Laski, Maxton and Strachey.

WALTER GREENWOOD   *Love on the Dole* (1933, paperback 1969)
J B PRIESTLEY   *English Journey* (1934)
G D H COLE   *The People's Front* (1937)

G D H & MARGARET COLE   *The Condition of Britain* (1937)

GEORGE ORWELL   *The Road to Wigan Pier* (1937, paperback 1970)

ELLEN WILKINSON   *The Town that was Murdered* (1939)

FENNER BROCKWAY   *Inside the Left* (1942)

G D H COLE   *A History of the Labour Party from 1914* (1948)

C L MOWAT   *Britain Between the Wars* (1955, paperback 1968)

ELIZABETH THOMAS (ed.)   *Tribune 21* (1958)

WAL HANINGTON   *Never on our Knees* (1967)

PATRICIA COCKBURN   *The Years of the Week* (1968, paperback 1971)

JOHN LEWIS   *The Left Book Club: an historical record* (1970)

NOREEN BRANSON & MARGOT HEINEMANN   *Britain in the Nineteen Thirties* (1971)

RALPH HAYBURN   "The Police and the Hunger Marchers" *International Review of Social History*, vol. XVII, part 3, 1972

Angus Calder
Labour & the Second World War

ANGUS CALDER *studied literature at Cambridge and took a DPhil in Social Studies at the University of Sussex. He is the author of* THE PEOPLE'S WAR *(1969), a history of Britain 1939–45; and has reviewed for* TRIBUNE *and the* NEW STATESMAN. *He lectured in literature for three years at the University of Nairobi. He now lives in Edinburgh as a free-lance author and as a part-time teacher for the Open University. He is currently working on a history of the British Empire.*

Even the Left has a tendency to see "great men" as the prime movers of history. With the Second World War, luckily, no danger of this heresy arises. There is no hero to canonise, no Wilkes or Hardie, and no exotic costumes or brightly coloured lights with which to mount a drama. And I hope that this deficiency of supermen will never be overcome; that it is characteristic of a new and positive trend in social history; that working class may, politically, have outgrown the need for heroes.

"There is a war on and it is a people's war as well as ours", remarked a Lancashire JP in 1942—exposing with rare innocence a problem about the conflict with Hitler which dismayed the ruling classes. In a war against the populous, ruthless and highly mobilised nation which controlled most of Europe, only total mobilisation by Britain could offer a hope of victory. This meant the terrors of state control of industry, and the still worse terrors of full employment. The First World War had offered a foretaste—coal nationalised for the duration, cantankerous shop stewards, wild promises of reform and prosperity made by the rulers to their dangerous dupes, and then belied by mass unemployment in the 'twenties and 'thirties. This time, and the ruling classes knew it, they wouldn't be let off so lightly. The people; who must be made to feel once again that this was their own war, couldn't be asked to endure an even longer conflict without a huge and sparkling display of political and economic concessions.

However, the British ruling class has always been remarkable for calm manœuvring under fire, and responded well to Quintin Hogg's suggestion that Conservatives should "lead and dominate revolution by superior statemanship" instead of opposing it. In spite of wild talk then and since about a "social revolution" in the 'forties, we can see that the politics of the decade maintained and even strengthened capitalism, at the expense of minor modifications to the class system; that socialism was not given rein, but was jerked back and confused.

And the question must arise : how highly can we now value the undoubted advances in the condition of the British people over that decade, when we set them against the loss of political direction without the Labour movement? That movement was compromised by its own leaders, with the willing connivance of most of those whom they led; it was almost inextricably committed to a pro-American foreign policy and to a "managerial" ideology.

The Second World War, when the top politicians of all parties arrived at an affable consensus in coalition, had a lot to do with these setbacks, though their origins may be traced as far back as the first. In Alan S Milward's words, the influence of the two wars combined was "not merely to produce the nationalisation of basic industries after 1945, but also to determine that that nationalisation would be dictated primarily by considerations of the optimum deployment of resources rather than by more radical aims". In plain language, Labour confused socialism with "efficiency," and set out not to destroy capitalism, but to preserve it. When Churchill brought the Labour leaders into coalition in May 1940, he was the agent of an intelligent section of the ruling class which recognised that the co-operation of the workers was essential if the war was to be won. His acceptance of Ernest Bevin, biggest and toughest of union leaders, as his Minister of Labour, was perhaps his most important domestic decision of the war. Bevin, while basically a committed Keynesian, was a man of large and humane vision who knew how to apply the managerial ideology which he shared with Herbert Morrison, with Stafford Cripps, and with the younger Conservatives, in such a way that it presented a smiling human face.

No man did more to further wartime "efficiency"—his handling of the drastic manpower shortage was of crucial importance —but no man did more to pay back the people for their trouble. Labour, in a situation of full employment, was in a very strong bargaining position, and Bevin, the great negotiator, used this to push through advances in wages for backward trades, improvements in working conditions, and his own committed view that efficient management was kind management and just management. I offer the terrifying observation that no Labour Minister in office has ever achieved more.

The famous report which Arthur Greenwood, as a Coalition Minister, commissioned from Sir William Beveridge, might seem remote from managerialism. But it wasn't really. Rationalisation of social insurance, merely on grounds of "efficiency" was as long overdue as reform in education and as the creation of a unified National Health Service. The notion that the welfare state was created by Labour after 1945 in accordance with socialist ideology bears no examination at all; Labour carried out proposals already agreed in their essence by enlightened managerialists of all parties.

Kingsley Martin observed in 1941 when the contours of the tightly controlled war economy were becoming plain, "if you press for a constructive programme of the highest production you will automatically expose the waste and inefficiency of capitalism". He thought this meant you would get socialism. But the war itself had exposed inefficiency so clearly that capitalists could see how they might correct it. The Amalgamated Engineering Union pressed strongly for Joint Production committees in the engineering industry, with workers elected to serve from the shop floor. Lord McGowan, chairman of ICI, gave his blessing in a letter to Churchill. True, "extremists" might get elected—but they would be moderated by "a place in the sun", and would lose influence with other workers. Thousands of such bodies were set up; some promoted efficiency, but none promoted industrial democracy.

But the Left wasn't simply conned. It obliged the ruling class by conning itself. And we must work out how it was that most of the Left talked about socialism, even revolution, while busily committing themselves to consensus.

Firstly, the Labour Party, which had been divided, weak and remote from power in the 'thirties, was for obvious reasons glad of the chance to display its "responsibility" in Coalition. Its leaders were delighted to find out how much they could actually achieve, in a direction which appeared "socialist", without provoking the Tories to counter-revolution. (To Lord Woolton, on the other side "the practices that would be normal under a socialist state seemed to be the only safeguards of the country"—but all he was talking about was temporary state control of the economy.) Similarly, the trade union leaders were given sergeant-major status in the home-front army. Weakened grievously by the depression, they were only too anxious to help. Habits of willing compromise were bred by five years of Coalition.

Secondly, this war was not a bleak confrontation of bandits like the first. If Churchill was a bandit, Hitler was much worse. I hope no ingenious analysis ever convinces any future generation that what the Communist Party implied in 1940 was true: that there was no real difference between Britain and Germany. There was, although less than people liked to think. It was, surely, worthwhile to fight against an imperialist power which suppressed trade unions and murdered Jews, even on behalf of one which conned trade unions and interned Indians.

It seemed to most socialists that the winning of the war was itself a socialist aim. The doctrine of "revolution by consent" propounded by Harold Laski was very insidious: to win the war, the ruling class would have to *agree* to a socialist revolution. The CP, then in love with Joseph Stalin, was hardly the body to keep socialists up to the mark; the Independent Labour Party was on its death-bed and Sir Richard Acland's Common Wealth Party, which won three by-elections in its three years of effective existence (1942–5) was almost entirely composed of naive middle-class newcomers.

Thirdly, few people yet understood Keynes, and no one had realised how dangerous his doctrines were. The best argument for state control of the economy, almost as an end in itself, still seemed to be the fact that the newspapers were full of letters from businessmen calling for *laissez-faire*. Over the years, "socialism" had been confused with "nationalisation", and only a few sharp eyes, like George Orwell's, had spotted the difference. "Nationalisation" hadn't yet been tried out and found wanting—and nor had the "tripartheid" system ushered in by Butler's Education Act of 1944, which most socialists supported at the time. One has to forgive people for getting excited about measures taken during and after the war which now seem inadequate and even harmful.

Labour didn't really "betray" anyone, even itself, in 1945–51. It put through a sizeable number of measures which most socialists at that time thought were socialist; it is hindsight which shows us they weren't. Even the direction of foreign policy may be understood, if not forgiven, when one recalls that Labourites as far Left as Bevan and beyond had been impressed and encouraged by Roosevelt's New Deal, so that America still seemed a progressive force in world affairs.

Finally, the decade was far from being all waste as far as socialism was concerned. The working class gained greatly in self-confidence. Full employment, after decades of insecurity. A redistribution of the national income in its favour, through progressive taxation. The sniping of the Tory press muted in the interests of "the People's War", and positive, flattering propaganda over the government-controlled mass media—not a minor matter this, since it meant that the dignity of labour was now officially recognised.

And in some areas, a new sensation of working-class power was experienced. The miners, whose earnings improved dramatically, were able to take revenge with large-scale strike waves for their humiliation between the wars. Skilled engineers, in very short supply, could, by lengthy overtime, achieve very high wages. They were now quite indispensable; so much so that, as in certain Coventry factories, they could ignore the management and run the production of aero engines much as they liked, and with great success.

More than ever before, the people were participants, even protagonists in their own history. They showed a sense of this not only in "war industry", not only in their momentously brave conduct as air-raid wardens and rescue-workers in the Blitz, not only by voting the prodigious Churchill out in 1945, but also, more amazingly, by their conduct in the armed forces. The educational reforms of 70 years had born fruit, and the depression years had provided the younger generations with a sound, if expensive, socio-political education. Now soldiers were no longer prepared to content themselves with the status of cannon-fodder, and the Army recognised this when it not only sanctioned, but encouraged, discussion of contemporary issues, through the Army Bureau of Current Affairs.

The people of Britain in 1945 were more alert and sophisticated, politically, than ever before in their history. Churchill's attempt, with his "Gestapo" smear, to repeat the successes of "the Red Letter" and "Post Office Savings", those efficacious "scares" of inter-war elections, fell far short of convincing the people. And if the growth of CP membership to 56,000 in 1942 reflected naive admiration for Russia more than anything else, it did in the long-run have the effect of spreading Marxist ideas more widely than ever before. If the 'forties had their own very special brands of political illusion and mystique, they gave everyone a better chance to understand what socialism was, and what it wasn't and what it might be.

If one had to find a single hero, I think he would be a modern version of the Unknown Soldier. Let us call him the Thinking Serviceman. He hoped against hope for "a better world after the war", but he wasn't taken in for long by any politician, especially after the Coalition Government had let itself seem lukewarm about the Beveridge Report. His experience of Army discipline sharpened his dislike of the British class system. His travels across the world to fight gave him broader horizons than most Britons had had before. ABCA discussions left him better informed and more argumentative.

Perhaps he didn't vote at all in 1945 (most servicemen didn't), but his radical, sardonic opinions were in his mother's mind when she went to the polling booth. The influence of this man and of his generation upon British life has been enormous, especially upon our cultural style. Thanks to them, Britain is now a much less stuffy and snobbish country than ever before, and "deference", praise be, at last shows signs of decline.

MASS OBSERVATION   *War Begins at Home* (1940)
MASS OBSERVATION   *People in Production* (1942)
CHARLES MADGE   *Industry After the War* (1943)
R B MCCALLUM & A READMAN   *The British General Election of 1945* (1947)
R M TITMUSS   *Problems of Social Policy* (1950)
P INMAN   *Labour in the Munitions Industries* (1957)
MICHAEL FOOT   *Aneurin Bevan*, vol. I (1962)
ALAN BULLOCK   *The Life and Times of Ernest Bevin*, vol. 2 (1967)
ARTHUR MARWICK   *Britain in the Century of Total War* (1968)
ANGUS CALDER   *The People's War: Britain 1939–1945* (1969)
ALAN S MILWARD   *The Economic Effects of the World Wars on Britain* (1970)
HENRY PELLING   *Britain and the Second World War* (1970)
NORMAN LONGMATE   *How We Lived Then* (1971)

Benn Levy

Looking Backwards & Forwards— The Labour Government of 1945

BENN LEVY *was born in London at the turn of the century and was educated at Repton and Oxford. He has written or adapted more than 25 plays, produced all over the world. He has also been involved in cinema and journalism. He is married to the actress Constance Cummings. He was a member of Parliament during the Labour Government of 1945 to 1950. He served on the executive of the Arts Council from 1953 to 1961 and assisted with the long agitation to abolish theatre censorship.*

I remember shocking George Brown during the 1945–50 Labour Government by making what seemed to me the rather platitudinous observation that Ernest Bevin was not a socialist. I don't know why Brown, who wasn't a socialist either, should have been so bewildered and indignant, for he must have known that the Labour Party throughout its history, from its inception down to today, has been composed both of socialists (namely, people concerned to achieve a non-capitalist organisation of society) and of others, almost certainly more numerous, who, like sections of the old Liberal Party, were concerned with the improvement of conditions and wages for wage-earners under the existing system. Because socialists were equally anxious about wages and conditions, a working basis for collaboration in the party has always been feasible.

But insofar as the initiative for socialist theory and action has originated, for the most part, not within the working class but among political defectors from the midddle class, an undertow of potential strain between the two components has persisted, though seldom surfaced. If Bevin, and people like him, were suspicious of "middle-class intellectuals", it was because he himself was born into the Labour movement as surely as Lord Salisbury, Sir Alec Douglas-Home and most of the peerage were born into the Tory Party. He wasn't in it solely from conviction like the defectors, who had joined against their own class interests and who, like all converts, took the articles of faith with a sometimes inconvenient seriousness.

Bevin was an able man and undoubtedly a born boss; but, born in different circumstances, would he have been a trade union boss or a boardroom boss? I myself have little doubt. After all, he was a man who vaunted his class loyalty.

In discussing the coalition aspect of the Party it is relevant to recall that, of the first two MPs returned as candidates for the Labour Representative Committee (as the Labour Party was then called), Keir Hardie was a socialist and Richard Bell was not. Even Hardie had previously sought nomination as a Liberal. The parents of the Labour Party were the established Socialist societies and the trade unions. The parliamentary candidates previously sponsored by the unions alone had called themselves not socialists but, avowedly, Lib-Lab. Many of our MPs are of the same genus today—but less avowedly. In those days and for many years after, the word socialist was opprobrious and damaging. It was a bogey word that some of us have regarded as an unearned compliment and others as an undeserved stigma, loaded upon us by unscrupulous propagandist cads like Beaverbrook and Churchill. But now that the word has lost its venom (long since transferred to the word communist), even non-socialists in the party use it freely and indeed eagerly, perhaps in order to colour their reformism with a label that still has revolutionary implications. I think the resulting woolliness attached to the word may explain George Brown's mystification. If I had said that Bevin was not a revolutionary, I doubt if even he would have dissented.

I have laboured the point because it seems to me that the party has reached a critical stage when some attempt must be made to chart its future. This means an attempt to find out who it was, who it is, who it might be and who it ought to be. The answers govern its capabilities and its obligations.

It is to the credit of Clement Attlee's Government that he responded to both elements in the party. Both socialisation and social services received an unprecedented boost. When his Government completed its term, 20 per cent of the economy was in public hands. The Bank of England, coal, railways, canals, road haulage, electricity, gas. hospitals, and the iron and steel industry were all removed from the vagaries of private ownership.

And, on the reformist side, the far-reaching Report on Social Services by the Liberal economist, Lord Beveridge, which Arthur Greenwood had had the foresight to commission during the war, was boldly implemented and supplemented. Old-age pensions, unemployment benefit, industrial injury compensation, free schooling without means tests, family allowances, free meals for schoolchildren, the raising of the school-leaving age and, above all, a free health service; these were among the massive social benefits initiated or improved by the Labour Government.

Moreover, while Churchill's rhetorical call to "set the people free" was still echoing vacuously, Attlee, a staunch anti-colonialist, was busy doing it—though in a manner by no means to Churchill's taste. He set no fewer than 500 million people free in India, Pakistan, Ceylon and Burma. When we remember how gravely his Government was harassed and embarrassed not only by the abrupt termination of "Lease-Lend" but also, like Wilson's administration later, by cruel short-term problems such as balance of payments, attacks upon sterling, threatening inflation and the ill will or at least mistrust of the international bankers and speculators with devaluation as an unavoidable consequence, it is a remarkable record.

It is on foreign policy that the record is vulnerable. Bevin's policy made him the white-headed boy of the Tory Party and was, on at least one occasion, actually and publicly initiated by the Leader of the Opposition! I am referring, of course, to Churchill's notorious speech at Fulton which hoisted the flag of cold war, duly to be saluted by Bevin with the Foreign Office firmly behind him—or perhaps before him. The Russians, whose well-tried scepticism probably led them to expect no less, were of course not slow to reciprocate in the mutual folly; and indeed no one can say that they themselves would not have run up the same flag if Churchill and Bevin had not beaten them to it. But it was hardly the line to be expected of a Labour Foreign Minister.

True, I am by no means sure that "a socialist foreign policy" is a meaningful phrase but, if it has a meaning, it certainly does not mean getting the country in pawn to American capitalism— nor of course to Soviet dictatorship, for the Labour Party was nominally opposed to both.

It might, therefore, have been expected at least to struggle for independence and for the furtherance of its own distinctive alternative. This would have meant a bid for European leadership and the backing of Commonwealth and undeveloped countries. If it had succeeded, there would have been no European vacuum later, to be filled by the EEC on capitalist initiative, and no calamitous temptation to participate, at the tail, in the wrong kind of Europeanism.

However, apart from foreign policy, the Labour Government succeeded in packing its five years tight with precisely the kind of legislation it had promised and which its supporters, both socialist and non-socialist, could have hoped for. During the whole of that five years it lost not a single seat at by-elections. Why, then, at the 1950 general election did the tide turn against it?

It may have been partly due to the misguided strategy of Herbert Morrison who chose to woo voters under a banner with the strange device, "Consolidation", a word which, if it suggested anything, suggested conservation or marking time or even "Safety First". These may be suitable slogans for a Conservative party but are unlikely to inflame the enthusiasm of progressive voters. The unspoken target, of course, was the floating voter, that disastrous will o' the wisp who has led us more than once to destruction. Pursuit of this seductive phantom means the alienation of our own traditional support. For a left-wing party, the demand for a non-committal mandate is fatal, as Harold Wilson found to our cost in 1970.

But there were other more general reasons. Paradoxically, a left-wing government pays electoral penalties for its successes. Insofar as it mitigates hardship, it reduces the ranks of the discontented, whose votes it normally collects. Measures of social equity bringing relative affluence swell the ranks of the petty bourgeoisie. Past grievances are soon forgotten—and past help!

Moreover, although social reform still has a degree of electoral appeal, socialism still has little. But since both parties have for years been veering towards the centre in pursuit of "consensus opinion" (first cousin to the floating voter), the resulting But-skellism has largely blurred the Labour Party's distinctive image even as the party of social reform.

The reasons that socialism proper has never been a winning electoral card are simple. It is, after all, a theory—and quite a difficult theory—of social and economic organisation, an intel-lectual blueprint for society. Its relevance to more tangible bread-and-butter matters is apparent only to those who study it, a per-manent minority even among the party's supporters. And there are many different blueprints for socialism; for example, national-isation, syndicalism, guild socialism—or even Russian commun-ism. The last commands little emulation and the first has for us by now a familiarity which has largely devalued its status as a "cause". Besides, to many workers in the nationalised industries, the change must seem little more than a change of bosses and Mr Heath lost little time in driving home the point that under a Tory Government they were particularly exposed to wage re-strictions and redundancies.

To the extent that nationalisation was planned not on the argu-ment of national needs too important to be left at the mercy of the profit-motive but on the argument of efficiency measurable in terms of profit and loss, disappointment was inevitable. But even on the plane of theory, socialism has suffered. Capitalism, as Tory doctrinaires are beginning to realise once more, works best when it is most ruthless; that is to say, when its twin dynamic, the carrot and the stick, greed and fear, is given the fullest play.

But what nearly all of us have come to subscribe to, Tories and Labour alike, though with different willingness, is capitalism tem-pered with mercy. National advantages have therefore been sacri-ficed (rightly of course) to the advantages of the weak. Every bar to exploitation, from acts against child labour to unemployment benefits, enforced by common humanity, have weakened the capitalist drive. Nevertheless, its dynamic, though impaired, does still operate at every level; the carrot and the stick. What we are beginning to recognise is that socialist theory has failed to suggest a convincing alternative. In the earliest euphoria it was vaguely argued that service to the community would be an adequate incentive. But few people now believe that this can suffice except in wartime. Russia, though relying mainly on the stick, has been forced to reintroduce a little carrot.

Is this, therefore, an analysis of despair? Was Hugh Gaitskell right in seeking to extirpate the socialist Clause Four from our constitution, introduced originally (by the way) by another middle-class intellectual, Sidney Webb? The Labour Party, perhaps for sentimental reasons rather than from conviction, resisted the attempt. Should we be satisfied to accept the role merely of an "alternative government", differentiated from our opponents only by a slightly stronger bias toward social reform? Should we acquiesce in the revisionists' arbitrary re-definition of socialism as mere equality of opportunity? If so, Samuel Smiles, that great Victorian champion of individual opportunism, of meritocracy, would be eligible for membership, if not indeed for leadership, of the Labour Party. Should we resign ourselves to a "mixed economy", formally as well as in practice? It is reassuring that at a recent party conference a demand for a further substantial instalment of specified socialism was carried, albeit against the platform.

This, I think, is one of the signs that should give us heart. But it is imperative as a first step that we should overhaul our socialist thinking, face up to its weaknesses and buttress them. The party should commission a high-powered working party of socialists to do just this and to decide what brand or brands of socialism should become official policy.

For my part, I incline to some updated version of the guild socialism idea, not merely because I am a fanatic for maximising self-government in all social organisms, not merely because there is a current leaning towards it, reaching beyond the region of the Clyde, but also because it may well be that in this area we shall discover the vital missing dynamic. Participation and involvement, the more direct the better, can engage men's interest and energies. Although state capitalism is obviously preferable to private capitalism, it is as remote as representative government is increasingly felt to be in a community of 50 million people. It does not democratise industry; which is to say it does not democratise our daily lives.

Concurrently and no less urgently, I should like to see the Labour Party initiate a fundamental re-appraisal of the political constitution with a view to discovering what forms of centralisation could make government more immediately and continuously responsive to the governed.

In short, if the party alignment became recognisably Tory capitalism *versus* democratic socialism (with positive commitment and a fresh specific meaning to both words) instead of an opportunist jockeying for the central position, the country, already disillusioned by the sense of a sham battle or at least a trivial one, could recover its proper involvement and the party system its vitality. And with such a two-pronged programme we would no longer need to fear the all too justifiable scepticism of the young! The best of them would be with us; even, one hopes, within our leadership.

R B MCCALLUM & A READMAN *The British General Election of 1945* (Oxford, 1947)

ROBERT BRADY *Crisis in Britain* (Berkeley, California, 1950)

HERBERT & NANCIE MATTHEWS *The Britain We Saw* (1950)

ARNOLD ROGOW (with PETER SHORE) *The Labour Government and British Industry, 1945–1951* (Oxford, 1955)

HERBERT MORRISON *An Autobiography* (1960)

CLEMENT ATTLEE (with FRANCIS WILLIAMS) *A Prime Minister Remembers* (1961)

RALPH MILIBAND *Parliamentary Socialism* (1961)

HENRY PELLING *A Short History of the Labour Party* (1961)

HUGH DALTON *High Tide and After, 1945–1960* (1962)

HARRY HOPKINS *The New Look, A Social History of the Forties and Fifties in Britain* (1963)

MICHAEL SISSONS & PHILIP FRENCH (eds) *Age of Austerity, 1945–1951* (1963)

HAROLD NICOLSON *Diaries and Letters, 1945–1962* (1968)

David Rubinstein
Epilogue: Reflections on Violence in British Social History

"If the people is violent, you say you must not yield to disorder; if the people is silent, you say they are contented; in either case the people get nothing."—W E Gladstone

How can meaningful social change best be achieved? Feeling on the left has always been divided over the effectiveness of militant action which leads to violence. In the late 1950's and early 1960's, at the height of the Campaign for Nuclear Disarmament, there was a profound belief in non-violence. Many of the most militant opposed the use of force, although they resorted freely to extra-legal methods. CND helped to alter the climate of opinion throughout much of the world. But capitalism remained strong, the bomb was not banned, and a Labour Government soon came to office, with little ambition to change either the nuclear or the social order. Peaceful methods seemed to have failed. Under such circumstances it is not surprising that in the thinking of many socialists the position of Parliament, central for so long, should be devalued. Nor is it surprising that much political energy on the left passed over to revolutionary groups of various kinds.

British history does not give a clear or simple verdict on the effect of force as opposed to consent. Yet it can certainly give us some idea of the dilemma and the solutions preferred by past generations, dealing with situations in many ways similar to those which face us. As Michael Foot writes in his introduction to this book, history is, in a sense, our only guide.

Most of the preceding articles demonstrate the alternation between peaceful and violent means which have characterised much modern British history. As A J Peacock points out, as soon as political organisation and trade unionism failed, there was a reversion to direct action. Thus the Luddite risings met a severe reaction; thrown off balance by unrest and by industrial changes which they did not understand or, in many cases, want, the ruling classes reacted viciously. During the same period eleven people were killed in the Peterloo massacre and more than 400 were injured. Repressive legislation was passed and for a time the democratic movement was halted. The ruling classes, always quick to condemn violence when used against them, have been equally quick to use it in their own defence. Normally, however, they have attempted to follow violence with conciliation.

Violence played an important role in the early 1830's. The Swing riots were again answered by severe repression which included hangings and transportation to Australia. Even so, the delaying of agricultural mechanisation showed that the rioters had some measure of success.

In the demand for political reform in 1831–2 violence was strikingly successful. Not only did those with money to draw institute a run on the banks to crush the opposition of the obdurate Duke of Wellington (with the cry: "To stop the Duke, go for gold!"), but riots in Derby, the burning of Nottingham Castle and the sack of Bristol were all parts of the process which led to the passing of the Reform Act of 1832. Significantly, many among the middle classes supported the violence from which they themselves were to benefit. Victor Kiernan, in a stimulating essay on "Patterns of Protest in English History (*Direct Action and Democratic Politics*, eds R Benewick and T Smith, 1972), argues that "At such times of excitement, it would seem that some subtle change of temperature, some hint of a relaxed attitude to order in respectable quarters, is enough to give a lower class the signal that the hour has struck. A lawless populace then constitutes the battering-ram that opens the breach for those above it. It is by such a combination of pressures that all 'peaceful' reforms, like that of 1832, came about." It was certainly how all such reforms had come about up to that date. But from that point on, with few exceptions, the working classes were on their own.

In the North of England, violence succeeded in delaying the application of the Poor Law of 1834, with its "Bastille" workhouses for a generation. Again, a considerable number of manufacturers and other middle-class sympathisers openly supported the working-class rioters.

The Chartist movement was poised between peaceful and violent methods. Both sides were non-Parliamentary in their strategy but aimed at Parliament as their goal, a situation which characterised many later movements. But the only event which threatened the security of the state was the Newport rising in South Wales in 1839, and it was ruthlessly crushed. Riots and attacks on factories in the North marked the Chartist upsurge of 1842, which had the tacit support of many manufacturers seeking support for the repeal of the Corn Laws. It was when the riots spread and appeared to threaten the middle classes that the Government was able to use armed force to restore order. Again in 1848, at the time of the Kennington Common meeting and petition, Chartism together with the danger represented by foreign revolutions seemed to menace the security of the state. The result was that the middle classes stepped forward in their thousands to enroll as special constables and the Chartist leaders were imprisoned in large numbers.

Fear of revolution or at least of civil disturbance was a powerful motive behind such social reforms as were instituted in Victorian England. This was notably true in the case of housing. The first semi-philanthropic housing reformers, in the mid-century, specifically intended to ward off revolution, and the motive remained constant. The fear of armed uprising receded but it never died. In 1883, for example, a pamphlet describing slum conditions was published with the striking title *The Bitter Cry of Outcast London*. It made a great impact, and reviewers stressed that housing reform could well be the means to prevent revolution. An article in *Macmillan's Magazine*, typical of many, argued that so long as the working classes lived in slums "there lurks a real danger which may involve society in an overwhelming overthrow". As late as 1908 Sir James Reckitt, opening the Hull Garden Village, pleaded with "people of wealth and influence to make proper use of their property, to avert possibly a disastrous uprising".

If the fear of risings and riots was a motive in social reformers' minds, the pressure of the working-class movement itself was more potent. A hundred years after the passing of the Reform Act of 1867, which gave the vote to large numbers of urban working men, controversy raged over its causes. A number of conservative historians, challenging Royden Harrison's views, have played down the importance of popular agitation in winning the vote, pointing to the part played by party machination and manœuvre. These latter were undoubtedly a significant factor in determining the terms of the Act. However, it is also clear that renewed working-class militancy, spearheaded by the Reform League, was the decisive cause of the Act's passage.

The 1850's and early 1860's had mostly been peaceful years, in which working men demonstrated only for foreign democratic leaders like Garibaldi or foreign causes like the American Civil War. Thus, when militancy in the form of marches, demonstrations and small-scale riots reappeared, the effect was all the greater and parallels with Chartism were uncomfortably drawn by those with something to lose. Lord Cranborne, who as Lord Salisbury was to be three times Conservative Prime Minister, strongly opposed the Act. In an article in the *Quarterly Review* in October 1867, entitled "The Conservative Surrender", he explained his view of why it had been passed. Many Members of Parliament had feared that "the pot should boil over. . . . The meetings in the manufacturing towns and the riots in Hyde Park had had their effect. The comfortable classes had no stomach for a real struggle."

The West End riot of February 1886 had important repercussions. Concessions were made to those without work and socialism made a significant if limited advance in public consciousness. However, had riots continued the forces of state repression would doubtless have mobilised. This is in fact precisely what happened on "Bloody Sunday", November 1887, when Tragalgar Square was heavily garrisoned, heads were broken, many marchers "skedaddled" (as Bernard Shaw, who was one of them, wrote) and prison sentences were freely handed out. Exemplary violence by the state was once again the solution. "This operation was the Peterloo probe again", Victor Kiernan comments, "with truncheon instead of sabre."

The hectic period before the Great War of 1914 was to see more violence and threatened violence than at any other period to date in the twentieth century. Violence by opponents of Irish Home Rule tragically delayed its application, suffragette violence made Votes for Women a prominent political issue for the first time, while trade union militancy and violence brought its suffering and its martyrs. The labour unrest saw violent incidents and major riots in Hull, Liverpool, South Wales and elsewhere. More than ever before the British working-class movement was led by militants and struck for more than purely economic reforms. For the first time syndicalism became a force to cope with and contempt for Parliamentary institutions was loudly—though far from universally—voiced. What was the effect of the strikes? A book called *The Social Unrest* was published in 1913 by a well-informed observer. He analysed figures of strikes and wage movements and came to this conclusion: "Demands backed by threats of war have been necessary before the share of Labour in increased national wealth has been improved. One's recollection of what has happened again and again in one's own experience is borne out by these figures, viz. that when prosperity returns Capital shows no voluntary disposition to share its increasing gains with Labour, but retains them for itself until forced to part with them." The observer was not normally found on the militant wing of the Labour movement; his name was James Ramsay MacDonald.

As for the suffragettes, the effect of their militancy has been variously interpreted. Fenner Brockway, politically active during the period, has suggested that militancy increasingly carried public opinion until it became violent, when a reaction took place. The leader of the constitutional suffrage workers, Millicent Garrett Fawcett, admitted before militancy became violent that the suffragettes had achieved more in twelve months than she and her followers had been able to do in twelve years. When some of the first women were arrested, in 1906, Mrs Fawcett wrote that their action had "touched the imagination of the country in a manner which quieter methods did not succeed in doing".

It may be that later violence made Asquith and his colleagues far more obdurate, that it roused antipathy among formerly friendly men. I can only say that on my reading of the evidence it was suffragette militancy that made Votes for Women a real issue after nearly forty years of fruitless debate and ladylike behaviour. The war, on this view, served as an excuse to give women the vote, but without earlier militancy the war would have gained them nothing.

Which methods, then, have worked best? Two tentative conclusions may be drawn. First, that meaningful social change has never occurred in British history without extra-Parliamentary, extra-constitutional action. The General Strike was called off after six days in 1926, but the strikers' reward was victimisation and defeat, though the strike may well have done something to prevent further wage cuts. The Labour Party behaved as constitutionally as Mrs Fawcett herself when faced by heavy unemployment between the wars and a virtual *coup d'état* in 1931. The result was, as Robert Skidelsky points out, "20 years of mass unemployment and sermonising without action". Only sporadic violence in the streets won sporadic concessions. Similarly, militant actions like those of the Upper Clyde Shipbuilders and the miners in the early 1970's have been crowned by success. We may well agree with words attributed to T H Huxley: "Though truth is great and in the long run will doubtless prevail, it is necessary to give it a kick from behind to be sure it moves definitely upon its road." It is a recipe for inertia to rely solely on Parliament and party politics.

The other conclusion is to some degree contradictory. It is that without the presence of revolutionary conditions, continual violence is likely to be self-defeating. Occasional spontaneous outbreaks, often for limited aims, have had considerable effect, but when repeated they tend to lead to repression. Working-class movements which coincided with the wishes of the middle class in the early nineteenth century achieved considerable success, but when isolated and dangerous they were crushed. One West End riot in 1886 was productive, but subsequent meetings were suppressed. Strikes which led to violence were successful, but when Tom Mann appealed to the army in 1912 "Don't shoot!" he was imprisoned.

The question is where to stop. When will violence be successful and when will it recoil on its users? Every generation faces its problems anew. Yet the diagnosis of Harold Laski, one of the great socialist teachers of this century, made in a lecture in 1932 called

"The Militant Temper in Politics", seems to me to remain entirely valid:

"In any society the tactics of a privileged order are always the same tactics. Declare, in the first place, that the demand is impossible; insist when it has been proved to be possible that the time for its translation into statute has not yet come; then when it is clear that there seems to be some urgency about it, say that the time is coming but that this is not yet the time; then when an angry clamour surrounds the demand, insist that you cannot yield to violence; and when finally, you are driven to yield, say that it is because you have been intellectually convinced that the perspective of events has changed."

Both British and Irish history stood behind Laski's analysis. Since he spoke events in India, Cyprus, many parts of Africa and again Ireland have supported his view. Although the French risings of 1968 were unsuccessful it would be hard to argue that they are of no significance in later years. It is unlikely that the lessons of militancy are outdated in Britain.